MW00815109

Tony's World

Tony's World

The Recollections of a Pilot, a Sailor, an Ice-boater, a Skier, a Bobsledder, a Winemaker, a Museum Director —and a Natural Storyteller

William E. Doherty, Jr.

Edited and Introduced by Charles Champlin

1999 · Fithian Press · Santa Barbara, California
For the Glenn Curtiss Museum of Local History, Hammondsport, New York

Printed in the United States of America

Published by Fithian Press
A division of Daniel and Daniel, Publishers, Inc.
Post Office Box 1525
Santa Barbara, CA 93102

Book design: Eric Larson

LIBRARY OF CONGRESS CATALOGING-IN-PUBLICATION DATA
Doherty, William E. (William Ellwood), 1917–1996.
Tony's world : the recollections of a pilot, a sailor, an ice-boater, a skier, a bobsledder, a winemaker, a museum director—and a natural storyteller / William E. Doherty, Jr.; edited and introduced by Charles Champlin.
p. cm.
ISBN 1-56474-290-3 (alk. paper)
1. Doherty, William E. (William Ellwood), 1917–1996. 2. Air pilots—United States—Biogrpahy. I. Champlin, Charles (date). II. Title
TL540.D57A3 1999
629.13'092—dc21
[B] 98-36879
CIP

Contents

The Beginnings

The War Years

Tony's World

Introduction

Near the end of his long and uniquely adventurous life, William Elwood (Tony) Doherty, Jr., began to write it all down. There was a lot to write. He had been a skier, an early bobsledder at Lake Placid, a sailor, a pilot during World War II, a winemaker and winery executive, a glider enthusiast and sales manager for a major sailplane manufacturer, an iceboater, a museum director and probably several other things I have forgotten or never knew about. He was part of a remarkable, colorful family and he was a wonderful raconteur, with a prodigious store of anecdotal memories and information about Hammondsport and its citizens past and present. His stories were great because he was someone (more than anyone I know) to whom or around whom dramatic things happened. As I read through his words, I realized that he had had more lives than a restless cat and many a hair's-breadth escape.

He and his word processor were not natural friends, but he fought it to a draw and by the time, in May 1996, when he was carried away by a swift and unbeatable cancer, Tony had created a large stack of first-draft pages, pecked out in occasional frustration and anger, but always sounding very much like Tony talking, as he wandered back and forth in recollection from early childhood to late maturity, and being lively and interesting wherever memory's eye fell.

He sometimes seemed to be writing at white heat, as if aware that his time was not unlimited, but wanting to set it all down. He used abbreviations and short cuts and sometimes skipped last names as if anyone reading him would know who it was he meant. Given time, he'd have gone back and polished up the prose and set it in chronological order. But he did run out of time, and I'm sure he had miles of reminiscence yet to go, particularly his life in the postwar years, including his long service to the Glenn H. Curtiss Museum of Local History, of which he was the director for several years.

There is, for example, a long and vivid portrait of his father (called Gink from prep school days) but little about his lovely mother, although every mention makes it clear that he adored her. On the other hand, he left an amazingly detailed and affectionate account of his childhood years in New Orleans as well as in Hammondsport.

Those pieces—building a tree house, fishing, trapping, climbing the glens, sledding, learning to sail, creating a diving bell—evoke a world I'm not sure exists any more, even in Hammondsport, which has withstood the changing world better than most larger places. He suggests Tom Sawyer and Peck's Bad Boy, with seasonings of Tom Swift and, yes, the Holden Caulfield of *Catcher in the Rye*; his world is not without shadows.

He piloted transports rather than fighters or bombers in the war, but his experiences are hair-raising enough (crash-landing in total darkness on a country estate) and his account of being on hand at the meeting of Yanks and Russians on the Elbe is, of all things, very funny. In war or peace, he is wonderfully descriptive of the experience of flight.

Tony was my first cousin, who became one of my closest and most cherished friends as well. His mother, Gladys Champlin Doherty (whom I called "Aunt Tommy" I think because I couldn't manage "Tony") and my father, Francis Malburn Champlin, were brother and sister. (My father is Uncle Kid in the memoirs, having been called Kid from an early age, as in kid gloves.) Tony and his brothers, Duane (Boog) and Peter, and my brother, Joe, and I grew up across Lake Street from each other. When the disastrous flood of July 1935 hit Hammondsport, Tony, then a sturdy eighteen-year-old, slogged through the rising waters at midnight to carry Joe and me (four and nine then) on his shoulders to the house next door, which was on higher ground. I admired him ever after.

For me, Tony's father, Gink, was a dashing figure with the deep mellifluous voice of a very good radio announcer. I think he would have been a *boulevardier* if Hammondsport had had a boulevard and bistros in lieu of saloons. I've always thought that much of Tony's charm and eloquence, as well as his love of flying, came directly from Gink. The easy charm was a family inheritance that came to Duane and Peter as well.

With its history of champagne and flying machines, Hammondsport became, it has always seemed to me, the most cosmopolitan village for its size and relative isolation of any village in the country. It is still a wonderful place to grow up, with its lake and glens and hills, and Tony did most of his growing up here. His descriptions of the village as he first saw it and came to love it and of its characterful citizens are some of the most eloquent and moving parts of the memoir.

Tony had been sharing his writings with me, piece by piece, for a decade or more. I loved them and felt strongly that they deserved a wide audience. After his death, I volunteered to put the pieces in shape for publication. This has mostly meant placing the vignettes in a kind of order (he wrote as the spirit moved him) and eliminating duplications (he occasionally did sections over but never threw anything away).

What editing I've done has been for clarity and continuity, and when I've had to clarify, or re-order, I've tried to hear Tony saying, "That's what I meant." The voice you hear is Tony's, all the way through. Reading the pages again and again has in fact been like hearing his voice, and in the mind's eye seeing him walk across the lawn or up the street with his characteristic side-to-side sway that reminded me of John Wayne's famous lope, but taken at a faster tempo. Tony lives again for me in these pages, and I hope he will for his readers, those who knew him and those who may be discovering him.

This book is for Tony's widow, Mardo Underhill Doherty, for Tony's son, Trafford, his daughter, Anne, and Tony's brother Peter. It honors the memory of Tony's first wife and the children's mother, the couragous Jacqueline Leigh-Mallory Doherty, and of Tony's brother Duane, both of whom died even as the book was going to press. And the book is, of course, for everyone in whose memory Tony lives.

CHARLES CHAMPLIN
Fall 1998

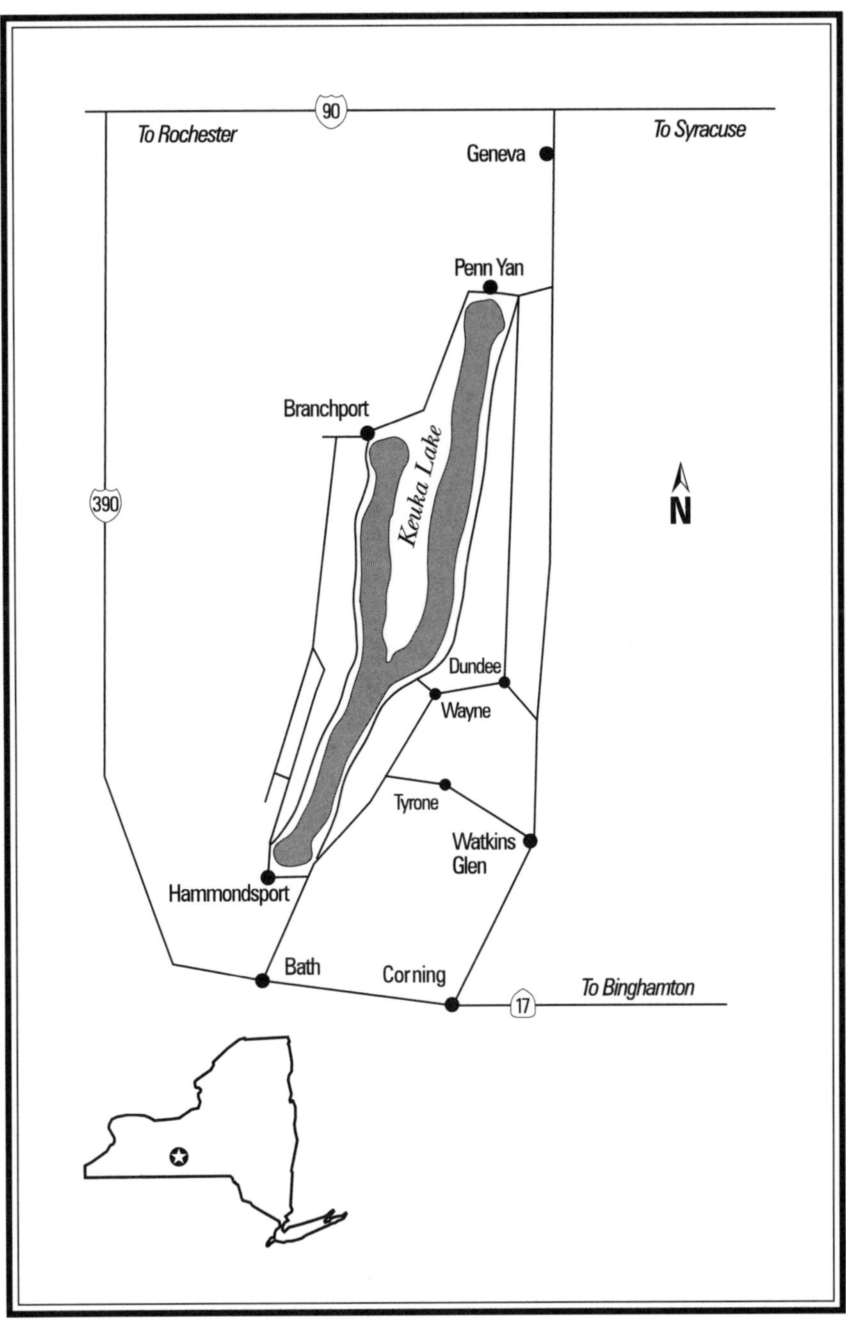
90
To Rochester
To Syracuse
Geneva
Penn Yan
Branchport
Keuka Lake
390
N
Dundee
Wayne
Tyrone
Watkins
Glen
Hammondsport
Bath
Corning
17
To Binghamton

The Beginnings

Early Days in New Orleans

1920

IN WHAT YOU would probably call its formative years, our family did what a lot of families did, moving from one place to another as the jobs dictated. Mother and Dad, who had been married in London and stationed for a while on the coast of Spain (but that's several other stories) had first set up domestic housekeeping in Marblehead, Massachusetts, and it was at their house on Pleasant Street that I arrived on January 22, 1917. Dad was then a test pilot for the Burgess Company, which Glenn Curtiss owned. When the United States declared war on Germany later that year, Dad was commissioned a naval aviator and we moved to Washington, where we shared a house with John Towers, who had learned to fly at Hammondsport along with Dad (and was a rear-admiral in World War II.) Dad was made commanding officer of the Anacostia Naval Air Station.

After Dad was "demobbed" by the Navy, he rejoined Curtiss as a sales representative, assigned to the New Orleans area. His staff consisted of a part-time secretary, a full-time mechanic and one Model E Curtiss flying boat. While Dad went ahead to arrange housing in New Orleans, Mother and I went back to Hammondsport to stay with her mother (Nano as we learned to call her) and there Mother awaited the birth of my brother Duane, who later on came to be called Boog. We moved to New Orleans in 1920 and lived first in an upstairs apartment on Napoleon Avenue. It was there I had scarlet fever—and also tasted Coca-Cola for the first time. It was there I also had my first plane ride, taking off and landing on Lake Ponchartrain. After two years we moved to a downstairs apartment on Walnut Street. It was on the municipal golf course (and thereby hangs another tale) and only a short walk from Audubon Park and the Mississippi River, both of which we found fascinating.

It was an exciting time. Dad bought a new car, an air-cooled Franklin touring model with a sloping nose instead of a standard radiator. On weekends we often drove out to the West End Yacht Club or to the bayou where Dad had a hangar for the plane.

One scheme Dad had for selling the Curtiss flying boats was to interest people who lived along the Mississippi and worked in the city. He figured they could commute by air, landing and docking their boats at the yacht club. In theory this was a great idea and he made many demonstration flights. It was fine when Dad was at the controls, but when the customers realized that they would be doing the flying, their enthusiasm cooled in a hurry.

Dad didn't sell many of the flying boats, but he made a lot of friends. He'd taken them up for plane rides, and they returned the favors with fishing trips and sailing on Lake Ponchartrain. Mr. Merrick, who was president of the United Fruit Company, would give us a full bunch of bananas every week, more than we could eat, and we'd have to call on the neighbors for help.

It was during the Walnut Street days that we began exploring the countryside. We spent a weekend at an ante-bellum plantation up the Mississippi. We made trips to Spanish Fort, Bayou Lafitte, and the War of 1812 battlefield at Chalmette, where Andrew Jackson defeated the British. One day we went across the river to watch an air show that featured ten or so Curtiss Jennies, with wing walking and parachute jumps. One of the pilots was an old pal of Dad's and he gave me a ride, my first time in an aeroplane.

Dad had had a landing area dredged out of a bayou outside the city for his plane. The hangar was located on a strip of land between the landing area and another bayou. One day he was returning to his base, low on fuel and flying in thick fog. He had one quick glance at his hangar as he passed over it and then straightened out to set down. He was just wide of the cleared area and the hull struck a submerged stump. The boat was reduced to kindling and Dad ended up in the hospital with cuts, bruises and a broken nose. In all his years of flying, it was his only crash!

The Curtiss Company decided that Dad should be assigned a territory with more potential. It may have been Alaska, but the family liked New Orleans and decided not to move. A good friend of the family persuaded Dad to join the sales department of the Miles Salt Company. He did and we stayed in New Orleans.

Miles was a large outfit and its source of salt was a mine located at Weeks Island, in the Cajun bayou country a hundred miles or so west of the city. On Weeks Island was a small settlement and a processing plant. Just outside the settlement was a large old plantation mansion, which had been converted into a guest house for company executives where their families could stay for a vacation.

Thus in the summer of 1924, Mother, my brother Duane and I were spending a week at the guest house on Weeks Island. Duane and I were five and seven respectively. Dad had driven us out from the city in our air-cooled Franklin. We had taken the ferry across the Mississippi and then driven many miles on sandy dirt roads. Dad spent the night but left for the city early the next morning, leaving Mother to cope.

It was really a fascinating place. We were poled in flat-bottom boats through Cypress Swamp with its black water and overhanging foliage. We were admonished to keep our hands inside the boat, and after seeing several water moccasins slithering by, we were only too willing to oblige.

Another unforgettable treat was when one of the foremen took us on a tour of the mine and the processing plant. Both were interesting, but going down in the mine was really impressive. We rode down in the large steel container that brought the raw salt to the surface. I remember the opening at the top growing smaller and smaller as we descended, until it was merely a pinprick of light. When we reached the lower level there was a great deal of activity. We were in a huge domed cavern with tunnels radiating out in many directions. The area was brightly lighted, and electrically-powered engines pulling cars loaded with salt would rumble up to a huge maw where large grinders chewed up the big chunks.

The walls of the great domed cavern were black from the smoke of the explosions. It looked more like a coal mine. But when we rode on an empty train to the end of the line or the face of one of the tunnels, it was like a fairyland, with the salt crystals sparkling under the electric lights. Several of the tunnels went well out under the Gulf of Mexico. They only blasted at night when the mine was empty, in case the blast opened a seam and flooded the works.

I remember one operation in particular: the production of salt licks for cattle. They were made in three colors, white, yellow (sulfur) and blue (minerals). I noticed that imperfect blocks (and there were a lot of them) on the conveyor belt were carried to a huge pile, which streams of water washed back into the Gulf. Salt was plentiful, and cheap.

The mine and the plant were wonderful, and the swamp trip was fun. But the place that had the greatest delight for us was a small pond alongside the railroad tracks, midway between the house and plant. It must been a hundred feet or so in diameter and two or three feet deep.

Our first project, under Mother's very anxious eye, was to roll some railroad ties down the bank and make a raft. I don't remember how we held it together, probably with pieces of rope, but using poles we had a great time cruising around.

Around the pond were a great many very large black grasshoppers, which we would catch and put in a jar. Somewhere along the way I had heard about Siamese twins. It might have been at a circus we had recently attended. One day I caught two grasshoppers that were joined together, just like Siamese twins, or so I thought. I showed them to Mother proudly, but I didn't understand her reaction. I think she was nonplused, and she made me throw them away. A few years later, when I knew a little more about a lot of things, I came to the conclusion that Mother had missed an opportunity to set me straight on some facts of life.

But the highlight of our vacation on Weeks Island came on almost our last day. Duane and I were cruising on our "ocean" when a train came along. It stopped right by the pond, and a man climbed down from the engine, walked a little way up the track, bent over and unlocked a padlock. He then lifted an iron bar with a block of metal on one end and swung it up and over. The train started moving and the man swung aboard as it passed him.

My brother and I watched this whole operation with great interest. Mother had gone back inside the house so we couldn't ask her what it was all about. So we went over to investigate for ourselves. I couldn't quite lift the block of metal, but Duane gave me a hand and between us we were able to swing it up and over. That was hard work but except for a very satisfactory clang there wasn't much to it. We went back to our raft and were happily cruising when the train came back.

It started going "clunk, clunk clunk." Three cars were derailed before it stopped. Several men appeared and there was a great deal of yelling and arm-waving. They stopped and looked at the two of us. We couldn't hear what they were saying, but one of them shook his head as if to say, "No way." But Mother had come out and she wasn't fooled for a moment. She wasn't sure exactly what had happened but she would have laid odds that somehow or other I was involved. For some reason, I developed that reputation early. What I had done was learned what a switch was.

Mother waved us ashore and took us back to the house to get cleaned up for supper. We were allowed to go back and watch the re-railing, which was very interesting. When Dad arrived to collect us the next day, very little was said about the railroad incident. But in later years it became one of those oft-told family stories that always began with, "And then there was the time the boys wrecked a train."

Our street in New Orleans stopped at the river just two blocks south of the house. The Mississippi was a major attraction. From the top of the levee we could watch ocean-going steamers, tugs pushing huge barges, and the wonderful many-decked paddlewheel riverboats. We were never allowed to go to the levee unescorted, but it was awfully tempting.

Over the levee was a large wharf where freighters unloaded hardwood logs for the sawmill on the riverbank. One afternoon Dad loaded Boog and me in the Franklin and drove to the mill, a very exciting place full of the noise of the great saws biting into the wood. Dad talked with the man who ran the mill and came back to the car carrying a piece of dark wood about three feet long. What was it for? Dad said, "Wait and see," quite mysteriously. A few days later he called us out to the car. The wood had been cut into a dozen pieces of various shapes. It was, I know now, Honduras mahogany. Dad said we were going to make a model sailboat. A wood-working friend of his had done the initial cutting and sawing, but we did the rest ourselves. I was amazed by Dad's patience, and his skill. The spars and booms were shaped by hand, the tiny blocks and cleats, all hand-shaped, were perfect. The model, always called The Mahogany Boat, was sloop-rigged, copied from the *Resolute*, which was then defending the Americas Cup, with a gaffed mainsail, topsail, jib, and staysail. Mother made the sails and they fitted perfectly.

We launched the boat one gala day at the West End Yacht Club. It sailed beautifully as it cut through the waters of Lake Ponchartrain. Even now, every time I look at The Mahogany Boat, I remember the patience and the skill with which Dad made it. Thirty years later, he showed the same skill and devotion when he re-rigged the boat as a schooner, for his grandson. I regret I couldn't match his skill or his patience when I readied the Mahogany Boat for his great-grandson.

Our last year in New Orleans was very active. Boog and I had started school when we lived on Walnut Street. (I was held back a year and Boog started a year early so we could be together.) But school began in earnest when we moved to Nelson Street. We attended the Robert E. Lee School, ten blocks from the house. It was in the school cafeteria that we both developed a taste for that great Cajun staple, red beans and rice. It was also at the school that I got in my first fight and suffered my first bloody nose.

We were older by now and could appreciate more fully the family outings and activities. A close friend of Mother's and Dad's was of the family that owned Antoine's, the famous restaurant, and we often went there on Sunday afternoons for dinner in the beautiful courtyard. We loved the picnics at Spanish Fort, a great gloomy brick place with tunnels and dungeons. We made a trip to Avery Island, where Tabasco sauce is made, and took boat rides through the bayous of Evangeline country.

We didn't know it at the moment, but change was in the wind. Late in the fall of 1924, Grandmother came to New Orleans to see us. She was in a kind of mourning. Her favorite son, Uncle Kid (or Francis Malburn Champlin), who had been living at the house, upped and eloped with Katherine (Kitty) Masson. Nano was shattered, even though her other son, Uncle Charlie, and his family were living near by. We'd never really gotten used to the humid New Orleans summer (no air-conditioning in those days). Mother had never cut her emotional ties to Hammondsport, and my father, never really at home in the salt trade, had never cut his ties with Buffalo, where he grew up. He'd been back there on several business-and-pleasure trips. So there were a variety of tugs from New York State.

Then a friend called Dad to say that Rolls-Royce was opening a sales office in Buffalo and would Dad like to head it? Darn tootin'. Another friend, the architect Duane Lyman, called to say he was building a big school in the Buffalo suburb of Williamsville and that there was a very nice house at the location that was going for a song. Would Dad like to buy it? He would and did, sight unseen, and we prepared to leave New Orleans for the north. As luck would have it, we were leaving the nice weather in New Orleans for New York in the dead of winter. But Boog and I didn't know what that meant, or what adventures lay ahead.

Northward Ho! New Orleans to Hammondsport

1925

IN CHICAGO WE changed trains from the City of New Orleans, that had brought us up from New Orleans, to the New York Central without incident, much to Mother's relief. Making the same trip two summers before, there had been a disruption as we passed through the main concourse of the station.

It came about because at that time we had been living on Walnut Street in New Orleans. Our house fronted on the municipal golf course and I had taken up golf, using my father's clubs, or "sticks," as they were called in those days. My course consisted of driving from the green to the previous tee. I had to hold the club low on the shaft and let the rest of it go under my armpit.

On my first outing, a very large policeman who patrolled the links asked me what I was doing. My answer must have satisfied him because we became good friends. After that, every time he saw me he gave me one or two balls he'd found on his rounds. As a result I'd ended up with a fine collection of golf balls, which were my pride and joy. My father had given me a small leather sample case and in it I packed my prize collection of balls. They filled it completely. That summer my mother's favorite aunt died and we went north for the funeral.

While we were crossing the concourse the latch on the sample case came loose and my collection hit the marble floor and bounced off in all directions. Mother gave a loud wail and I, being six years old, burst into tears. I understand that it caused a fair amount of excitement but for the most part people were sympathetic to Mother's crisis and gathered up the rolling balls and returned them. When we traversed the concourse this time, I still had my sample case, but this time it contained underwear and socks.

The big blizzard of the year caught up with us as we were leaving Chicago and it swirled and whitened the countryside as we traveled eastward. We arrived in Buffalo at the height of the storm and were very fortunate to get transportation to the hotel where we planned to spend the night. When we got there my brother Boog and I were plopped into a hot bath.

Boog and I were fascinated by all the white stuff that filled the air and lay in large piles on the ground. The next day we were confined to the hotel but spent most of our time glued to the windows watching the men struggling to clear the streets. I don't remember any plows, only men with shovels, and horse and wagons and a few trucks. I also don't remember being cold, but we should have been since we'd just left the very moderate temperatures of New Orleans.

The next morning a taxi took us to the Lackawanna Station for the train ride south to Bath. The storm had passed through but we were fascinated by the snow-covered countryside. We had seen such sights only in pictures and on Christmas cards. Years later we'd have said Currier and Ives prints.

At Bath, Grandmother was there to greet us with her Essex, driven by "James," who was sixteen at the time. The cars didn't have heaters then but Grandmother was prepared. There were hot soapstones wrapped in newspapers in the floor, and piles of robes to wrap around us. The Essex had chains on the rear wheels, and they made a rumbling, whirling sound as we drove along. As I remember there seemed to be more horses and sleighs than cars on the road. The road to Hammondsport, eight miles down the valley, hadn't been plowed, and we slipped and slithered slowly along while Grandmother brought Mother up to date on the latest news from the village—who'd done this and who hadn't done that. Boog and I were still enchanted by all the snow.

When we arrived in Hammondsport and pulled up in front of the house on Lake Street next door to the Episcopal Church, we were hustled out of the car and we hurried gratefully into the warm interior. I remembered it from our visit two summers before but Boog, who was only a year old at the time, had no memory of it at all. There was a fire in the living room fireplace and that really fascinated us because it was the first one we'd ever seen. I couldn't get over how good it felt, and how much it enlivened the homey atmosphere of the room.

It's difficult to separate our impressions of the house when we first arrived from those we formed over the fifty years we were associated with it. I do know that our two favorite rooms were the living room with the fireplace and the overstuffed chairs and sofa, and the kitchen with its large, black coal range. On it was done all of the cooking. Besides heating the back part of the house, it heated a large tank of hot water.

It was in the kitchen that Nano, as we called my grandmother, worked her culinary magic. She was a superb cook, but one who would make today's dietitians despair. The two basic ingredients for her cakes, cookies, casseroles, and desserts were butter, eggs...and more butter. Under normal conditions she used a five-pound crock of butter every two weeks. The crock would be delivered to the house by a dairy farmer from back in the hills.

It was a big house now, but when our grandparents (Charles Addison Champlin and Georgia Malburn Champlin) first moved into it in 1884, it had only four rooms and had been one of the earliest frame houses in the village. But it had grown like Topsy—a room here, an addition there, until Uncle John Davis warned Nano to forget the idea of adding a third story. She did like to add on and remodel.

There were two areas of particular interest to Boog and me, but they were off-limits to us: the front cellar and the attic. The front cellar was under the original portion of the house. During one of Nano's expansions, another cellar was excavated for the furnace and the coal bins. We weren't too excited about that part of the cellar, because there was always coal to be carried in a scuttle up to the kitchen range, or shoveled into the furnace.

It was the front cellar that intrigued us. It lay behind a heavy door which was secured by a massive padlock. Just before Prohibition fell like a dark shadow on Hammondsport and the vineyards and the wineries, carpenters from Pleasant Valley, the family winery, had built a number of large cupboards in the front cellar, each named for an adult member of the family and each with its own heavy padlock.

Before the Feds literally locked the front and back doors of Pleasant Valley (as of all the wineries), each member of the family made a list of the wines they wanted, and the quantities. I suspect that every family connected with a winery did the same thing, and those with friends at a winery did, too, but probably not so efficiently as was done under Nano's direction.

Not all the closeted vintages were consumed. Fifty years later, I had the depressing and arduous task of emptying those cupboards. It was sad but our local dry wines didn't have the legs to be palatable after all those years. (In fact, worldwide, very few do.) I carried bottle after bottle up the cellar stairs to the curb, to be collected by the rubbish man. Interestingly enough, any of the sweet wines would not only have withstood the passage of years but would have improved greatly. Obviously the family was well aware of this. There was no sherry and no port to be found in the cupboards.

When we arrived on Grandmother's doorstep that snowy February day we were greeted with open arms. It had been an empty and lonely house the past few months. My grandfather had died a few years before, but when we visited two summers earlier, my younger uncle, Malburn, or "Kid," was still living at home. He was not yet married and, since the winery was barely functioning at all, he had turned to agriculture and was running what remained of the family farm and in conjunction with it, operating a dairy and a milk route. That earlier summer I often accompanied him on his rounds and delivered the smaller orders to his customers' back stoops.

This same uncle played golf, and when he saw my collection he persuaded me to sell them to him for a penny apiece. His room was next to the nursery where I was deposited for a nap every afternoon. He actually had two connected rooms. The front one he used for his office, and the old roll top desk he used was usually covered with change from his milk route. At that time Indian head pennies were still in circulation and they fascinated me. I could relate to Indians but I wasn't familiar with Lincoln. I would go to the desk and take the Indian heads for my collection. The other coins meant nothing to me; money had no meaning for me. Yet. Ah, youth.

Later I discovered that my new hobby was causing all sorts of problems. Uncle Kid couldn't balance his books. Nano, who was a pretty shrewd individual, solved the mystery when she found my hoard of Indian heads in a cigar box in a drawer. I was given a stern lecture on never touching anything that wasn't mine. Luckily my transgressions were forgiven by Uncle Kid and I continued to accompany him on his milk route.

That first February day we arrived in Hammondsport to stay, we weren't allowed to go out. Our blood was too thin; we had to be acclimatized. Boog and I could only go from window to window, marveling at the snow-covered landscape and watching the cutters and sleighs and the odd car go by.

The next day would be the one to remember. After a very hearty breakfast in the big, warm kitchen, we were told we were going "over town" to get some suitable clothing. The expedition was not as simple as it sounded. James the chauffeur was summoned and at the back door Nano gave him a kettle of boiling water, which he carried out to the barn where the Essex was housed. In those days, anti-freeze was almost unheard-of, and if you operated your car in the winter, you drained the water from the radiator while it was still warm, and filled it again the next morning.

The blocks of soapstone were heated for our feet, and there was a great deal of rummaging in closets and cedar chests for heavy winter garments, all smelling powerfully of mothballs. We were thoroughly encapsulated. James honked to signal that the Essex was at the front door and we carried the newspaper-wrapped soapstones to the car for our feet.

Our first stop was Smellie's Drug Store, which also sold newspapers, and Nano picked up her copy of the *Buffalo Courier-Express* (now, sadly, extinct). But our main destination was M. Cohn & Sons clothing store just down the block. I can still remember the aromas of wool, leather, rubber, and cotton. The first stop was for underwear—cotton long johns (luckily not the adult sizes, which came in scratchy red wool). Next came heavy wool stockings, wool trousers, felt boots, and rubber overshoes that buckled. Then shirts in both flannel and wool, a wool hat and—the crowning glory—sheepskin coats. We were ushered into a dressing room where we put on our new gear. We could hardly walk, but we were ready for twenty below.

When we left Cohn's we were allowed to walk back to the house, escorted by Nano. But we discovered we weren't going to be turned loose. Our acclimation to northern weather would follow a definite schedule—supervised by Nano. We could spend a little more time outdoors each day, for the most part walking over town on a specific errand. But that was the way I made my acquaintance of Hammondsport and the village shops that were on the main street and around the village park. In those days, everyone shopped at the village stores, including the farmers, who came to town on Saturdays on their horse-drawn wagons or in winter sleighs.

Nano's house was on Lake Street next to the Episcopal Church, St. James's, and diagonally across the intersection of Lake Street and Main from the stone schoolhouse. In the middle of the intersection stood the Civil War monument to the Grand Army of the Republic, the Civil War veterans. It was very impressive, with its granite column topped by the statue of an infantryman with his rifle. It was mounted on a circular grass-covered base that contained two cannons and two tiers of cannon balls. Unfortunately, as traffic increased, the monument grew smaller. The grass disappeared and the cannons and the cannon balls were moved to Pulteney Park (the village square), where they remained until World War II, when they were melted down to help win another war. Then, with the influx of very long tractor trailers, the monument itself took refuge on the lawn of the old schoolhouse.

Leaving Nano's house, you turned left and went around the church onto Main Street. The next street was Sheather, on which many of the village stores were located. You turned right, past two homes and came to Frey Opera Block, an imposing brick building four stories high and containing a real opera house as well as stores, apartments, and offices. Unfortunately because of fire safety rules the opera house was padlocked about the time of the First World War and never used again.

The Post Office occupied the first store space in the building. It has been moved twice since and is now at the other end of the village square. Next door was Frey's Dry Goods and then Grimes's Bakery. E. R. Wooding's millinery shop was next, then the A&P and after it a two-lane bowling alley. Next was a large, white shrine-like edifice. It was the Honor Roll, listing all the men from the village who had served in World War I, with gold stars beside some of the names. When I'd visited Hammondsport two summers before, there had been a barber shop in that spot, but it had burned down and been replaced by the Roll of Honor.

The store below the Honor Roll was Neff and Leighton's, the jewelers, who also sold magazines and papers. The establishment next door was one I never visited. It was the American Hotel, run by Fred Frey. Today it would be called a bar and grill, but this was during Prohibition, and speakeasy says it all. An alley next to the place led back to a row of stables where farmers left their teams and wagons while they shopped. Beyond the alley was the Village Building, a white frame structure. Upstairs was a large meeting room and downstairs were parked the village's fire-fighting equipment, consisting in those days of hand-pulled hose and ladder wagons and a motorized fire engine that was said to be impossible to start.

Next door was an establishment we would all get to know and love over the next thirty years and more. It was Smellie's Drug Store, "The Medical Hall," owned by "Pop" Smellie, who was later succeeded by his son Jim. Not only was it a full-fledged pharmacy, with many shelves of patent medicines, it also had a soda fountain and was the Western Union office. Many of the news stories about Glenn Curtiss's early exploits were filed from Smellie's. It was also famous for its sodas and had been a popular hangout for many of the young men who were students at the Curtiss Flying School in the years before the first World War.

The Masons had their rooms upstairs over Smellie's.

The next store was another one that became a special favorite of mine over the years: Freidell and Lacher's Hardware. When you went into the store you were greeted by the most wonderful blend of aromas, metal, oil, wood, and others you couldn't quite identify but that were typical of a real, old-time, hardware store, as it was, with a wall of drawers running from floor to ceiling along one wall, and attached to the front of each drawer was a sample of what the drawer contained: screws, bolts, hinges and so on. There was a roller-mounted ladder so the clerks could reach the highest drawers.

The appeal of Freidell and Lacher's was that it really was a complete hardware. There were the customary nuts, bolts, nails and screws, but many other fascinating items that were featured with the changing seasons. In the fall there would be a display of corn stalks, stuffed pheasants and partridges, shotguns and shells, clay pigeons, and hand traps. The store took great pride in its window, and rightly so.

At our ages, Boog and I were much more enamored of the pre-Christmas displays, especially the very popular Flexible Flyer sleds that came in all sizes. There were also ice skates, both kinds, the ones that clamped to your shoes and the absolute ultimate, skates that were attached to shoes. There would also be several pairs of skis, and a toboggan, all made by Northland.

We would wander around the store, past the case with the Daisy Air Rifles, the shotguns and the rifles and the cases that held the ammunition. At that time our primary interest was in downhill equipment, the sleds, skis, and toboggans. Mr. Freidell and his clerk, Chub Benham, were very patient with us. They knew that with Christmas coming, their store would be high on our list.

There was another grocery next to the hardware, the Cash Food Store, run by a Mr. Stever. And next to it was the Park Inn, the oldest building on the square, dating back to 1863. It had a dining room, and some sleeping accommodations upstairs. It was also the most popular bar in town, a favorite with the aeroplane pilots of an earlier day, who made pilgrimages to it whenever they came back for a visit.

Emmett Donnelly's meat market was next to the Park Inn, and, like the hardware, it was the real thing, only meat products and nothing prewrapped in plastic. A white tile floor sprinkled with sawdust. and a big wooden butcher's block behind the display cases with their sausages and weenies. Emmett was not only the town's leading butcher, he was a real entrepreneur and somebody said later that he had more irons in the fire than a four-armed blacksmith.

Cohn's, where we got outfitted for winter, was next to the meat market. It occupied two store fronts in the Union Block, Hammondsport's other skyscraper, a three-story brick building. The building's stairway was flanked by Cohn's on one side and the Gent's Club (two-chair barber shop, pool tables in the rear). It was a number of years before I was sent to the Gent's Club for my haircuts, and could listen to the tales of World War I told by the proprietor, Arthur (Swarty) Swartwood, who did his war service at Camp Yaphank on Long Island. He ran the local American Legion post for years.

The last outpost of the Union Block was the Park Pharmacy, which like Smellie's was essentially a drug store, but with a soda fountain. Later on it was Hammondsport's main source for pulp magazines, including "G8 and His Battle Aces," a favorite of mine.

On the second floor of the Union Block were some offices, one occupied by Dr. Donald Gleason, our dentist, a close family friend and the extremely popular Scoutmaster.

The third floor consisted of two very large rooms, occupied by the village's volunteer firemen. The Citizens Hose Company had one and the Hook and Ladder Company the other. There were folding doors separating the two and for dances and other major social events, they were thrown open to create a very large space. It was within a few years in the Citizens Hose room that my brother and I were introduced to the intricacies and social graces of ballroom dancing, under the elegant tutelage of Bob Hallenbeck, the blacksmith's son.

Mechanic Street, which runs perpendicular to Sheather, was a brief extension of the business district. Just behind the Park Pharmacy was The Fair Store, one deep room that was part of the clapboard home of Mrs. Veley, who owned the store. It was a catch-all kind of store that stocked everything from toys to dishes to knickknacks and cap pistols, caps, and holsters. Veley's was very popular, partly because nothing in it was too expensive.

Across the street was John Cameron's meat market, which like Emmett Donnelly's had sawdust on the floor and offered very good meat, particularly his lamb. On the Park side of Cameron's was George W. Fay's Feed Store, which adjoined his grocery store on the corner. Fay's was an independent market and consequently had more of a general store atmosphere. A lot of things that are sold packaged now were still sold in bulk in those days, and the beans and other foods gave it the most interesting aroma of any of the stores. Because of its feed store alongside, it did especially well with the farmers.

Across Sheather Street from Fay's stood the Hammondsport Hotel, a three-story wooden building, with a wide balcony overhanging the Sheather and Mechanic Street sides, creating covered sidewalks in bad weather. The lobby had large windows looking out on the village park. The lobby itself had a white tile floor. Its small six-sided white tiles looked a lot like those in Donnelly's meat market, which may have been a coincidence, although Emmett Donnelly owned the hotel too. The lobby was quite austere with some uncomfortable oak and leather chairs and a pair of potted palms for decor. The customers could sit and watch the passing parade, including the village watering trough, which was at one edge of the park. On the north side of the hotel was a kind of lean-to attachment that housed the bar.

Next to the Hammondsport Hotel was the Central Hotel, which as far as I knew was really just another bar. But beside it was one of our favorite destinations, the Park Theater, the village movie house. When we were very young we were allowed to attend the Saturday matinees. It was a while before we could attend the evening shows, and then only on Friday or Saturday nights. And no movie was complete without a visit to the establishment next door: Grimaldi's. It was an ice cream parlor, and they made their own delicious ice cream. Their milk shakes and sodas were sublime and they also carried a wide variety of candies. In later days, Mrs. Grimaldi's chocolate cake put Betty Crocker to shame forever.

Across the street from Grimaldi's stood "Pop" Love's popcorn stand that he operated from late spring to early fall. He was especially busy on Saturday nights, when all the farmers came to town to do their weekly shopping and all the townsfolk came down to hear the weekly concerts by the town band in the ornate bandstand in the park.

Pulteney Street ran alongside the park, parallel to Sheather Street. At Grimaldi's corner it angled left and became the state road along the west side of Keuka Lake. Just beyond Grimaldi's to the right was another bar (still there) and to the left was the blacksmith shop. The clang of the hammer on the anvil and the roaring forge were irresistible magnets, particularly when the horse being shod stepped on Mr. Hallenbeck's foot or kicked him. But we were seldom permitted to visit Mr. Hallenbeck because of the uncouth language that was occasionally (or frequently) to be heard.

On the corner across from Grimaldi's was Jim Jones's barber shop, where for a number of years we had our hair cut. It was more "genteel," which meant it had no pool tables. The Joneses were one of the two black families in Hammondsport. Mr. Jones's shop was slightly behind the times, and pleasantly so. There was always an aroma of tobacco smoke. But both Mother and Dad smoked regularly and after dinner Nano would regularly produce a gilt tin of Shepard's gold-tipped cigarettes from S.S. Pierce in Boston, so we were so well inured to tobacco smoke we really didn't even notice it.

The barber shop was long and narrow, with windows facing the street and on the right side, so it was well-lighted. There was only one chair, the proprietor's own, but the shop had a unique feature: a rack of personal shaving mugs. In earlier times, the town's leading citizens would go to the barber shop for their daily shave, and their individual mugs carried suitable designs and the owner's name handsomely inscribed. The cabinet must have had fifty spaces, but only half still had mugs in them—a symbol of changing times.

One of Mr. Jones's customers stays clearly in my mind. His name was Talmadge and he came in nearly every day for his shave. He was said to be well-off, but what intrigued me was the way he smoked his cigars right to the bitter end. He would stick a toothpick through the butt so he could savor the last few puffs. When he climbed into the chair he would toss the butt into the cuspidor, where it expired with a most satisfactory hiss.

Directly behind the barbershop was Mike Candeloupe's garage. In those days it was more important to know someone who could keep your car running than someone who sold gasoline. Mike did both and I never got a haircut without stopping to watch Mike take someone's motor apart or put it back together. My association and friendship with Mike lasted through seven decades.

Next to the barber shop was Smitty's Shoe Repair. It's probably another sign of changing times, but in those days it seems to me you kept shoes for quite a long time, although they needed re-heeling or re-soling fairly frequently. Today's shoes seem to go out of style before they have a chance to wear out. Smitty was a good repairman and his shop was another one of those places with a distinctive aroma. I love the smell of leather, and the special sharp tang of shoe polish. As a matter of fact, I think in those days I could have gone into most of the shops in town blindfolded, and identify where I was by the their special smells. Harder with meat markets and grocery stores, but the others would be no problem.

Conveniently next to Smith's Shoe Repair was the "Billy Will Use You Right" Shoe Store, owned by Billy Reynolds, whom we always called Mr. Reynolds, a bustling and very cheerful little man who was very fond of young people and showed it. It was one of our favorite stores to visit.

Next door was I.E. Eckert's grocery, with its own meat department and, so Nano always said, slightly higher quality merchandise (including gourmet items) than the chain stores carried. I always thought it was Carl Eckert's supply of soft soap that made the difference.

The next store was different from the others, which were mostly of frame construction. This one was small and made of rough-cut stone. It used to be a bank, and looks like it. (It is now a liquor store.) It was then J.O. Moore, Inc. "Postage Stamps for Philatelists." The shop was owned by "Uncle" Lad Seely, who was formerly the European sales manager for the Curtiss Aeroplane Company. Mother stayed with the Seelys in London in February 1916 and they hosted Mother and Dad's wedding at that time. Later I became an ardent stamp collector and a regular after-school customer at the Moore establishment, looking through the "penny specials."

Above Moore's were rooms that had had a varied career: as a restaurant, a bar, a grocery store, and again a restaurant. Next door was a large frame building that housed F.C. Faucett's Furniture Store and Undertaking Parlor and alongside it was Amy and Roma Marsh's Beauty Parlor. The last building, then being used as Faucett's rug and carpet annex, was a significant village landmark. It was the wooden building that had housed Glenn Curtiss's bicycle repair business when he began his career, with the support of Pop Smellie and other local backers. The career led on to motorcycles, speed records, lightweight engines, then the pioneering airplanes like the June Bug and at last a permanent place in history as "The Father of Naval Aviation" and a man who helped change the nature of the world.

Diagonally opposite the former bicycle shop was what seemed to be a private dwelling but was actually the home of the *Hammondsport Herald*, our local weekly, whose editor and publisher was the same Lad Seely who'd been a Curtiss sales manager and who owned the stamp store. The *Herald* was another fascinating place, with its own distinctive aromas and sounds: the smell of the ink and the hot lead in the linotype machine, the rumbling thump of the big presses when the weekly was being printed and the rapid clatter of the job press doing envelopes or letterheads. I was occasionally put to work folding and stuffing, or running errands.

At one time I was also a cub reporter for the *Herald*, covering local and school news. I was reimbursed five cents an inch for anything that could be deciphered from my rough notes (and was thought fit to print). My major journalistic coup was a story about one of the sailboats that had sailed its final race and was moored to a piling at the head of the lake, firmly surrounded, when I wrote my piece, by thick ice. Uncle Charlie had made me a present of it, as it was and where it was. For weeks I'd been cajoling my pals to walk over to the head of the lake with me and help me chop around the hull to keep the ice from crushing it. I wasn't as persuasive as Tom Sawyer with his fence-painting scheme and very shortly I had no pals to help me.

Then I got the idea of selling it and wrote an ad (the price was $25), thinly disguised as a news story for the *Herald*. I was the proud author of a five-inch article called "The Old Skidoo." Unfortunately the editor cut out the last paragraph with the sales pitch and the request to call me. Nobody did.

The village's only really new building in those days, the Bank of Hammondsport, stood next to the *Herald* on the south side of the village square. It was a single-story brick structure with shiny brass railings on the steps and ornamental lamps. God and Mammon existed side by side, because alongside the bank was the handsome Presbyterian Church with its tall, slender steeple containing a four-faced clock.

Turning right and heading back up Sheather Street there stood three houses. The first was the home and office of P.D. (Doc) Green, the village's second dentist. Next was the office of Dr. John Lawrence, the village's second doctor. On the corner lived Melville Chapman, who was the town's Chevrolet dealer, destined to be Hammondsport's last new car dealership.

Diagonally across Main Street from the Chapman home lived Ben Casterline, who operated the Texaco gas station just across the Bath and Hammondsport railroad tracks at the lower end of Main Street.

Ben's house was another village landmark, because it had been Lulu Mott's boarding house, a legendary place where my father and many of the early students at the Curtiss Flying School boarded.

Next door to Ben's house stood a beautiful, one-story house in the Greek Revival style. (An itinerant house-builder with a taste for the Greek Revival style had paused in Hammondsport in the 19th century and several houses bear his "signature.") It was more common later to move houses than to demolish them, and this house had originally stood where the bank was built. It was owned by Walter Drew, who was the town's only lawyer.

I'd made the acquaintance of the Drews on our first summer visit. They lived in back of Nano's house, and they were such good friends that when Nano built an eight-foot-high fence along the back yard, she had a door cut into it so she could visit the Drews without having to walk around the church, and vice-versa.

The Drews had no children of their own but they were wonderful foster parents to all the children in the neighborhood. There were always freshly-baked cookies and glasses of milk to be had. And Mrs. Drew gave me an unforgettable treat: my first ride in a horse-drawn buggy. We drove around town and then across the valley to "the Farm," the wonderful place Uncle Charlie had just bought from Charles Kingsley.

On our ride we passed "the water wagon." This was a huge cask, containing five or six hundred gallons of water, pulled by a team of horses and used to sprinkle the village streets, nearly all of which were still dirt. Automobiles raised the dust as horses and carriages did not. The wagon refilled at the village hydrants. Mrs. Drew knew the operator of the water wagon and arranged for me to be picked up at the hydrant in front of the church the next morning. I was there bright and early and spent a glorious time sitting high behind the horses and feeling quite important.

That was the last year there were steam boats operating on the lake, and although I never rode on one I remember sitting on the dock and watching them arrive and depart. But the next year the state paved the road up the west side of the lake and a contractor paved the village streets. So that when we moved north two years later, both the steamers and the water wagon were already history.

Nano's House

DAD WAS STILL winding up his affairs in New Orleans and the house in Williamsville was going to require extensive remodeling, so Mother and Boog and I stayed on in Hammondsport. We entered the local school, which was diagonally across the intersection from the house, instead of a ten-block walk away, and there we would finish the term.

There was a lot of getting-used-to in our new situation. For one thing, it was a household dominated by women: Mother, Mildred, the nurse and sitter, and Black Eva, handywoman and beloved permanent fixture. And Nano. As someone once said, Nano had a whim of iron. She was a strict disciplinarian and she punished all infractions of her orders with a heavy dusting with a leather riding crop. She was very good with it. I knew, and still remember. Boog and I didn't realize it at the time, but we missed Dad's leadership and his assumed authority. He and Mother were a good team. She gave the orders in our world and, when and if it was necessary, Dad administered a razor strop.

We did have a favorite male visitor—Uncle Charlie, who stopped by every morning for a second breakfast on his way to the winery. Occasionally on a Saturday he would pick me up and take me to the Cellar, as we called the winery, with him. I still remember those walks through the cool vaults, filled with thousands of cobwebby bottles and smelling faintly of sulphur, which was burned to keep down mildew.

Uncle Kid, Nano's younger son, was just back from his elopement with Kitty Masson, a great crisis in my grandmother's life, as she saw things. Kid would appear, hat in hand like a penitent, and receive a pretty frosty greeting. It was some time before Kid and his bride were welcomed back, but eventually they were.

There were various pleasures that helped Boog and me cope with our new regime. One was the excitement of a new school and new pals. There were also the big barn and the mysteries of the house with its many padlocked doors. Not only the wine cupboards in the front cellar, but the attic door (a heavy brass padlock and chain), two tool rooms, what had been the groom's room in horse and buggy days, and the upstairs of the barn. Nano carried a ring of keys that would have done the turnkey at the Tower of London proud.

The forbidden areas naturally acted like magnets on Boog and me. I discovered that there was just enough play in the chain on the attic door so that I could squeeze between the door and the jamb. One day I did and tiptoed through a wonderland, actually composed of broken toys and ancient athletic gear. I was savoring my triumph when I heard the click of the padlock and the rattle of the chain on the door at the foot of the attic stairs. I ducked behind the soft water cistern and under a table. The lights came on and Nano came in and I figured my goose was cooked. But no, she found something in a drawer and went back downstairs. I was safe. But when I got to the door I found that Nano had tightened the chain and I couldn't squeeze through. I stood there peeking through the crack when, surely enough, Nano reappeared with her ring of keys in one hand and her faithful riding crop in the other. I received a very good dusting.

Grandmother Champlin was an interesting person. With her strong will she certainly took after her mother, Helen McDowell Malburn, who in 1869 divorced her husband in Illinois, packed up her children, Georgia (Nano), then six, and Will, aged one, traveled by covered wagon to Colorado and settled in Colorado Springs. Her uncle, A. Cameron Hunt, was governor of the territory, but my great-grandmother didn't try to capitalize on the relationship. She opened a restaurant at the Colorado Springs stage stop and before she was through, she was operating restaurants at all the stage stops between Colorado Springs and Pueblo.

I put more of Helen's story together in the 1970s when I visited the Colorado Springs Historical Society and read through their thick and fascinating file on her. One of the clippings recorded the fact that Helen's daughter, Georgia, was leaving for the east to attend St. Agnes School in Albany. Georgia had another uncle, John Davis, who lived in Hammondsport, and it was while visiting him from school that she met Charles Addison Champlin and so commenced what you might call my part of the family history. Nano, incidentally, was also descended from the Brewsters, who were on the Mayflower's passenger list.

She was, all in all, quite a package, and my feelings about her after all these years are mixed. I was proud that she came from such sturdy pioneer stock. I admired her love of the outdoors. She was a fine gardener, and she helped me develop a love for these things. I enjoyed long walks with her in the woods and up the glens that surround Hammondsport.

Looking back at the past, it is difficult not to let your emotions color your views of it. Its almost too easy to remember long, sunny hours and to forget or to suppress other episodes that were pertinent, and not so pleasant. It would take an experienced psychologist to help me sort out my feelings. It might even have been better not to have said even this; then again maybe it is as well that I do. The hours were not all sunny in Nano's house.

Gink

1886–1954

MY FATHER, William Ellwood Doherty, was born in Buffalo, New York, in 1886 and it was his home for nearly twenty-five years. His father, a first generation Irishman, was for many years the police commissioner. His mother was born in Costa Rica to an internationally respected English financier and the daughter of an aristocratic Spanish family. Both of his parents were active in civic affairs, his father in politics, clubs, and fraternal orders (he was a thirty-second-degree Mason). His mother was active in the symphony guild, the library, and the museums.

When he was sixteen, my father went to Ridley College and from there to the University of Toronto. It was during the summer vacation between Ridley and the university that Dad landed his first job. It was as an engineering test driver with the Thomas Automobile Company. He was always interested in anything mechanical, and delighted to be paid for doing something he admired so much.

Many years later he was driving Duane and me to Ridley and we were descending the hill down the Niagara escarpment into Lewiston. He remarked that he'd driven the hill many times in the past: it was part of the test for a Thomas car. They had to make it up the hill in high gear to pass the test. It was quite a hill and I wondered how they made it in those days.

One day in June of 1911, during his test-driving days, Gink learned that a former classmate at the University of Toronto, John A. D. McCurdy, would be giving a flying exhibition just outside Buffalo. McCurdy had been a member of the Aerial Experiment Association, which had been founded by Alexander Graham Bell. Shortly after the death of AEA member Lieutenant Thomas Selfridge—he was a passenger on an Army test fight piloted by Orville Wright and became the first aerial fatality—the AEA was dissolved and McCurdy joined the Curtiss Company as a member of the exhibition flying team.

Gink drove one of the Thomas cars to the field where the exhibition was to take place. When it was over, Gink offered to drive McCurdy to the DL & W station for the train to Bath and the connection to Hammondsport. They were running late and would have to hurry to make the train. In conjunction with his test work, Gink had done some auto racing, and he was now speeding through the city to get to the station. They came to an intersection where two trolley cars were approaching from opposite directions on the cross street. Instead of stopping, Gink sped up and passed between the two streetcars, as in a silent comedy. When McCurdy opened his eyes again and saw that Gink was quite unconcerned, he said, "With that sense of judgment and timing, you should go into aviation. Come on down to Hammondsport and we'll teach you to fly."

"Great!" says Gink. He parked the car at the station, called his boss at Thomas to say where he'd left it and caught the train with John McCurdy.

When he reached Hammondsport, he enrolled in the Curtiss Flying School. John must have told G.H. (as Curtiss was called) about the trolley episode, because Curtiss taught him personally, possibly to keep a close eye on him. Gink took a room at Lulu Mott's famous boarding house, where "Spuds" Ellison and Jack Towers (US Navy pilots No. 1 and No. 3) lived, along with Charlie Whitmer and McCurdy himself.

After graduating from the Flying School on July 11, 1911, Dad joined the Exhibition Flying Team. Although he learned to fly on land planes and flew them with the Exhibition Team, Gink became very interested in "water flying" and became a very skilled seaplane pilot. At that time Curtiss was in the early stages of developing the flying boat. Following a series of successful experiments with hydroplanes at his winter operation near San Diego, Curtiss built a special hydroplane for the Navy, which had been delivered in 1911.

In the late spring of 1914, Gink was back in Hammondsport

testing the Model E Flying Boats. More importantly in his career, the Smithsonian Institution had sent to Hammondsport the Langley Aerodrome. (This was the catapult-launched aeroplane designed by Professor Samuel Pierpont Langley. On its crucial experimental launch it had sunk in the Potomac.) Curtiss would conduct tests to prove or disprove that Professor Langley's aeronautical theories were correct.

There were two reasons for testing the Langley craft in Hammondsport. The "Old Guard" at the Smithsonian wanted to vindicate Professor Langley by a demonstration that his machine could indeed fly successfully. At the same time, Curtiss was embroiled in patent disputes with the Wrights. He wanted to see the "'Drome" flown successfully and thereby prove that it antedated the Wright Flyer as a lighter-than-air craft, and incidentally void some of the Wrights' patents.

Gink always claimed that only minimum modifications were carried out in readying the Langley craft for the flight tests. Three floats which weighed about three hundred pounds were installed so it could operate from Keuka Lake. Some extra bracing was needed to support the floats. Because of two previous dunkings in the Potomac, the Manly engine would only develop forty-five horsepower instead of the original fifty-two. Because of the value and the fragility of the engine, tests of it were held to a minimum. It is my understanding that only two actual flights were attempted with the Manly engine. Curtiss himself piloted the first one, when the "'Drome" lifted clear of the water. Gink piloted the second test. Following these runs the Manly engine was removed and an eighty horsepower Curtiss engine with a tractor propeller was installed.

The Langley flight tests continued all summer, using the Curtiss engine and the tractor propeller configuration. Adjustments were made which changed the angle of attack of the wings. There were no ailerons for lateral control. Professor Langley felt that by having about twenty degrees dihedral for each wing the "'Drome" would be self-stabilizing as the upper wing would develop less lift. At the same time this complicated making a turn because the outer wing would be traveling faster and thereby developing more lift. This resulted in banking into the turn, but unless the pilot was careful the turns would start to tighten, causing what we know as a spiral dive. A lot of altitude can be lost, and since the Langley never flew much higher than fifty feet, there wasn't much margin for error. Consequently what turns were made were very shallow and covered a wide area.

One flight in particular caused a considerable amount of comment. Some adjustments had been made in the rigging, and it was to be a short hop to see the effect of the adjustments on the take-off run. There was a fairly strong north wind blowing. The "'Drome" took off quickly and wanted to continue to climb. When the throttle was retarded, up came the nose and only by maintaining full throttle was it possible to maintain level flight. (One of Harry Benner's best shots of the Langley clearly shows Gink piloting the machine with the control column against the center brace.) He attempted to throttle back several times but each time with the nose pitching up. He continued on down the lake until he reached Bluff Point. He flew into its lee, where the wind wasn't so strong and the waves were smaller. Throttling very gingerly, Gink kept the plane in a nose-high attitude until the stern float touched water and slowed the plane down until it came to rest on all three floats. The crash boat soon arrived and took the plane in tow. They decided it wouldn't be smart to try to fly back until they determined what caused the peculiar flight characteristics.

G.H. was very much interested in Gink's reports on the flight. The other pilots kiddingly suggested that Gink had really just been heading for the Keuka Hotel and some refreshments, and the crash boat just got there too soon.

Gink obviously found the Langley a most unusual aircraft to fly, with its limited maneuverability and its wide turning radius. But he was also impressed with its size. It had a wingspan of forty-five feet and an overall length of sixty feet, dwarfing all the Curtiss planes except the new America, the mahogany-hulled flying boat Curtiss had designed for Rodman Wanamaker.

The pilot's seat in the Langley's original configuration was below the forward wing. This proved very unsatisfactory. On two previous attempts in Washington, the pilot, Charles Manly, had ended up in the water, beneath the machine. The first flights in Hammondsport, with the original engine, were made with the seat still under the wing. But when the engines were exchanged the pilot was perched on an orange crate (as Gink called it) above the entire structure and very much exposed. Gink always said that the Langley test flights were some of his most interesting experiences in aviation.

After the successful flights of the Langley Aerodrome at Hammondsport, the Smithsonian published a pamphlet affirming that the Langley Aerodrome was the first powered aircraft capable of human flight. This of course infuriated the Wrights and it took thirty years of negotiations before a truce was achieved and the original Wright Flyer was returned to the U.S. and displayed in the Smithsonian.

In the fall of 1914 Gink and J. Lansing (Lanny) Callan were dispatched to Italy and loaned by Curtiss to the Italian Naval Air Service, which had taken delivery of a number of Curtiss "F" Flying Boats. Gink and Lanny would be responsible for training the naval operators and would be based at the big Italian naval base at Taranto. There were British and French ships there as well, which resulted in some jolly international get-togethers.

The training wasn't easy, either for the pilots or the mechanics who had come from Hammondsport with them. It was easier for the pilots, because any movement of the controls produced a definite result. It was harder teaching the Italian mechanics how to keep an OX-5 engine running like a sewing machine, or to convey the mysteries of setting the right gap on a spark plug.

The student pilots were generally quite adept but inclined to be overconfident. At first the instructors informed the students the night before they were to solo. This was a mistake. The next morning the ramp would be crowded with family members eager to see their boy make like big bird. One of them decided to show what a magnifico pilot he was—until he caught a wing in the water and cartwheeled into the bay. Thereafter the students got no overnight warning but somehow a gala group would always be waiting. The crash boat was always alerted and the crowd wasn't often disappointed.

The work was arduous and occasionally tragic, but Gink and Lanny had compensations (including a per diem of $90 a day). There were parties, and occasionally days off in the best hotels in Rome.

But their duties weren't confined to instruction. They saw no reason why their young pilots shouldn't help the war effort by flying submarine patrols, since the Germans were active in both the Mediterranean and the Adriatic. Gink himself flew patrols and on two occasions caused what would be called flaps in World War II.

The first incident was on a Monday, after a particularly active weekend in Rome. Gink was out in the Adriatic, looking for a U-boat that had been sighted in the shipping lanes. His official report said that after a short time his engine began to overheat and, since there was little wind and the sea was calm, he landed and shut down the engine so it could cool off. His confidential version for Lanny was that, after the hard weekend, the drone of the engine was making him sleepy. He thought it might be a good idea to take a short nap to revive himself. He did, and was soon sound asleep. He must have overslept because back at the base he was overdue and presumed down at sea. Rescue actions were launched, but before they were underway Gink, refreshed by his nap, cranked up, continued on his patrol until his fuel ran low and he flew back to base.

The official report was accepted by the top brass, but the unofficial version also made the rounds. And so it was that on another Adriatic patrol a few days later, Gink developed real engine trouble and had to put down in the water. This time no search and rescue efforts were launched and Gink spent a very uncomfortable thirty-six hours on a rainswept, choppy sea, going from wingtip to wingtip to keep his plane afloat, and bailing like mad. On the afternoon of the second day he was spotted by an Italian destroyer and hoisted aboard. When they returned to Taranto, the appearance of both the aircraft and the pilot after the ordeal forestalled any facetious remarks anybody might have made after the first incident.

The Italian experience was a mixed bag—pride in training young pilots and creating a new service, sorrow when one of the trainees was killed, pleasure at the parties that let you forget petrol and castor oil fumes and the stress of responsibilities. And there were adventures, like Gink's own, and the time a storm came up quickly when one of the flying boats was not ashore but anchored in the bay. The surf was too rough to beach the aircraft. The solution was to swim out, clamber aboard, start the engine and, by carefully coordinating the throttle and the controls, hold the plane into the wind and keep it level, to prevent the anchor mooring from tearing loose from the thin wooden hull. The squall passed through and the plane, unharmed, could be beached.

Another storm had a very long after-history. Gink was returning from another Adriatic patrol and saw a heavy line of storm clouds building up between him and the base at Taranto. Storms in general were to be avoided, especially one of this magnitude. He spotted a small, sheltered bay that had a sloping sandy beach. Up from the beach was a cluster of tents. He landed without incident and taxied to the beach, to be greeted by a number of men speaking English. They were just about to have their tea, and would Gink like to join them. They were British anthropologists from the British Museum, on a dig for Etruscan artifacts. After tea they showed Gink their findings to date, beautifully preserved and decorated earthenware from the third and fourth centuries B.C.

The storm passed and Gink thought it wise to head to base before he was reported missing again. He thanked his hosts and asked if there were anything they needed. As they pushed his plane back into the water, they confessed that they had a crisis: they were out of Pimm's Pink Gin. As it happened, Gink and Lanny had made many Royal Navy friends in Taranto and Gink had no trouble appropriating two cases of the stuff. He flew back to the bay with the Pink Gin on the passenger seat.

The story ends something like fifty years later. I was cleaning out the lower level of the Champlin barn, preparing to remodel it into an apartment for my wife and myself. I uncovered a very large wooden crate, banded and sealed so tightly I had to use a crow-bar to loosen the boards. It was tightly packed with wood shavings and some paper-wrapped objects I took in the house and showed to Gink. "So you found those," he said. And with some coaxing, I learned the story of the Pink Gin and the artifacts. There were twenty-six pieces, from a small oil lamp to winged vases sixteen inches high, from the fourth century B.C. After Gink died, Mother wanted the collection to be given as a memorial to him. So the collection is now in the Thompson Museum at Cornell. One piece, an Apulian kantharof, is in the W. Ellwood (Gink) Doherty Display at the Curtiss Museum in Hammondsport.

Both Lanny and Gink were decorated by the King of Italy, Victor

Emmanuel, and made Chevaliers of the Legion of Honor by the French. The students they trained became the leaders of the Italian Naval Flying Service through the rest of the war and for the next two decades. One of their students, Italo Balbo, in 1933 commanded a flight of Savoie-Marchettis, very large, twin-hulled float boats that circumnavigated the earth and landed in Chicago at the 1933 World's Fair.

The Curtiss operation in Italy was phased out in 1916 and Gink and Lanny went to England for a spot of leave. London turned out to be a reunion town, a kind of Hammondsport UK. Lad Seely, the sales manager for the Curtiss company, was there with his wife, Peg. Jack Towers, USN, who learned to fly in Hammondsport, was an observer attached to the U.S. Embassy. Cyril Porte of the Royal Navy, who had flown the Curtiss flying boat *America*, was a frequent visitor to London. And, perhaps not too surprising, Gladys Champlin, also of Hammondsport, was visiting Lad and Peg Seeley.

A social highlight of the London season took place on February 16, 1916, in St. Margaret's Church, Piccadilly, when Gladys Helen Champlin was married to W. Ellwood (Gink) Doherty.

Gink's next assignment was to repeat the Italian program with the Spanish Naval Air Arm, and in February what could be finer for a honeymoon than the sunny coast of Spain. The Spanish navy base was located near a fashionable seaside resort, and the newlyweds set up housekeeping in a waterfront hotel. From their balcony they had a wonderful vista of white sand beach and the sparkling blue waters of the Mediterranean beyond. Spain was technically neutral and it was pleasant to leave the anxieties and austerities of England and Italy. It was hard to believe that an overnight train ride could transport you to a completely new world.

Gink left in the early morning for the base and didn't return until early evening. So the bride kept herself busy with shopping, walking on the beach, and reading. She usually ended up having tea on the veranda. There was another woman, obviously an American, who was also a regular for afternoon tea. Before long the two met and began taking tea together. The other woman was from Philadelphia, very beautiful, but quite reserved. She and her husband had recently arrived from Philadelphia, but she didn't volunteer anything more specific.

Gink was meantime quite satisfied with the progress of the program. The fact that Spain wasn't at war eliminated some of the pressures and tensions, There was even a siesta after lunch, although Gink never adopted the habit and used the time for exercise instead. He'd always been interested in contact sports, boxing especially, because of a bit of family history.

His father, as I've said, was a tough Irish politician, police commissioner of Buffalo, but his mother was of aristocratic Spanish descent, with tastes to match. She dressed her son in Little Lord Fauntleroy suits of black velvet, with a wide white collar and white knee stockings. It doesn't take a lot of imagination to hear the hoots of scorn and derision he got from his contemporaries on the street—"young toughs," in his mother's view. Many a time, his father would return from the office to be greeted by an indignant wife and a bruised, bloody and weeping young Ellwood.

One day, he took Ellwood as if to the office, but stopped instead at a gym run by an Irish friend of his, Paddy Something-or-Other, who had been a better-than-average welterweight. The father handed Ellwood over to Paddy said, "Teach this kid to fight; he's getting the s— kicked out of him."

And so it was that Ellwood became a pretty good scrapper and eventually a very clever boxer. Their neighborhood toughs got their comeuppance and he continued boxing in school. At the university he became Intercollegiate Lightweight Champion. It was at this time that he was nicknamed Gink and shed the accursed Ellwood. [Tony didn't like "Ellwood" either, but found it less accursed with a single "l," and spelled it Elwood all his adult life.]

It was because of his history in boxing that he was fascinated to learn that an American heavyweight had a training camp nearby. His name was Jack Johnson, and he was in fact the heavyweight champion, the first black to hold the title. Johnson was not a popular champion—among whites—and when he eloped with a white society girl from Philadelphia, all hell broke loose and the ostracized couple took refuge in Spain.

Gink went to Johnson's camp and introduced himself and they

became good friends. In the course of time Gink actually got in the ring and sparred with Johnson. He was quick enough so he wasn't there when Johnson threw one of those big blockbusters of his—or so Gink said. They did develop a good friendship, and the first time they got together for dinner, they were surprised to learn that their wives were already good friends, from their afternoon teas.

A Change in Plans

1925

IT IS APPARENT that I didn't adapt readily to that male-less household. Dad was settling into his new job in Buffalo and working with the architect and contractors on our new house in Williamsville. He could only spend the occasional weekend with us, and when he did he, too, was a guest. When he was in residence it actually felt good to be reprimanded by a male voice, although I do remember that I would catch myself looking over my shoulder to see if Grandmother might countermand what he'd said.

There was one glorious event I remember very well. I accompanied Mother to Buffalo to inspect the progress on the new house. Mother was well along with her pregnancy with our brother-to-be, Peter. Dad met us at the station with his new Mercer roadster, a very sporty vehicle with a rumble seat. We had dinner at the Saturn Club, where Dad was living until we moved into the new house. The architect, Duane Lyman, Dad's closest friend, and his wife "Aunt" Bessie joined us for the evening, and she and Mother discussed patterns, colors, and other boring stuff.

The next morning we went out to inspect the house. I was very impressed with the house itself and the spacious grounds. There was even a small stream on the property. There was a big attic (no lock), where I was told I could set up my Lionel train. There wasn't room at Grandmother's.

The next afternoon we met Uncle Duane at his office to pick up the final version of the blueprints to show Grandmother. I remember being very impressed with the main drafting room. I'd seen blueprints on construction sites I used to visit (and get ejected from) in New Orleans. That weekend in Buffalo, seeing the almost-completed house and watching plans for new structures being created in the office, was the beginning of a love affair with architecture that has lasted all my life.

At dinner the night before Mother was bubbling over with enthusiasm and anticipation. After years of gypsying from city to city, rented apartment to rented apartment, we were going to have a house of our own. The happy mood on the train ride lasted until we were back in the house at Hammondsport. Grandmother did not jump for joy at Mother's descriptions of the house, or the fact that it was nearly completed. Her response was really an ultimatum: there would be no moving to Buffalo until the baby was born and old enough to travel.

The summer of 1925 started pleasantly enough, as I've said. What I didn't realize at the time was that all the events in the household revolved around the arrival of the new baby. For reasons I've never understood, Nano took me to Niagara Falls a day or two before the baby was to be born. She had lived there for several years following my grandfather's unfortunate demise. We actually had a great time, visiting her old friends and familiar places.

When we got back to Hammondsport, everything had changed, and the household revolved around the new baby. We tiptoed up the front stairs past the nursery, if we were brash enough not to use the back stairs as we were supposed to.

At eight, I wasn't really aware of the situation that was developing in the house, but I could feel the tension, especially when Dad drove down from Buffalo and brought up the timing of the move to Buffalo. Our furniture from New Orleans and our belongings from Marblehead (which had been in storage in Boston), were all temporarily stored in Grandmother's barn, awaiting shipment to Buffalo.

Mother and Dad had planned to be in Buffalo before the new school year began. But in late August, although I don't remember the actual circumstances, Grandmother took to her bed with a mysterious but debilitating ailment. Due to circumstances beyond our control, as they say, the move to Buffalo was not to be, just then. Actually the house wasn't yet quite ready. But Dad owned some commercial properties, including apartments, in Buffalo and wanted to move us into one of them, reuniting the family at last.

It was only in his and my later years that I realized there was an unusual factor that made Dad reluctant to live in Hammondsport. One was that the Curtiss student pilots, of whom Dad had been one, were attractive and dashing young men who made a great hit with the townspeople—and the town belles. The local swains apparently developed a resentment of the pilots that never entirely went away. No former flight student was ever invited to join the exclusive all-male Glenwood Club, for example. Memories die hard.

As the months went on, we settled into a routine that was neither fish nor fowl. We loved the outdoor activities possible in Hammondsport (not to be had in Buffalo, as Grandmother once pointedly reminded us). But the uncertainty about the move kept Boog and me off balance, as I'm sure it did Mother, torn between duty and desire.

The summer that Dad took me to summer camp on Georgian Bay (I was bitterly homesick but made what turned out to be some lifelong friendships), Mother met me in Toronto and Dad met us at the Buffalo station. We drove out to Williamsville to see the house. It was finished at last, but empty.

The next summer Dad took Mother and Boog and me to Marblehead. It had been their first home. Mother had always spoken of it with great nostalgic fondness. They'd made many friends and we visited with some of them. Starling Burgess was the marine architect who had designed the last two J boats to win the America's Cup. He headed the Burgess Aeroplane Company, where Dad had been a test pilot. Frank Payone was also a marine architect, who had designed and built the *Yankee*, another J boat contender. We dined at the Eastern Yacht Club, where Dad and Mom had been members.

When we got back to Hammondsport, though, there'd been no movement toward Buffalo, and the situation was beginning to tell on me psychologically. I started to get into trouble at home and at school. When Dad came down from Buffalo, we'd drive over to the cottage and have a man-to-man talk, with Dad holding a written list of transgressions reported by both Mother and Grandmother. Boog and his friends were into sports, baseball particularly. My pals and I preferred hiking and fishing (we were too young for hunting licenses). What we did was energetic, but it didn't require the discipline of sports and it didn't provide an adequate outlet for my pent-up frustrations. I got into fights, disobeyed orders all too often, and was thoroughly unpleasant.

Uncle Charlie was aware what was behind my rebelliousness and tried to help. When he was working on his A boat, the *Deltox*, he would let me ride the tow down to Keuka. One Christmas Dad gave me a Winchester Special .22 rifle, adored by Boog and me, loathed by Grandmother. Uncle Charlie solved the problem by letting me keep the rifle in the gun cabinet at the farm. I could shoot it any time he or Dad were around to accompany me.

Boog and Jack Seely accompanied me to the Georgian Bay summer camp that one summer, when I proceeded to get in one scrape after another, if not for fighting then for swiping candy bars in the tuck shop. It's a miracle I wasn't tossed out.

In fateful 1929, there was a moment of glory just before everything went sour. Dad shook up the town a bit by arriving in one of the agency's Rolls-Royces. He surprised the family even more by disclosing that he was dickering to buy Boericke's Point, one of the widest and finest on the lake. The Boericke house, almost a mansion, was a fascinating barn of a place, built in 1886. A 1918 Pierce-Arrow limousine was included in the asking price: $15,000. The family lived in Philadelphia but had been pioneer cottagers on the lake. Some of them must have died off. We drove down in the Rolls, met the caretaker and inspected the place. Boog and I were fascinated, naturally, but I think Mother was a little dubious. Dad told me years later he'd gotten to the point where he decided, "If you can't beat 'em, outflank 'em."

The Rolls was black. Perfect symbolism. A few weeks later the stock market crashed. Not long after, Rolls ceased their production in America; their Buffalo agency closed and Dad was on the street. Closer to home, the family winery, already suffering under Prohibition, began to suffer more.

After Uncle Harry Champlin died, Uncle Charlie and Kid started an operation that was just inside the law. The Taylor Wine Company was selling grape juice that with a little help and encouragement would turn into wine. The uncles went several steps further. They began marketing a blend of champagne juices (the cuvee, actually) that with help would turn into wine but that with more skilled help would turn into champagne. The skilled help was usually Uncle Kid, who went to homes and performed the necessary procedures. These had to be performed over a period of time; the service did not come cheap and unfortunately the majority of the customers were severely damaged if not ruined by the stock market crash. And so a source of vital income for the winery dried up.

I don't know how much Dad had invested in the market (or had bought on margin like everybody else). But he was mortally wounded financially by the crash. The commercial properties went first. The house in Williamsville had been rented to a stockbroker who suddenly couldn't pay the rent. Dad let stay him on in the house anyway, until the bank foreclosed the property. I didn't really understand what was going on, but I was shocked, stunned, by the idea that the house—our house—was gone. Mother was devastated, as I learned later. Only Grandmother wasn't.

What it meant to the Dohertys was that our stay in Hammondsport was no longer temporary.

To the casual observer, our household wasn't a divided camp. When Dad began working for the winery, he naturally joined us at Grandmother's. By now I don't think there was ever any hope that we would have our own home. The situation became even more strange. While there was never any outright unpleasantness, there were definite tensions, and not too far below the surface, either. Sometimes icy politeness is crueler than sharp rebuke, as I realize looking back. All in all, it wasn't a comfortable atmosphere, but it was generally tolerable.

In the circumstances, the cottage at the head of the lake was a godsend. As soon as school was out, Mother, Dad, and we three boys, and a couple of dogs, would move to the cottage for the summer. We all loved it; we were a family again, minus Grandmother's presence.

Actually, those last several years before World War II are pleasant to look back upon. They now seem years beyond recall, or recalling. They were good years, too, from the standpoint of the family. There were still undercurrents of tension, but somehow we'd all learned to adjust our goings-on to minimize the chance of open hostility. It was a kind of artificial or thin-ice tranquillity, but it let us enjoy some golden days and ignore the gathering storm clouds in Europe.

A Change of Schools

1930

THERE WAS NO summer camp for us in 1930, no trip to Marblehead. I cobbled up a sailboat from a rowboat Uncle Charlie had given me and I spent a great deal of time on the lake. Ironically the boat figured in my first brush with the law—and my last, I might add.

That spring a man from Corning had asked and received permission from Uncle Charlie to pitch a small tent and camp at the head of the lake. He camped there for several weeks and then disappeared, and in time the tent collapsed. In September, Charlie Snell and I were sailing past and Charlie spotted the tent and said it looked like it had been abandoned. I agreed and said I was sure Uncle Charlie would be glad to have the unsightly mess removed from the beach.

This we did, loaded it in the boat and later set it up in the gully behind the Curtiss factory. We spent several weekends camping out in it. One afternoon I came home from school and was told that Billy Leary, the chief of police, wanted to see me at his office in the Municipal Building.

When I got there, Ed Percy and his father, Archie Squires and his father, and Charlie Snell were all there, looking very serious. It seems that Ed and Charlie, who lived not far from each other, had decided to move the tent from its inconvenient location in the gully to Ed's front yard. There its owner, the man from Corning, spotted it and went to the police chief. My buddies had all decided that I was to blame for their predicament, and I had to agree. When I owned up to it, Mr. Percy said, "Officer, he's telling the truth." The owner was glad to retrieve his tent and did not press charges. But for a while I was blacklisted by my pals' families and under virtual house arrest at home.

I delayed going home as long as I could, walking around the block, stopping in the barn and sitting on a furniture crate to think about my dilemma. I realized there was nothing to do but face the music. Actually I got off relatively lightly, for the moment. Uncle Charlie came over and we had a heart-to-heart talk about honesty, and then my house arrest began.

The episode put me in the family spotlight, and every transgression, however slight (there were some), got full-blown family attention. My deportment didn't seem to be improving, so it was decided that enrolling me in a military school might do me a lot of good. A local man, Louis Rose, was attending Carson Long Institute near Harrisburg and was a very well-mannered young fellow. Perhaps it could work miracles and civilize me.

So on a cold February day, Uncle Charlie loaded me and my trunk into Grandmother's Chevy and deposited me on the doorstep of the school. (Dad had gone to New York and was trying to get back into aviation with the American Aeronautical Corporation, which was actually an Italian firm selling Savoie-Marchetti flying boats and headed by one of Dad's Italian students from wartime.) Dad had been dead against the military school idea, but to no one's surprise, he was outvoted.

My term at CLI was a kaleidoscope of adventures and misadventures. I was big for my age and clumsy, which was no help. I got in trouble with my class advisor. We were to research and deliver an oration. I chose either "The History of Military Aviation" or "The Future of Military Aviation." Nothing doing. He, or the school, wanted a more patriotic subject—the Constitution or its equal. For once I bucked authority. I didn't get a licking (they were fairly common) but I was confined to campus for two weeks. But I did graduate (from eighth grade) with my class.

I have to admit that my most cherished memory of CLI was my fight with Benny Woodhouse. Benny was the class bully and had all the boys completely cowed. One day, leaving the mess hall, Benny came up behind me and tried to trip me. Somehow we both went down and I landed on top of him. I was horrified and beat a hasty retreat. I'd just gotten to my room when Benny arrived with several followers and demanded satisfaction. I thought, What the hell, you've been beaten up before. So when he took a swing at me I waded in and the next thing I knew Benny was sitting on the floor with a bloody nose and an eye that was beginning to close. Three years later I made a visit to the school with Louis Rose, and he heard one of the boys say, "That's the guy who beat up Benny Woodhouse." It was my claim to fame at CLI.

Years later Uncle Charlie said he'd been unimpressed with the appearance of the school, but that it had done wonders for me. I couldn't agree with him and what I said surprised him. What put me on the track back to civilization was a sailboat and his daughter, my cousin Caroline. He had asked me to teach Caroline to sail and one day we were out in a very light breeze. For whatever reason, I made a very coarse and very unnecessary remark. Caroline was offended and she told me so (told me off) in no uncertain terms and very plain words. That's all it took. She never had to reprimand me again.

By the time that the summer of 1931 was over, you could say that I had decided to rejoin the human race. I had entered high school and was associating with my role models, the team athletes. I made the soccer team, and it was the beginning of an interest in sports that never left me. I would earn a fair number of team letters and athletic awards. To the family's disappointment, I confess I never made the honor roll.

Tensions at home eased a little. Grandmother was convinced CLI had knocked some sense into me and I did nothing to disillusion her. We didn't see Dad very often because he was working in New York. When he could he took the DL&W from Hoboken to Bath, where Mother would meet him.

In the summer of 1933 we had an unusual family diversion. Dad had had a bad bout of pneumonia in New York. His University of Toronto roommate, Alex Spencer, was building a large country house in London, Ontario, and he invited Dad to come to recuperate and serve as clerk of the works for the estate. There was a nice brick tenant house on the grounds and Alex thought the family might enjoy spending the summer there. It was a chance to be a family again.

It was a very pleasant summer. The one disadvantage was that there were no boys our age around (no girls either). So Boog and I were left to our own devices. I helped Bill Fraser, a former Royal Canadian Mounted Police trainer, with the horses early each morning. "Uncle" Alex gave me a few jobs, one of them was to paint Bill's new house down by the stables. Most afternoons Boog and I went down to the river, the Thames, to swim or to explore it on a raft we put together. The big thing was we were a family again, headed by Dad. We didn't know that events in the near future meant it would be ten years before Dad would be head of the household again, after Grandmother's death.

Back in Hammondsport, I got my hunting license at long last and Uncle Charlie loaned me my grandfather's 12-gauge shotgun. I was the center forward on the soccer team, so things were good, for the most part. Prohibition was over but wine sales resumed slowly. People had evidently gotten used to the hard stuff. Prosperity hadn't returned yet. The London house had been completed and Dad was again looking for a job. As it happened, Uncle Kid, who was the chemist at the winery, was in poor and failing health, and Dad was asked to be his assistant. But first he had a role to play with Boog and me.

The Glens

The Early 30s

I HADN'T BEEN in Hammondsport from New Orleans very long before I began to discover and explore the glories of the glens. There was one, the excitingly large one, just at the west edge of town. The other was in the hills on the other side of the valley.

The stream of the village glen descended nearly a thousand feet from its source before it flowed into the lake. Meandering through meadows in its early stages, the stream became very spectacular when it entered the gorge. There was a series of waterfalls and rapids, framed by both wooded banks and sheer rock cliffs that rose as much as three hundred feet. As my pals and I grew a bit older, it was the thrill of climbing those falls and cliffs that lured us.

From the top of the first falls to the meadows above, large evergreens formed a canopy above the stream. The trees were so inaccessible they had thankfully been spared the lumberman's ax. The sunlight filtering through the branches created a cathedral-like atmosphere. There were a number of large, deep pools up there, and even on the hottest summer days, the water was very brisk. It was wonderful to strip and take a dip in one of the pools and then dry in the sun on the warm rocks.

Climbing the glen was easier than going back down, so we usually returned along the top, either by Dead Horse Trail (so-called because of the scattered remains of the skeleton of a horse that had been found along the path), or down the Pine Grove Trail that came out on Reservoir Hill (where we went sledding in the winter).

Considering how young we all were, and how nervy, it's amazing that there weren't any serious accidents. The falls were wet, slippery, and vertical. The shale that formed the falls and the rocky cliffs was likely to have been loosened and weakened by winter frosts. But we all loved the challenge of climbing, and once in a while our ambition got the better of our good sense. And yet I can only remember one accident that required a doctor's services.

On a cold January day when Arch Squires and I were about ten, we were climbing the wall above the Boy Scout cabin, which stood at the foot of the falls. The wall consisted of a steep bank with a series of small shale cliffs about ten or fifteen feet high.

We had navigated one of the cliffs and were just starting to climb the second when Archie stepped on some snow-covered ice and began tumbling. We had rope but we weren't tied together. He hung on to the rope and I tried to hold him, but I didn't have very solid footing and the next thing I knew I was also tumbling head over heels down the steep slope. The strange thing was I could see snow and debris whirling before my eyes. Then I was aware of flying through the air as I reached the first cliff and tumbling some more and coming to rest in the top of a small tree.

I wasn't hurt and I climbed down from the tree. I could see Arch lying on the ice-covered stream in a widening pool of blood.

When I reached him he was groaning, so I knew he wasn't dead. But he had a sizable gash on the top of his head. I used my handkerchief and some snow to staunch the flow of blood. I helped Arch to his feet and we made our way to the doctor's house. When his office door opened, I pushed Arch inside and then beat it for home as fast as I could run. My blood-spattered and bedraggled appearance prompted several phone calls to Mother. (There is nothing like a small town for fast reporting.) By the time I reached the house, she was ready with a very serious lecture on common sense and caution.

In later years we almost surely did use more discretion, but the glen remained a strong attraction. Scrambling up the steep falls is a bit beyond me these days, but I still visit the more accessible areas at the top and the bottom. And on certain days and nights, there is a unique flow of air—cool and moist, hinting of fresh leaves and plants and the sweet decay of dark woodsy places—that wafts out of the glen and reassures me that that wonderful place is still there, not much changed from my boyhood days.

Cold Brook Stream

The 30s

ITS OFFICIAL New York State name is Cold Brook, a wonderful trout stream that arises south of the artesian wells at the Fish Hatchery and joins a branch that comes out of the Mitchellsville Glen. Together they flow north through Pleasant Valley, broadening out as the stream passes through a marsh, and feed at last into Keuka Lake along the eastern boundary of the village. Actually, almost nobody calls it Cold Brook. It's either the Inlet or, as you move away from the lake, the Creek (pronounced Crick, naturally).

By any name, it became important to me almost as soon as I was able to leave the house unescorted. Like the lake itself, and the glens, the Inlet was a year-round source of pleasure, excitement, and adventure. In late fall it froze over well before any of the lake did. After supper and on weekends it became the village skating rink. If there was a lot of snow, we dragged car tires along the ice to "shovel" it away. The tires were unusable casings that Ben Casterline let us have. He ran the Texaco station, which included a retreading operation, right beside the Inlet. The tires also made a good fire, at least if you stayed upwind.

At first we struggled with skates that clamped to your high-tops like roller-skates. But with only one blade they were very frustrating and hard to keep on, and they usually came off when you were well away from the fire. In the attic I found a pair of shoe skates Uncle Charlie had used at Mercersburg Academy. When I tried them on, I couldn't believe the difference they made. Unfortunately Uncle Charlie spotted them in the hall and claimed them. I had to shovel a lot of walks and carry many an armload of firewood to earn enough to order a pair of my own from Montgomery Ward (Hockey Specials).

Snap the whip was a favorite game with the skaters. We formed a chain like a conga line and then the leader tried to wheel so sharply the last person couldn't hang on. Tag was another game. We skated around the clumps of rushes in the marsh to shake our pursuers. One evening Danny Hodge was It and chasing me so I led him down the Inlet and out into the marsh to try and lose him around one of the clumps. It was a good maneuver, except that when I rounded the clump the ice had broken off and floated free and—SPLASH!—I ended up in four feet of very cold water, with Danny right behind me.

As I surfaced, I could see Danny, silhouetted against the lights of the village and the bonfire, trying frantically to stop. But he couldn't, and in he came, and tagged me, which was the least of our worries. We scrambled back on the ice as fast as we could and headed for the fire. It couldn't have been more than a couple of hundred yards away, but we found ourselves moving slower and slower as our clothes began to freeze solid. We must have looked like robots as we stiff-legged the last few feet to the fire. We received a jeering reception as we got there and commenced to drip and steam. So far as I remember, neither of us caught pneumonia, or even a sniffle. Thank heavens for Ben and his tires.

As the winter went on, we continued to go down to the Inlet to skate, but by then the head of the lake had frozen solid, too, and we had a much greater expanse of ice to enjoy. About then, we could look for Bill Chadeayne to arrive with a long bundle which he transformed into the first skate-sail we had ever seen. He would soon be skimming back and forth over the glassy surface.

Mr. Chadeayne was a very interesting man. The story was that at an early age he had run away from home and gone to sea on sailing ships. He was quite short, and stocky, and it was easy enough to picture him standing barefoot on a pitching deck. If Mr. Chadeayne wasn't the first man to ride a Curtiss motorcycle clear across the country, he was surely one of the first. In some places, he used to say, the roads were so bad they rode the railroad tracks on the ties!

He became associated with Glenn Curtiss and was responsible for purchasing the lumber used in the flying boats being constructed in the Curtiss factories at Buffalo and Garden City, Long Island. Bill Chadeayne had liked what he saw of the village, and when the local Curtiss plant closed down in 1919, he moved to Hammondsport and joined Henry Kleckler, the engine designer, and other local men in establishing the Aerial Service Corporation, which became Mercury Aircraft, and he was with the company until he died.

His daughter and I were in the same grade and she was my first crush, partly because she had a mahogany hull, like the one from the flying boat *America*, in her backyard for a playhouse. (I had a lot of competition for her attention). At some point Mr. Chadeayne had a cage with a small live rattlesnake in it, the first most of us had ever seen, although once in a rare while someone would spot a rattler in the hills.

When we weren't ice-skating, the Inlet was great for trapping and fishing, frog-catching and rowing, and above all for trout-fishing. On the opening day of trout season in April, the banks of Cold Stream on both sides above and below the bridge at Pleasant Valley would be lined by anglers shoulder to shoulder. On quieter days, I learned to fly fish, with Uncle Charlie as my mentor.

Cold Stream, glens, and the lake—there was never a shortage of things to do, and I don't know why we ever wanted to grow up, but of course we couldn't wait.

The Chicken Shooters

1894–1925

WHEN MY UNCLE Charlie was nine years old, his father, C.A. Champlin, presented him with his first shotgun. It was a .410 gauge, single barrel model, made in Belgium. The shells had brass cases. Regulations regarding guns and hunting were a little more lenient than they are today, but Charles was not allowed to use his shotgun without permission, and this usually meant that he had to be accompanied by an adult as well.

About this time a backyard feud was evolving, featuring my grandmother, Georgia, or Mrs. C.A., and Mr. Sanford, whose property was directly behind the Champlins'. The item of contention was Mr. Sanford's chickens. His chicken enclosure ran right along the back of Grandmother's very elaborate flower garden. Mr. Sanford's run was not escape-proof and his chickens were always heading for greener or prettier pastures, which meant Grandmother's flower beds. The last straw came when four of the feathered fugitives were discovered having a good scratch in a freshly planted area.

Grandmother, accompanied by her hired man and young Charles, quickly rounded up the strays and hurled them over the wire fence. Mr. Sanford, hearing all the squawking, rushed out to see what was going on, and found himself confronting Grandmother, who was really fired up. Fix that fence, she demanded, or the next time she saw one of his chickens in her yard, she would have it shot.

Not long afterward, Grandmother was entertaining two ladies at tea and enjoying a bit of gossip, when young Charles burst into the room excitedly and cried, "Mother, Mother, one of Mr. Sanford's chickens is in the yard. Can I shoot it?" It seems likely she hadn't really listened to a word he'd said. Hardly turning his way, Grandmother said, "Yes, yes, Charles, run along."

A moment later the tea party was interrupted by a loud boom in the back yard. Very shortly there was a loud pounding at the back door, and it disclosed a very irate Mr. Sanford, holding a dead chicken in one hand and a very scared young Charles in the other.

That evening Grandfather paid a visit to the Sanford residence. The terms of the settlement were never disclosed. Years later Grandmother solved the chicken problem by having an eight-foot-high board fence built along the back property line. She even bullied Mr. Sanford into painting the back of his barn to match her fence.

By the time we moved north from New Orleans, thirty years had passed since the affair of Mr. Sanford's chickens and Uncle Charlie's marksmanship. Mr. Sanford still lived in the same house, and was now the village postmaster, and he still raised chickens, which stayed home thanks to the board fence.

But now I had just acquired my first BB gun, a Daisy. I could shoot at cans and bottles but not at song birds. I was up in the loft of the barn one day looking for promising targets. I discovered that the back window provided a swell birdseye view of Mr. Sanford's chicken yard.

As I watched, the chickens would come up to the water dish and drink. For the heck of it I shot a BB into the water, just in front of a chicken. The result was spectacular. When the BB splashed in the water, the chicken let out a squawk and jumped a foot in the air. This was so exciting that I kept on shooting. I don't know whether I got careless or whether one of the BBs was undersized or misshapen, but I can still picture that BB curving to the right and hitting the chicken in the head. That chicken also squawked and leaped in the air, but it landed on its back in the water dish and was very still.

Now I was in for it, and what to do? For some reason, the first thing I did was hide the BB gun. Then I went to the Sanfords' front door. I don't know where I got the courage to do that, but it was my own idea. When Mr. Sanford came to the door, I blurted out, "I just shot one of your chickens."

We went down to the chicken run, and no miracle had transpired. The chicken was still feet up in the water dish. It was one of his prize birds, Mr. Sanford said, and he was going to have to report me to Bill Leary, the village policeman.

I went home and told Mother what I'd done, and I got quite a lecture. The next morning I packed a lunch and took to the woods. It was a long day and I covered a lot of territory, but I knew I had to go home eventually, and besides it was getting near to dinner time.

When I got home, the atmosphere was cool but not hostile, as I feared it would be. I didn't say anything or ask any questions, and Mother and Grandmother let me stew in my own juices for a while. Then, just before the meal, Mother told me that Mr. Sanford had called. He had decided not to have me arrested, he said, because I'd been man enough to come and tell him what I'd done. He did add a remark about that kind of thing seeming to run in the family. That brought a snort from Grandmother.

Radio and The Seelys

1928

A GREAT MANY people now can't remember a time when there *wasn't* a television set in the living room and probably in the bedroom as well. But I can remember very well the first time I saw a radio, and heard one.

Until then the after-dinner entertainment found us gathered around the fireplace in the living room, listening to Mother or Grandmother read aloud. Grandmother's taste didn't run to *The Teenie-weenies* or *Tom Swift,* so Mother usually did the reading. But we also got a dose of the classics, *Jason and the Golden Fleece* and the *Arabian Nights.*

Then one day I was visiting the Seely house. Lyman J. (Lad) Seely and his wife Peg had seven children—Bill and Hank, the older boys, Mary and Margo, the older girls, Jack, who was closest in age to me, and Connie and Betty, the youngest of the kids. Lad invited us into his den, which was off the billiard room (probably the only one in Steuben County) at the back of the house.

There was a whole assortment of weird-looking equipment: cabinets with dials and meters, and a maze of wires running down to a large accumulation of batteries on the floor, and what were called trickle chargers to maintain power in the batteries. Uncle Lad was wearing earphones and fiddling with the dials. He suddenly smiled and handed the headphones to Jack and me. I heard a man talking and then there was some music. I was astounded; to me it was a miracle. Uncle Lad said we were listening to KDKA in Pittsburgh, two hundred miles away!

I returned home eager to prattle on about this new invention, and I was disappointed by the family's lack of enthusiasm. As a matter of fact, it was two years before there was a radio in the house. Until then we had to be content with our wind-up Victrola playing "Cohen on the Telephone" and "Over There" and Caruso singing on Red Seal Records.

Then Uncle Charlie and Uncle Kid gave Grandmother an Atwater-Kent for Christmas. It had a crackled metal finish, a separate speaker and a single dial. It was installed in Grandmother's bedroom, but she didn't warm to the idea of radio, and she couldn't find anything she wanted to hear anyway, so it didn't get much use.

Once in a great while she would invite the family in and turn the dial until a strong station came in, and we would listen to whatever the program was, no matter if it was a report on farm prices or a lecture on what to do about termites.

Fortunately, a couple of years later her sons gave her another radio, a cabinet model that she thought was too large for her bedroom so it was installed in the living room. That put a crimp in the reading aloud, but it opened up a whole new world of entertainment. As luck would have it, we were getting far enough along in school so that the homework was piling up and the family edict was that the homework got top priority and if we were lucky we might get to listen to one or two programs as a treat.

I'm not sure but what the Seelys were more interesting than the radio in those days, anyway. With all those lively children, they could have starred in their own version of "One Man's Family." They lived in the only house in town that could really be called a mansion. It was a three-story stone house at the corner of Lake Street and Bauder Avenue. It had been designed and built by Dewitt Clinton Bauder, who had been manager of the Pleasant Valley Wine Company and was related to Mother's family, the Champlins. Sadly, the house was torn down when the new school was built in 1933 on the hill behind the house.

Lad Seely had been a newspaper reporter in Rochester, sales manager for the Curtiss Company, and, later on, publisher of the local newspaper and a wizard philatelist. He was a connoisseur who imported his cigarettes from Dunhill of London, and he was a superb raconteur. One of his favorite stories involved his years during World War I as the European sales representative for Curtiss in London. The British government ordered a large number of Curtiss JN-4 Jennies. Lad cabled Curtiss to see if the delivery schedule could be met. Curtiss wired back, "Only on payment of a hundred thousand dollar advance." Lad so advised the First Lord of the Admiralty, Winston Churchill, of this request. Churchill told him the check would be ready the next morning. It was, but it was for a hundred thousand pounds, then worth about five hundred thousand dollars. Lad had forgotten to specify the currency.

I owe a special debt to the Seelys. During the war, Mother went to London to stay with the Seelys. My father got leave from his work in Italy, training Italian pilots, and the Seelys made the arrangements for my parents-to-be (a few years later) to be married in the fashionable St. Margaret's Church in Piccadilly.

All that, and radio, too!

Goose Island

1930

I SUPPOSE MY first visit to Goose Island must have been in about 1930, in late November. Goose Island was a lovely place, high above Hammondsport and stretching back from the top of the Glen. In summertime the "island" was a meadow with the stream flowing through it that led to the Glen. On one flank of the meadow was a wooded hill and on the other there were steep, pastured slopes. At one end of the meadow, just before the deep gorge of the Glen began, was a stand of hemlock trees, about an acre in size. The trees were a very popular place for picnics and camping. The local Boy Scout troop used to camp out there at least one weekend every year. Sadly, only a few years later the flood of 1935 devastated that section of the hilltop, washing out many of the big trees and cutting gullies through the hemlock grove.

But that was yet to happen. My introduction to Goose Camp came from "Uncle" Lanny—J. Lansing Callan, one of the early Curtiss pilots who had returned to the village after service as a Navy pilot in World War I to help operate Airships, Inc., a Hammondsport company that produced inflatable rubber life rafts and gas cells for dirigibles.

Uncle Lanny stopped at the house one day and said he was looking for volunteers. Years before, up at Goose Island, he had built an Adirondack lean-to, a three-sided structure open at the front, which was defined by two trees. The sides were formed by poles about a foot apart. Then, in a way similar to the construction of tropical hut, the roof and the sides were thatched with hemlock boughs. Eight or ten feet in front of the open side was a semi-circular fireplace made of large boulders banked at the back with earth. Above the fireplace was a frame from which the cooking pots were hung. Uncle Lanny had Jack Seely in tow that day and promptly drafted me, too.

We drove up Reservoir Hill, parked just above Goose Island, and followed an old logging trail down to it. At the bottom we spotted the lean-to through the trees and it looked pretty decrepit. Last year's boughs were dry and much the worse for wear. That was our project, to remove the old ones and replace them with fresh ones. We were supplied with knives, hatchets and a big ball of binder twine. Lanny located some low-hanging hemlock limbs and cut and hauled them to the camp while we were cutting down the dried boughs.

The roof went on first, naturally much thicker than the sides to be as rain-proof as possible. We also laid a fresh carpet of boughs on the floor. It took us two days to finish the job, but it was really worth it. There was hardly a weekend it wasn't in use, sometimes by two or three families, not just one. In winter we almost always walked up Reservoir Hill, dragging our toboggans and carrying our food in Adirondack pack baskets, or in World War I knapsacks, of which some of us were the much-envied owners. It was several miles up to the camp, but the company was always good, and the anticipation was half the fun. For the younger generation, snow was a prerequisite for a winter trip to Goose Camp, but luckily the camp was about a thousand feet higher than the village, so we were rarely short of snow.

The first arrivals were responsible for gathering wood and getting the fire started. As a good conservationist, Uncle Lanny was well ahead of his time. Only dead trees and limbs could be cut, and we all took turns with the buck saw on the larger logs. No indiscriminate loosing of small boys with hatchets to flail away as they would. Water was dipped from a small side creek and was hung over the fire in a big iron kettle.

After the fire was going well and the knapsacks and baskets had been unloaded, the next order of business was to head for the slopes with skis or the toboggans. The pasture side of the Island was nice and smooth for good runs. After a session on the slopes we were usually cold or wet or both, and that big fire pit felt wonderful. There was usually also a pot of hot chocolate at the fire. The adults favored something less hot, but stronger, usually brandy from a local distiller (this was still Prohibition) and when it was really cold the adult menu included a hot brandy toddy.

The meals served at the camp were always wildly popular. A stew cooked in a kettle over the fire was a favorite. But there might be a pot of baked beans and hot dogs on other occasions, or steaks broiled over the fire and served with potatoes baked in the fire. The potatoes were usually served with butter and honey, and sometimes gravy. No one person did all the cooking. The men took turns doing the honors, and there was a fair amount of good-natured ribbing if the beans stuck or biscuits were burned.

The outings at Goose Camp are some of my favorite childhood memories. There was the good food, and the sports, but what was best of all was the camaraderie and most particularly the closeness between the generations, the children and the adults. Not a gap in sight, and at the time we had no reason to know how lucky we were.

Tony's Tree House

1930

AT ONE STAGE in their lives, a lot of boys who live in small towns or in the country share a common urge—to build a treehouse or a cabin. Anyone who's walked in a woods is apt to have come upon the remains of a shanty. It's an interesting point that very few were ever completed. I suspect that the enthusiasm runs out before the roof goes on.

There's something mystical about a tree house. I think Boog's and my imaginations were first awakened when Mother read us *Swiss Family Robinson* while we were still living in New Orleans. We used to climb the huge live oaks in Audubon Park and at Spanish Fort (ideal for tree houses) and we even built a treetop platform at our last house, on Nelson Street.

In Hammondsport the subject of tree houses came up unexpectedly one evening when Ellen Bardine took me on a hike up Reservoir Hill to the huge black tank that contained the village water supply. We walked down a trail that led past an old red building called the spring house that had been part of an earlier water supply system. Uncle Charlie dropped in for dessert that night and Mother asked him about the spring house. I don't remember what he said about that, but I perked up when he said that was where Uncle Kid and Jernie Richards had their tree house. It was a large, sturdy structure of white pine boards and they'd actually slept in it, but in some way Charlie and Kid's father found out that something was not quite kosher at the tree house. The hired man was sent to investigate and found smoking materials, playing cards, poker chips, and dice. The tree house came crashing down.

The tree house idea surfaced a few years later, around 1930. A shipment of furniture had arrived in a huge plywood container, four by four by six feet. It had been adapted into a playhouse for our kid brother, Pete, but he had outgrown it and it was about to be junked. It would obviously make a great tree house, but not at Nano's on Lake Street.

Uncle Charlie had the endearing habit of being enthusiastic and supportive of our useful projects, unless they seemed wildly impractical or dangerous, in which case he skillfully diverted us to some other project. He thought the woods up behind the Farm, where he lived, would be a good place for a tree house.

The smart thing would have been to have taken the playhouse apart and reassembled it in the woods piece by piece. So much for hindsight. We made do with the two crucial ingredients, youthful enthusiasm and boundless energy.

Initially the treehouse was the joint brainchild of myself and my friend Bob Richards. Brother Boog and my cousins Harry (Champ) Howell and Jack Horne came aboard at various stages, not too often to cool their interest. Once we got underway, our problems all involved logistics—a word I didn't know the meaning of until I was flying ammo, fuel, and other supplies to the front lines fourteen years later.

One big problem was that the packing crate that had become a playhouse was at the barn, a long mile across the valley to the Farm. Here we got a big break. Grandmother was having the barn cleaned out and had hired Charlie Brown and his Reo truck to haul the stuff away. Between trips to the dump we persuaded Charlie to carry the crate to the Farm.

Behind the barns was the lumber shed, and behind it was a good-sized pile of lumber scraps. Uncle Charlie's hired man, Howard Robinson, helped us pick out some timbers and a pair of old doors for a platform. The trees where we intended to build the house were still several hundred yards away. The solution to all our transport problems was to visit Pilgrim's Boat Works, which was almost next door to our cottage near the head of the lake. They let us borrow a lightweight, two-wheeled boat cart (using Curtiss motorcycle wheels).

Enthusiasm and energy are fine, but they can only take you so far.

That's where ingenuity comes in. We were all becoming interested in things mechanical at that point in our lives and *Popular Mechanics* was our favorite magazine. We were fascinated with blocks and tackles, and fortunately Howard let us borrow a couple at the Farm.

We found two perfect trees, each a foot in diameter, a hundred feet up the bank from the highway. There were smaller trees in front but they didn't block the view. One problem was that the lowest limbs were twenty feet above the ground. We solved this by borrowing a ten-foot ladder and shinnying the rest of the way up. The tree on the left, a hemlock, had a strong level limb facing the lake. We ran a beam between the two trees, level with the limb, securing it to the trees with spikes and wooden blocks. A second beam was fastened to the other tree, a pine, and then to the limb. We fashioned a makeshift bosuns chair and swung in it while we were getting those beams in place. Getting the doors in place for the platform was easy, and the day of truth arrived.

When the gang was at full strength, we loaded the packing crate/ playhouse on the cart and pushed and pulled it down the road. When we got below the trees, we used the blocks and tackle and did a great job of hauling the crate up the bank and through the second growth to "our" trees. That was enough for one day.

The hoisting was an affair to remember. We did a lot of planning as to where to place the blocks and guide lines, and with a lot of groaning and panting, it was suddenly there! We tied the "cabin" in place so it couldn't blow away. Our budget wouldn't allow for a rope ladder, the usual approach to a tree house. We built a ladder that went part way up, then we made steps from spikes and wire for the rest of the way up. We hid the ladder when we weren't there.

We sat on the platform and admired our panoramic view, which took in the valley, the village, and the lake as far north as Bluff Point. We added finishing touches. The plywood wasn't waterproof, so we liberated an old, heavy canvas tarpaulin from Airships, Inc., the balloon factory in the old Curtiss plant, and covered the top and the back and also attached it to a frame to make a roof over part of the "porch," which had a railing on two sides. We added a hinged table that dropped down to make room for sleeping. We had a kerosene lamp for light and a Sterno stove for cooking and we slept in the treehouse many a night in that summer of 1930, when I was thirteen.

But the enthusiasms of young men never stay still. The next year Uncle Charlie bought a sailboat for his daughter, my cousin Caroline. He asked me to teach Caroline to sail, and we went out every day. Occasionally, tacking toward the cottage, I would look up the hill and see through the trees the now-abandoned treehouse.

On an October afternoon in 1995, I was standing on the road above the cottage, discussing the placement of a new culvert with the state highway people. I glanced up the hill and caught sight of two very large evergreens, a pine and a hemlock. Between them I could make out a length of gray and weathered timber. It was one of the beams of the treehouse. All I could think of was, "Good heavens, how in the world did we do it?"

Learning to Sail

The Early 30s

AS BOOG AND I grew older, the lake took over from the glens (with their minnows and crabs and shallow pools) as the greatest natural attraction for us. In a way, my own active introduction to the lake was also my first lesson in horse-trading.

Dad brought up the subject of buying me a rowboat. We were at Pilgrim's boat shop watching them build their famous Keuka Lake fishing boats. They were a graceful design with cedar planking over steam-bent oak ribs. Charlie Pilgrim was the owner and he had three sons who helped him: Lawrence, Floyd (who was in my class at school), and Leo. They were all fine craftsmen, even as boys, but Floyd was the best of the lot.

On one side of the shop, we noticed a small rowboat, built of flat boards and about eight feet long. Charlie was with us and he said it had been built for Floyd and Leo but it was too small for them now and he was going to sell it.

"How much?" asks Dad.

"Five dollars," says Charlie.

"Give you two," says Dad.

"Five," says Charlie.

"Give him five!" I cried.

"Goodbye," says Dad, and we left.

On the way home, Dad gave me a lecture on the psychology of horse-trading. A couple of days later we drove over to Pilgrim's again, and in a very short time I was the proud owner of my first vessel—at a bargain sale price of three dollars.

I rowed it the quarter-mile from Pilgrim's back to the cottage, one very pleased boy. So began the love affair with the lake that would last sixty years.

With its side only eight inches high (eight inches of freeboard, I'd learn to say later), the *Goop*, as I christened it, was not very seaworthy. Even a mild north wind would swamp it. And of course there were new regulations and restrictions. I was only a dog-paddle swimmer, so I wasn't supposed to cruise in water over my head, or take passengers without supervision. The only life jackets were some adult-sized cork life preservers left over from the lake steamer days, and when I put one on I couldn't move, let alone row. Still, the *Goop* was a great tutor of seamanship. I became very familiar with the shallows at the head of the lake and used to row quite a way up the Inlet. It also became my first experience under sail.

The family had always been nautically inclined, you might say. Both Grandfather Champlin and Uncle Charlie fished the lake for years. In the early 1900s, Grandfather had given both Mother and Uncle Charlie Peterborough canoes. After his courting days, Charlie modified his with seats and oars, for bass fishing, and it survived for fifty years until it was destroyed when the barn at the Farm burned in 1954.

Mother's canoe had a shorter but very colorful life and gained a niche in aeronautical history. Glenn Curtiss was experimenting with hydro-aeroplanes and asked if he could borrow the canoe for an experiment. It became the main float on a pusher aircraft (which has gone into history as the canoe-hydroplane). It made several successful flights. There wasn't enough left of the canoe to return, and Mother said, "Glenn was very grateful for the loan of the canoe, but since he didn't return it, I've always thought a share or two of Curtiss stock would have been nice."

Uncle Charlie kept his canoe on the beach at our cottage, and one day he arrived with an armful of poles, canvas, and wire. We were enthralled as he installed a mast, leeboards, and a sail, and away he sailed. That was for me! I went down to Pilgrim's and conferred with Floyd. We raided several storage sheds and came up with an old jib, a couple of poles, and a lot of baling wire. Floyd was very handy, and in a relatively short time, we had stepped a mast in the *Goop* and attached an oar lock on the transom so I could use an oar as a rudder. Mother was on hand during the construction and was a bit apprehensive about the whole thing, but since there was only a light breeze she allowed me to take my maiden sailing voyage.

One thing Floyd and I had overlooked—a keel or centerboard. We went almost as rapidly sideways as we did forward. I had watched Uncle Charlie come about so I had an idea how that was done, but in the meantime the wind had freshened, the waves were higher and I was shipping water. I was only about twenty feet from shore when we swamped and capsized. Mother dashed into the water up to her waist, grasped the bow and between us we concluded the *Goop*'s ignominious maiden voyage.

My next craft was a sixteen-foot, double-ender Uncle Charlie gave me. What had happened was that he had taken several pictures and sketches and a set of dimensions to Charlie Pilgrim at the boat yard. He wanted a so-called St. Lawrence skiff, a lightweight double-ender with gently rounded bows. What he got was as if the Pilgrims had put two of their boats, with their sharp prows, end to end. It didn't resemble a St. Lawrence skiff, nor did it handle like one. So Uncle Charlie continued to fish for bass from his canoe, and I inherited the double-ender.

It was sitting in the basement of the Keuka Hotel, eight miles up the lake from Hammondsport. Early one Saturday I hitched a ride to Wayne (the highway along the east side of the lake, now Route 54, hadn't yet been built) and walked the three miles down to Keuka Village. I got there about noon and saw Derb Young, who ran the hotel with his colorful mother, Bessie. With the help of one of his men, we got the boat out of the basement and down to the water. Derb was dubious. He said it hadn't been in the water and would probably leak like a sieve. It did, and filled right up. There was nothing to do but moor it and let it soak up. I walked the eleven miles back to Hammondsport on the lower lake road. It was a long day, but I had a new boat.

The following Saturday I got a ride to Keuka. With Derb's help, we beached and emptied the boat and re-launched it. It was tight as a drum and rowed easily and I started on the long pull to the cottage. There was a south wind so I was going into the waves; last week there'd been a north wind. I was soon raising a crop of blisters and when I got to the Seely cottage I saw signs of activity and decided to take a break. I was given dinner and the promise of a ride home (after I'd called to assure the family I was OK). I completed the double-ender's maiden voyage the next day.

For a while I settled for oar power, but the boat was not very maneuverable. The problem was partly the length, partly the fact that the Pilgrims had installed a three-inch keel. It was easy to see why Uncle Charlie preferred the quick responsiveness of the canoe. One day at the cottage I asked him what kind of a sailboat he thought the double-ender might make. "Let's find out," he said. So we borrowed the mast and sails from his canoe and jerry-rigged them on the rowboat. Using a paddle for a rudder we set out. It performed surprisingly well. Uncle Charlie said, "I think with a larger sail and a jib you could steer this by just trimming your sails and shifting your weight fore or aft." And that's what we did.

Uncle Charlie suggested the height of the mast and length of the boom and helped me lay out a rigging diagram. I went to the Meadowcroft Balloon Company and for five dollars (those were the days) they made me a main-sail and a jib.

I went up in the woods behind the Farm and cut down a straight hemlock. I trimmed off the branches and peeled off the bark with a drawshave. Grape wire used in the family vineyards served for the stays and rings that held the sail to the mast and clothesline was used for the sheets and halyards.

The contrivance worked out very well. Sailing it alone, as I usually did, was quite demanding when you were trying to go about. The idea was to get to maximum speed, spill the jib, and haul in the main, all the while moving yourself forward and, if there was a strong wind, trying not to capsize. As you came into the wind you backed the jib and moved your weight aft. At first it took several attempts before I mastered the knack of it, and consequently I didn't try it too close to shore. It also required a little luck to bring the double-ender to a good landing.

But I sailed the double-ender for nearly two seasons and learned more about the basics of sailing than I did in the next twenty. On spring days after school I would go down to the dock where it was moored and with the prevailing westerly wind sail across to the head of the lake. It would take until almost dark to beat my way back to the mooring. The double-ender wasn't a speed demon but she was all the fun I could ask for.

Sailing, Sailing

Keuka Lake, September 1939

COMING OUT OF the movie, we stopped and sniffed the air. It was late in the month, but the air was soft and warm, a gentle reminder of a memorable summer, just ended.

Since it was Sunday evening and the work week started early the next morning, I dropped my date and stopped at the house to say goodnight before heading for the cottage. I also picked up Herman the hound, who often kept me company. I remembered that I had one final chore before bed. We'd been sailing that afternoon and the sails on the *Mystery* had been lowered but not stowed.

Driving over to the cottage, I realized, as I hadn't before, just how bright the moon was. When Herman and I walked out on the dock, everything was bathed in moonlight—the willows at the head of the lake, the hills rising behind the village, and the *Mystery* with a cockpit full of sails. When I pushed the rowboat into the lake, Herman jumped in and settled himself on the stern seat. I rowed out to the sailboat and made fast.

There was just the hint of a west wind, so I said to Herman, "How about a quick sail across the lake and back before bed?" Herman did not seem to object. I raised the sails, secured the rowboat to the buoy, and cast off.

Trimming the sails, we headed across the lake toward the village, moving along very nicely. But suddenly our nice little zephyr started flexing a bit of muscle. When the first gust hit, we heeled way up. I literally threw the sheet into the main and levered myself outward as I put down the helm. The jib was cleated with a slipknot but beyond my reach. Consequently we came into the wind very, very slowly. But we didn't go over. Not that time, I thought to myself.

I could see Herman, his front feet on the lee combing, ears blowing in the wind, watching all the activity with great interest. We came into the wind and straightened up, the sails slatting and snapping. We were in the middle of the lake and had lost steerage way. Since the west winds tended to shift frequently in strength and in direction as they came over the hills and out of the glens, I thought it would be best to run on a reach. One person and a dog just couldn't ballast forty feet of boat and five hundred square feet of sail. So off we went, on our quarter and making knots.

The nervous part was that the lake season was over. The summer residents had closed their cottages and returned home after Labor Day. If we capsized, it would almost certainly be all the way and mast down, and nobody around to notice in the moonlit night. I was particularly concerned about Herman, not at all sure how he could cope if we did go over. And as far as Herman was concerned, there was something else to consider. The bottom had an unusual finish. It had been varnished and, while still tacky, had been dusted with powdered graphite for a super slick surface. It would not be exactly an ideal surface to boost a dog up on, and hope for a paw-hold. It began to look like a long, uncomfortable night.

With a west wind, I knew that it would be quite calm in the lee of the hills on the east side of the lake. Unfortunately we weren't making much progress on a reach. When we did reach the lee calm, it was in the south cove of Boericke's Point, three miles north of town. Once in the calm, I dropped the jib and stowed it below.

The lee calm had given me a false feeling of security. We went about and headed for the cottage. The wind was waiting for us as we came out of the shelter of the hill and away we went. On this tack we crossed the lake and made it to a cove between Gateway and Rye Point, perhaps three miles north of the cottage. Close to shore the wind was quite light so we were able to come about easily. We made Two Mile Point on the next tack and Willow Point on the next.

And so it went. Just when we were on a heading that would get us to our anchorage, along would come a fierce gust and I would have to fall off and lose what we'd gained. This little game went on for what seemed like a very long time. The lake was lovely, with the waves and the spray sparkling in the moonlight. But I had had enough nocturnal beauty for a while. Herman had curled up and was snoozing on a couple of spinnaker bags.

But we finally did make the cottage and moored. I stowed and covered the sails and headed for bed, by no means as early as I'd planned.

Keuka Lake, July 1940

I am susceptible to beautiful nights, like the one on which Herman and I had our little adventure. This was another beautiful night, the kind you experience about three times over an entire summer. There was a full moon just rising over the far hill; the lake was like a mirror, reflecting the lights of the cottages on the other shore. The temperature was perfect.

I was sitting on the roof deck of our houseboat. The previous winter cousin Jack Horne and I had decided to build a houseboat, and by damn we had. We'd literally started from scratch—a pencil sketch on one of Grimaldi's paper napkins. The materials and equipment we couldn't borrow or scrounge, we had to purchase from cousin Bob Howell's lumber yard.

She was a solid vessel, twenty-four feet long with a ten-foot beam. There was a galley, a head, and a main cabin with two bunks. For power we relied on an elderly twenty-five horsepower Johnson outboard that gave us a top speed of about six knots.

On our maiden cruise, we had the company of good friends, a well-provisioned larder, and an ice-chest stocked with champagne. We cruised north to Boericke's Point on the other side of the lake. It was then one of the few unspoiled points left on the lake. The Boericke family (who lived in Philadelphia) weren't in residence that summer, so after the maiden voyage we decided to anchor in their south cove for a couple of weeks and commute to work.

Getting from the shore to the boat and vice-versa was a minor problem. We only had brother Peter's canoe, which, I might add, was uncommonly tippy. But we devised a procedure that worked well. The first one to arrive would take off his clothes, place them in the canoe and swim out to the boat, leaving the later arrival to come out to the houseboat in the canoe, with the clothes.

On the evening in question, I got to Boericke's first and, following our drill, stripped, left my clothes in the canoe and swam to the boat. I'd gone up to the top deck, where I was sitting in the moonlight, enjoying the lovely evening. I heard a car approaching and slowing and I saw that it was Jack. From my perch on the deck and with the bright moonlight, I had a grand ringside seat on what followed.

As he walked down to the beach, it was clear that Jack had been having a very jolly evening indeed. He was happy with life and feeling no pain. With an air of supremely confident savoir-faire, he launched the canoe and sprang into it. But as I've mentioned, the canoe was wickedly temperamental, wouldn't stand for such treatment, and didn't. It slid gracefully out from under Jack and deposited him in the water.

I heard a number of gurgling expletives and there was Jack, sitting waist-deep in the water while the canoe, pushed by the gentle offshore breeze, moved slowly out into the lake. Jack noticed this and, holding his left arm out of the water to keep his watch from getting any wetter, started wading in pursuit. The canoe was outdistancing him, so I dove off the roof and intercepted it.

He was a bit miffed with me, but I couldn't see how I could have done anything different, and in no time the miff had passed and he was able to detect the humor in the situation. We toweled off and went back up on top to enjoy the beautiful night.

A Bell for Keuka

Keuka Lake, July 1932

IT IS SAID THAT necessity is the mother of invention, and so it was with Jack Horne and me. Jack and I had been building a float for swimming, using some uncommon materials. For flotation, we'd acquired a supply of five-gallon tin containers, which still held a pungent aroma of alcohol. This was Prohibition and the tins had contained grain alcohol (hopefully pure). We used thirty of these tins, six long and five across.

With Uncle Charlie's blessing we had taken enough pine from his lumber storage area to build the deck and the outside frame. And what pine—six inches wide, seven-eighths of an inch thick, and not a knot in sight.

The other part of Uncle Charlie's generosity was the loan of his tools. Our record for returning tools was slightly spotty, and he had Howard Robinson, his hired man, make a list of our borrowings, and if they weren't all returned, there'd be no more tools, regardless of the project.

We built the main structure at the Farm and hauled it to the lake, where we attached the tins. We floated it down to the cottage and anchored it. All that remained was to attach the ladder. Jack was in the rubber dingy, holding the ladder while I nailed it in place. On the very last nail, the hammer slipped out of my hand and went flying into the lake. Disaster!

We weighted a piece of string and dropped it where we thought the hammer had landed and began diving for it. The lake was about twelve feet deep, and the bottom covered with a grassy seaweed. We dove and dove, but no hammer.

But necessity is the mother, etc., etc. That evening we were sitting on the porch at the farm pondering our dilemma when we happened to see a row of five-gallon glass demijohns at the edge of the vegetable garden. The bottoms had been cut off and they were used to protect the tomato plants from frost in the early spring. What if, we told each other, we could submerge one of them like a diving bell. It would take some weighting; how to do that?

A working farm is a wonderful place for would-be inventors. In short order we found a ball of binder twine with which we could weave a net around the jug. In the scrap metal pile we found some ancient stove-top laundry irons, just right for ballast. There were plenty of burlap bags at hand to wrap the irons in and baling wire to secure them with.

One problem was the sharp edges where the bottoms of the demijohns had been cut off. But we solved this by splitting a short length of old fire hose and attaching it to the rim with adhesive tape. We designed our binder twine net with four loops at the bottom, two on each side, from which to hang the weights.

We were about to insert a cork in the neck of the demijohn when we had a divine inspiration. We drilled a hole in the cork and inserted a four-inch long pipe nipple, and to this we attached a garden hose. We had to visit the blacksmith to have a tire valve welded to a hose fitting. An automobile tire pump, the traditional double-action kind, completed the project. Total cash outlay: fifty cents for the welding.

Our first test run was unforgettable. It worked! The launching was done very carefully—the main structure was glass, after all! One of us held the jug while the other attached the weights. The jug just floated; our calculations were right.

Jack manned the pump while I ducked underwater and very gingerly came up between the weights. My head displaced enough air so the unit settled on my shoulders.

I was transfixed! It was a completely new world. The water was crystal clear with rays of sunshine lighting an underwater meadow. Fish swam toward me, seemingly unafraid. The only sounds were the hiss of the incoming air and the gurgle of the air exiting around the bottom. It was as though I were in a bubble of air. I could see in all directions and everything seemed to move in slow motion. The water level rose as I breathed in and fell as I breathed out. My breath fogged the glass and at first I tried to splash water with my hand. But I discovered the answer was simply to duck my head, take a mouthful of water and squirt. I knew I had to come up and give Jack his turn, but I was very reluctant to leave my new world.

We only had fifty feet of hose, so I hadn't gone very far. Returning to the dock, I ducked out from under. Jack was very excited; since I hadn't drowned, the thing must have worked!

Then it was his turn and when he ducked under I started pumping. The water was so clear it was easy to see him moving slowly along the bottom. But in a minute his head reappeared. "I'm not getting any air!" he said. No wonder. I was so fascinated I'd forgotten to keep pumping. I assured him it wouldn't happen again, and he returned to the depths.

Rather than be tied to the dock, we took the pump out in a rowboat with a third person rowing. The whole area in front of the cottage was quite flat as it had once been a meadow before the level of the lake was raised for the Crooked Lake canal in 1830. Consequently it was easy for us to go exploring in our new element. It took us several days to remember that the real purpose of our invention had been to find the lost hammer. We quickly found it within a few feet of the weighted string marker.

One lesson we soon learned was that "the Lord looks after you." We hadn't considered all the factors involved with our diving bell. We made quite a number of dives over the next couple of weeks with no problems. Then one day we were diving off the steamboat dock by the B&H railroad station. The jar was floating by the ladder when somebody dropped a stone. The jar shattered and down it went. If Jack or I had been inside it would have been impossible to escape the sharp shards of glass. As strange as it seems, we'd never thought about that obvious danger.

But that didn't by any means dampen our enthusiasm for our underwater explorations. The next time we went down we had a helmet made from a steel hot water tank. Within a year, there must have been half a dozen homemade diving bells exploring the lake.

Days at the Races

1933–1945

Tony researched a long and useful history of the Keuka Yacht Club, a valuable addition to the Club's archives. For the purposes of this book, it has been edited to concentrate on Tony's own long association with the great days of the "A" boats.

BECAUSE OF OUR tender ages, my contemporaries and I were not allowed to sit in on the formative meetings of the Club in 1926. This was a great disappointment to us, for in addition to the lively discussions in the Anchor Room of the Keuka Hotel, there was the first slot machine I'd ever seen. Cousin Emily Howell was a very loyal devotee and played it with much gusto and a jangling of bracelets.

Although the fleet was newly organized, the boats themselves were quite elderly, several dating back to the 1890s. The years in storage had not been kind to them, and they all had a tendency to leak. Each boat had a large bilge pump which my pals and I were "allowed" to work while the meetings were in session and the boats tied up at the hotel's old steamboat dock.

In the second season, Uncle Charlie and Uncle Kid acquired *Skidoo* from Uncle Bob Howell. By the third season in 1928, the Champlin brothers had moved on to the *Deltox*, a light weather boat. Uncle Kid, who skippered the *Deltox*, lost the club championship that year to Bob Howell on a protest.

Although we were too small (and light) to qualify as crew members, and the demise of the *Skidoo* ended our bilge pump chores, there was one activity of the A's that provided a great deal of pleasure.

This was the Sunday morning tow when the boats were collected at their moorings and towed to the race site, usually Keuka or Gibson.

The morning began when I hitched a ride to the Farm. Uncle Charlie and the other white-garbed members of the crew would be on the front lawn pulling the spinnakers from their respective bags and stretching them on the grass. They were putting them up in stops. This involved gathering a sail together and securing it with wool yarn at eighteen-inch or so intervals. It could then be hoisted from its bag, set and with a pull on its sheet would blossom forth with a most satisfying whoomp. Unfortunately you could only work it once in a race.

After the spinnakers had been stopped and bagged again, we loaded up and drove down to the cottage where the *Deltox* was moored in the south cove. The crew was rowed to the boat, where, after the cover was removed, I was handed a small bilge pump and a sponge and told to dry her out.

About then Charlie Pilgrim would come along with his heavy-duty motor boat and take us in tow. We would return to the Pilgrim boat yard to pick up Uncle Bob Howell's truly beautiful, year-old *Privateer*, with its slender lines and curved mast. It was always hauled out of the water between races, to keep it light. Bob wasn't taking any chances after the close call of the previous season.

We'd head north to Willow Point, where Spink Taylor and his crew were getting the *Caprice* ready. Hitching it up for the tow involved a bit of juggling because Uncle Bob wanted to have *Privateer* at the end of the tow to eliminate any undue strain.

Once underway to the race location, where Commodore H. Allen Wagner had anchored the committee boat, Cousin Harry (Champ) Howell and I would go boat-hopping and check out the various proceedings.

The *Deltox* was a picture of tranquillity. Uncle Kid, who was the skipper, Uncle Charlie, the tactician, handling the main sail, and Curtis Maltby, on the leeboards, would be reading the *New York Times* or *Herald-Tribune.* Sam Balcom, the jib man, would be napping on the sail bags, recovering from the night before or getting ready for the next.

Not much happening, so Harry and I would go back to the *Caprice.* Spink ran a casual ship, and a wet one. There was always a bottle of lime rickeys being passed around. Besides Spink the skipper, his crewmen were John Frey (the main sheet), Larry Green (the leeboards) and Bill Seely (the jib). There was always a lot of good-natured joshing going on. Spink would bet John on how many last drops of lime rickey he could shake out of the bottle. He usually won. The conversation was the liveliest but usually over our heads. Not always. One Sunday we were going along the west shore, bound for Gibson, when we spotted a scantily-clad couple in the bushes. They tried to scramble out of sight when they caught sight of us. John said, "I like the action, but I prefer privacy."

On *Privateer*, the atmosphere was entirely businesslike. Skipper Bob was usually at the helm since, being last on the tow, the ship tended to wander. On his crew were Jim Smellie, the town druggist (main sail), Arnold (Doc) Gleason (leeboards) and his father, Dr. Don Gleason (jib). Like Uncle Bob, that crew took its racing very, very seriously.

Ironically, *Privateer* was ultimately responsible for the demise of the A boat fleet. The boat's advanced design and construction, combined with Bob's racing skills, made it just unbeatable. The *Privateer* would give the fleet a twenty-minute headstart (usually longer by the time Bob flushed his crew out of the bar) but it nearly always won anyway.

One time Kid Champlin, who was quite ingenious, attached two lengths of wire to an old coal scuttle. While a pre-race meeting was being held, Jack Seely (on Kid's instructions) swam out and attached a wire to each rudder. When the race got underway, all the other boats were faster until Bob felt the scuttle banging on the bottom of the hull. He was not amused.

The combination of the Wall Street crash, and the ongoing economic drought of Prohibition, made it impossible for most of the owners to start again with other boats, although the international Star class was already on its way to being the Club's most active and successful fleet.

The last scheduled A fleet race was to be at Gibson on the last Sunday in July, 1933, a day now remembered or acknowledged with horror by anyone who knows or sails Keuka.

Actually the race was canceled by lack of wind. The day had been oppressive, with no sun but very hot, and the flat-calm water of the lake looked oily. The Champlin brothers *Deltox* hadn't come down that day, but Charlie Pilgrim had towed the others to Gibson, including Art Connelly's *Lark*. Now, with the race called off, Charlie had assembled the tow to start back south to Hammondsport.

The tow was made up of *Caprice*, *Privateer*, and the *Lark*. There were only two people riding the tow, Dr. Don Gleason on his *Privateer* and Art Connelly on the *Lark*.

Several hundred yards in front of the Gibson dock, Bob Cole, a lawyer in Bath, was at the helm of his Star, *Chanticleer*, with Larry Woodside as his crew. They were trying to drift their way to Bob's cottage, which was just south of Gibson.

Suddenly and with no warning, a tremendous storm roared over the hills and down Pulteney Notch from the west. The gale-strength winds and sheets of rain obscured the lake from those on shore. The wind hit the tow, snapping the tow line and lifting *Privateer* out of the water and smashing it down, splintering the mast. The *Lark* capsized and Art Connelly was thrown into the water. Art couldn't swim, but always wore a life jacket while racing—but not while on tow.

Since no one on shore could see anything, what happened next must be conjecture. Don Gleason was the local Scoutmaster, an excellent swimmer and in excellent physical condition. The assumption is that Gleason, knowing that Art couldn't swim, went to his rescue. The rain and the wind whipped the surface of the lake to a foam, making breathing impossible. When the two men's bodies were recovered, Dr. Gleason had a grip on Art's shirt.

When the storm hit Bob Cole's Star, it was knocked flat and started to fill. Until then the only Star known to have been swamped and sunk had been on the ocean. When *Chanticleer* started to fill, Larry Woodside dove overboard and started swimming to shore. The foam and the turbulence defeated him and he drowned.

Just as the storm struck, Charlie Mummert was approaching the Gibson dock in his motorboat. He saw the squall hit Cole's Star and knock it flat. Then the rain obscured everything, but Charlie headed out in the lake in the driving rain and wind. He found Cole just as the Star was disappearing below the surface. Charlie pulled Bob into the boat but was unable to locate Larry. Charlie was awarded the

Carnegie Medal for Bravery.

The tragedy effectively closed down one generation's A boat activities and passed them on, with a different emphasis, to the next. In 1934, we Champlin-Howell cousins began sailing the *Deltox*. There was no thought of racing. We were primarily interested in not tipping over (and not wholly successful at that).

With the previous generation, racing was the primary reason for owning an A boat. They went out to practice occasionally, but never just for the fun of it. For the next generation of us, racing was just one aspect of our enjoyment of the big boats. We did a lot of social sailing, gathering a group of congenial pals and a good supply of refreshments and taking off—especially if there was a good wind. The winds blowing over and down the steep hills and out of the glens surrounding the lake can be erratic and difficult to judge. They add to the challenge and excitement of sailing the A's, and we became quite proficient that first summer.

The next year Obie O'Brien and his self-styled Corning Rum Dums bought the *Caprice* from Spink Taylor and joined the fun. About that time Commodore Wagner presented the *Mystery* to cousin Caroline Champlin, Uncle Charlie's daughter, and she promptly sold the *Deltox* to one of her beaus of the moment, De Forrest van Lieu, leaving us free to sail the *Mystery*.

The A's raced again in the summer of 1937, but the fleet was only a shadow of its former self, consisting only of: *Caprice*, *Deltox* and *Mystery*. The *Mystery* was a heavy weather boat, the *Caprice* did best in light conditions and the *Deltox* liked light airs. We won the championship that year with the *Mystery*—not because we actually won the most races, but because we completed them all. When we won in a big wind, the *Deltox* or the *Caprice* had tipped over.

There is a postwar coda to my romance with the A's. It was the first week in September, 1945. I had taken off from Kellogg Field near Battle Creek, Michigan. It was my last official day with the 52nd Troop Carrier Wing, with whom I had flown for many months in Europe. We had been posted to Kellogg Field for a refit. We would be brought up to strength, issued new C-46 Curtiss Commandos and would then fly to Okinawa to participate in the planned invasion of Japan. But then the A-bombs had been dropped, and the war was over.

The next day I would head back east and report to Ft. Dix, New Jersey, to be discharged. But I had decided to take a final flight, for the fun of it. We hadn't been issued the new C-46s. The only plane available was the general's bright and shiny refurbished C-47, so I borrowed it.

I had decided to pay the home town a visit, and headed east. We were a bit low on fuel, so I landed at Buffalo and also picked up a couple of milk shakes for lunch. Climbing out from Buffalo, the view was spectacular, we could see the Falls and Lake Ontario. Over Dansville, we could see the westernmost of the Finger Lakes. Then, well ahead of us we could make out a large white barn with a deep valley behind it. It was the D.W. Putnam farm, and the Keuka Lake valley. I throttled back and started our descent.

The familiar Y shape of Keuka came into view, and the orderly rows of vineyards on the steep hillsides. We swung down over the lake. There was a strong west wind, evidenced by the dark cat's paws on the surface. We flew rather low over the village, then on up the valley and buzzed the airport. The air was quite rough so we turned and flew back toward the lake. At the head of the lake we dropped down and went past the cottage and in the relatively calm air on the east side we motored along, past all the familiar landmarks of a lifetime, the Gateway Cottage, the Howells' on Tanglewood.

We started climbing when a familiar sight caught my eye. Between Keuka and the Bluff was an A, bottom up. I could tell from the black hull that it was the *Mystery*. There were figures sitting on the upturned hull and several motorboats coming to the rescue. "They'll learn the hard way," I thought to myself, "that you don't let an A go all the way over." We circled the end of the Bluff and as we climbed I took another look at all the familiar landmarks. We headed west and I turned the plane over to "George," the automatic pilot, and sat back and reminisced about all the great times and great people I'd known on the shores and the surface of that wonderful body of water.

An Interrupted Journey

Keuka Lake, July 1934

WHEN WE WERE younger, nothing daunted us, although the impossible tended to slow us down a bit. And so it was one marginal day in July. Jack Horne and I had met two very attractive young girls at the Farm, Uncle Charlie's home, the day before. They were from Corning and were spending the week at a cottage near Penn Yan, twenty-two miles north of Hammondsport.

They invited us to visit them and even proposed that we sail down and give them a ride. Well, why not! We would take the *Deltox.* It was a Class A Inland Scow, forty feet long, sloop rigged, with the mainsail and jib totaling nearly five hundred square feet of canvas. When the A's were being raced, they were manned by a crew of four. The crew had two main functions: to handle the sails, the leeboards and the backstays and, since there was no keel, to serve as ballast to keep the boat upright.

The day we had picked for the expedition was not ideal. There was a north wind and a hint of rain. Jack and I went down to the cottage, rigged the boat and set out for Penn Yan. We planned an intermediate stop just above Tanglewood Point to pick up Joe Swarthout, who was joining the party.

On Keuka Lake, north winds are the steadiest and most reliable. West or south winds tend to get riled up when they come over the hills or out of the glens. But we got off to a good start and made the four miles north to Tanglewood in just over an hour. At that rate we would hit Penn Yan about dusk. We were facing a twenty-two mile beat into the wind. But we weren't concerned about that. At that moment we were discussing the best place to land and pick up Joe.

He was staying at the old Hammondsport Club that belonged to his grandfather. It didn't have a very large dock, but as it turned out, we needn't have worried. While we were looking shoreward and contemplating a landing, a sudden unnoticed increase in the wind heeled us up past the point of no return, and over we went.

This was our first experience in tipping over, and it was a devil of a shock. The boat was big to begin with, and with its mast and sails in the water it approached the size of a football field. The main danger was that if it went mast-down, it would be very difficult to right, and there was the possibility of breaking the mast. Sitting on the topside, we were amazed how high we were above the water.

Our first priority was to get the sails down. With the wind pushing against the big expanse of the boat's bottom, the sails acted like a plane, slicing deeper and deeper into the water. We worked our way forward until we were above the leeboard. When we landed on the smooth, aluminum surface we both slid off into the lake. We climbed back on the board and our combined weight very slowly brought the boat back so the mast was level with the surface of the water. So far, so good.

I swam around the bow to the base of the mast and was uncleating the main and jib halyards when Jack called, "Need more ballast!" So back I swam, and again we were able to bring her back level. Returning to the mast, I was able to pull in the sails, and I returned to the leeboard. For the moment, we were all right; it was now a matter of waiting for someone to help us.

We were just about in the middle of the lake and even with Tanglewood Point. Help was soon on the way. Moving slowly was what appeared to be someone rowing a very large boat. It was Joe. He had observed our plight and had gone down the beach a couple of cottages to Cousin Emily Howell's to borrow a boat. There were two available, but for some reason she insisted he take the outboard, with oars. Thus his slow pace.

When Joe did reach us, I got in the stern and he rowed me around to the top of the mast, which I picked up and started lifting until the boat was almost balanced. We called to Jack on the leeside to swim clear, and up she went.

We had one problem that slowed us down—my hand. I'd had an operation a couple of weeks before and wasn't supposed to get my hand wet, so I had it enclosed in a large rubber balloon, courtesy of Doug Meadowcroft at the local balloon works. It was watertight but cumbersome.

We put up the jib and with Jack spelling Joe at the oars (my hand eliminated me) we made steady progress, although both the wind and the rain were increasing. But we finally made it to Joe's and went up to the Club and, hopefully, a little warmth.

Inside, Joe's mother, Laura, had watched our drama unfold, and greeted us with towels and blankets. She even offered us a hot toddy. In those days there was a chocolate mix like cocoa. Naive fellow that I was then, I was quite disappointed when she handed me a glass of hot water laced with whiskey. But it didn't go to waste; Joe drank it.

We hung our clothes by the fire and soaked up the warmth. It had stopped raining so there was nothing to do but call it a day and sail back down to the cottage. But there was a slight hitch: the boat was gone. We rushed out, thinking it might have broken away and floated ashore. But it hadn't. The people in the next cottage told us that a motorboat had picked up it and headed back down the lake with it.

It turned out that just after Joe had appeared at Cousin Emily's in quest of a boat, Emily had called Aunt Jessie at the Farm. In turn, Aunt Jessie had called Charlie Pilgrim at the boat yard. Charlie in turn had dispatched his son Floyd to the rescue. Floyd, of course, had arrived after the crisis had been resolved, but not wanting to return empty-handed (or possibly operating under Aunt Jessie's orders) had taken the *Deltox* in tow.

As a result of all that, Jack and I had to hitch a ride back home and, adding insult to injury, had to pay the Pilgrim establishment five dollars for the tow.

We never did sail all the way to Penn Yan, but the day wasn't a complete loss. We had gained a lot of valuable experience. And there was an amusing sidelight to the story. In those days all the cottages shared a party telephone line, and listening in was a popular pastime in days before soap operas (you always knew whose ring had been rung). After Emily's call to Jessie and Jessie's to Pilgrims, everybody along the line knew a drama was being played out and it enlivened a rainy afternoon. The cottage dwellers reminded me of the episode several times over the next couple of years.

Canoeing in the Adirondacks

Long Lake, New York, August 1934

THE DAY HADN'T started out too well. We hadn't gotten a very good night's sleep. This was the third day of Joe Swarthout's and my canoe trip through the Fulton Chain of Lakes that began at Old Forge and ended at Saranac Lake in the Adirondacks. I was seventeen and Joe was fifteen.

It was our first undertaking of this magnitude and we'd learned a lot while paddling over lakes one through eight and carrying the canoe and our duffel over three portages, each more than a mile long. The big lesson was that we had packed too much stuff. While it rode nicely in the canoe, it quickly became very heavy when we had to carry it. We were prepared for any situations—a change of whites in case we met up with a party; two mattress pads and, this being before the days of the two-pound down sleeping bag, two blankets apiece, plus our tent and ground sheets. There were unnecessary luxuries adding to the load.

We had reached Raquette Lake the day before and after a stop at the village had paddled on, looking for a good camp site. Several miles up the lake we pulled in on a nice sandy beach. There was a small tent pitched back from the shore but there was no one in sight so we set up camp a respectable distance away. After a swim and our supper we were sitting around the fire watching the sunset and enjoying the peace and quiet.

Just as it was getting dark a canoe appeared and landed on the beach. Two couples debarked. They seemed in very fine, high spirits. When they saw us, they waved and shouted greetings. That was the end of our peace and quiet. Amazing how sound travels over water: splashing, giggling, laughing. It did sound like a lot of fun. When we got up and broke camp the next morning, all was quiet in the other tent, and no wonder.

Our next portage was from the north shore of Raquette Lake to Forked Lake and then another from Forked Lake to the Raquette River. That was a long one—four miles—a real test of endurance. We got a break when we were getting our gear together for the carry to the river. As we were loading up a man came along with a team drawing a light wagon. He drew up and asked if he could give us a lift—the gear, not the canoe, which wouldn't fit in the wagon. Joe got aboard to handle the duffel, I carried the canoe.

The road, or tract, was soft sand and although my load was considerably lighter than usual, walking in soft sand is not easy, and it was a hot day. We also weren't sure how far we had to go, and I think neither of us had a watch. After a while I began to worry that I'd missed the entrance to the river, so I put down the canoe and walked toward the river. I came to the top of a cliff and there, a hundred feet below, was the river, flowing serenely along.

Aha! thought I. The end of the carry could be up stream and I have gone too far or, because the bank is so steep, it is down stream. I'll put the canoe in the water and either go up or down stream and surprise Joe. So, holding the canoe with one arm and slip-sliding from tree to tree with the other, I reached the river. Just up stream and around a bend was a fairly good-sized falls, so I unshipped a paddle and headed downstream. It was a beautiful stretch of river, canopied by large trees. A pair of wood ducks herded their family away from the strange interloper. But the tranquillity didn't last long. Around a bend there was a new sound—a muted roar, and the speed of the current increased. I paddled ashore, beached the canoe and walked downstream. I didn't have to go far to see an even larger fall, and no way over or around it.

The bank here was higher and, if possible, steeper than the one I'd scrambled down. But there was no alternative, so with the canoe slung over one shoulder and using both hands, I clawed my way up the damned cliff. At the top I flopped down to catch my breath, then shouldered the canoe again and continued down the track. It wasn't long before I came to a sign with an arrow pointing to the river. And there, at the river's edge, was our duffel, but no Joe.

I sat down with my back against the bedrolls, and the next thing I knew Joe was shaking me awake and asking, "How'd you get here?"

After he'd arrived at the arrow pointing to the river and unloaded our gear from the wagon, he decided to go back up the trail and give me a hand, but he had obviously passed me while I'd gone down to the river and taken my ill-advised "short cut." Despite the good fortune of getting a ride, Joe had plodded eight miles along the sandy track.

It was well past lunch time but we were starved and decided to invade our emergency rations—a half-pound bar of chocolate and some cookies. Unfortunately we'd packed the chocolate with the First Aid kit, spare batteries and two bars of Palmolive soap from the Ferns Hotel in Old Forge. The chocolate now smelled of Palmolive. The taste was peculiar but not objectionable and we ate it gladly.

We loaded the canoe and paddled down the river and into Long Lake. We spotted an ideal camp site on a sandy beach on the north shore and set up the tent. Someone had camped there a night or two earlier and had made two beds of spruce boughs. Six-inch twigs are stuck in the ground vertically. It takes hundreds of twigs and a long time, but the results are extremely comfortable.

We had a swim and thought about supper, but Joe complained that his stomach didn't feel quite right. He was burping the taste of Palmolive and nothing in the larder appealed to him. I was concerned because I did most of the cooking and I was afraid something besides the chocolate ailed him. I thought a good, square meal would fix him up, but where to get one?

We'd noticed a white hotel on the far side of the lake with signs of a lot of waterfront activity. The hotel might serve us dinner.

We dug into the duffel bags for our wrinkled but clean white shirts and trousers, slicked up as best we could and paddled over. I explained to the desk clerk that my companion wasn't feeling up to snuff and a well-prepared meal would do him a world of good. The clerk said we'd have to wait until the resident guests were served, and would we adjourn to the veranda.

We watched the other guests, fairly formal in coats and ties, and they must have eyed us with some curiosity. After quite a wait, we had yet to be summoned and went back inside to ask the clerk what was happening. He seemed rather evasive about why we hadn't been called, something about the dress code, possibly. In the end, we ate in the kitchen with the help, but we got the full four-course treatment, soup, salad, ham with pineapple and pie for dessert and our tab was a dollar.

We walked back to the canoe, where Joe suddenly divested himself of the chocolate plus the ham and all the trimmings, but then announced just as suddenly that he felt swell again. We got back in the canoe and paddled a mile along to the village of Long Lake. The local movie house was playing *Tarzan and His Mate*, with Johnny Weissmuller and Maureen O'Sullivan. One scene remains indelibly in my memory. It was shot underwater, tinted green, and the stars were swimming along wearing only their loin cloths. It was really very lovely but rather risqué for a pair of teenagers. We would have stayed for the second show but we had to paddle two miles back to our camp and we decided to wait and hope the show came to the Babcock in Bath. We did stop at the local soda fountain for a couple of sundaes. Joe was completely recovered.

We were breaking camp the next morning when a canoe with a young couple in it approached our point. The girl sitting in front was well-endowed and wearing one of the new two-piece bathing suits. We finished loading and shoved off and they waved and called goodbye. I had the feeling they were glad to see us go.

Joe was quite subdued as we paddled away. I asked why, and he said the girl had said "Bon voyage!" and he couldn't remember the French for "Thank you."

We went right to the village dock at Long Lake. We'd seen the station with a Railway Express sign. We made a tidy bundle with one of our ground sheets, enclosing the mattresses, the whites and a few other expendables. We sent it back to Hammondsport, $4.75 collect, and, lighter and wiser, we continued on our way.

Ridley

1936–1986

IT WAS OUR Fiftieth Class Reunion at Bishop Ridley College in St. Catharine's, Ontario, and we were sitting around the hospitality room doing a little reminiscing. "Remember the time at morning chapel," Bill Scandrett recalled, "when the Headmaster said, 'Will Tony Doherty and his gang of rowdies please remove the cannon from the front steps of School House before classes begin?'"

"Ye Gods," I wanted to say, "but that was fifty years ago." Actually it didn't seem all that long ago. As a family, our roots at Ridley go back more than ninety years—three generations as I write this. My father was an Old Ridlian, Class of '03, my Uncle Kid was '08 and I was '36.

I suppose I should give Rudyard Kipling as a Ridley ancestor as well. I became acquainted with Kipling while we still lived in New Orleans. Mother would read to Boog and me during supper. We were introduced first to *The Jungle Book*, the beginning of a long and pleasant relationship. But the book I associate with Ridley was *Stalky and Co.* The adventures of those boys at an English public school established a setting that I later met in real life at Ridley.

The indoctrination I received about Ridley from my father and my uncle wasn't quite fiction. But I think they may have embellished the truth at least a little. Dad, for example, told of the time the original School House on the east bank of the old canal burned down. The fire was at the further end of the building from Dad's room, which was on the second floor. Dad gathered all his clothes into a bedsheet, tied the corners, tossed the bundle out the window, then slid down the drainpipe to the ground in his nightshirt. But when he ran to the spot where he'd dropped the bundle, it was gone. His less enterprising classmates were putting on his clothes.

I expect if the stories Gink and Kid told me were compared to the ones I told my son, they'd be remarkably similar, all about high jinks and athletics, and very little reference to scholastic achievements.

I first saw Ridley on a late June afternoon in 1927. Dad was driving Jack Seely and me up to Onondaga Camp on Georgian Bay, and we stopped off to see Ridley. We drove onto the campus and up the long drive. I saw a large expanse of closely clipped lawn and several buildings of vine-covered brick. There was one that drew our special attention. It was the Chapel, a very striking Gothic structure built of light sandstone. Dad told us it had been erected in memory of the Old Ridlians killed in World War I. Later Jack and I went inside the Chapel. The light streamed through the stained glass windows, softening the gray of the stone walls. Standing outside and looking at the Chapel silhouetted against the sky, you felt that the Old Boys who lost their lives had been given a beautiful tribute.

We saw a number of older boys, dressed in white, playing a game that involved a ball and a wide bat but that didn't resemble baseball. It was cricket and the large lawn was the cricket crease. Dad parked the car and led us over to a man with dusty red hair, sitting in a folding chair and carefully observing the match. This was Dr. Griffith, who had been a student at Ridley the year it was founded. When Dad was there as a student, Griffith was a master and coach of the rugby team on which Dad played and which won the '03 championship in its league. The next year Dr. Griffith returned to his alma mater, the University of Toronto. as head coach of the rugby team. He urged Dad to enter the university and play rugby. Dad did, and made many friendships that were to influence his later life in significant ways. Now Dr. Griffith was back at Ridley as headmaster.

Talking with Dr. Griffith, it turned out that I had shared a cabin at Onondaga Camp with his son Adam and another Ridlian, Tony Cassels, both of whom were returning in the fall. As a matter of fact, Jack's brothers, Bill and Hank Seely, were both at Ridley. Bill was on the first rugby squad, Hank on the second.

There were obviously all kinds of forces that were drawing me to Ridley. Early in September Dad had arrived from London (Ontario) and announced that we were going to attend Ridley. He had stopped in St. Catharine's and told Dr. Griffith that he had a pair of potential rugby players, and when did he want them? The sooner the better was the answer and we were on our way in a day or two.

There was a ritual when you went through customs at Lewiston, just before the bridge to Canada. When you were asked where you were going, you said Ridley and were waved right through. On the first trip, Dad stopped before customs and gave us a serious piece of advice (the same one he had given us before we went to Onondaga Camp). "Just remember," Dad said, "the Americans did not win the war. They just helped."

We stopped at the headmaster's house and were talking to Dr. Griffith when a boy named Hugh Glasgow walked by. Dr. Griffith reached out, grabbed him, and tugged his hair. "Haircut, Hughie," he said. I concluded that very little escaped the headmaster's notice, and I was right.

I was assigned to School House under the tender care of Terry Cronyn, a cousin of the actor Hume Cronyn. Duane went to Gooderham House under Mr. Hamilton. That first year, I was assigned to 6A, the top form, and Duane, as I remember, to the 4th. We were amazed at our schedules: seven or eight subjects a day in thirty-minute classes and an enforced study hall six nights a week. But the quality of the athletics made up for all the studying. I was on the rugby seconds squad, although the nearest I'd come to football before was an occasional game of touch. I had dreams of playing in the backfield but my father had been one of the best ends and surest tackles in Ridley history, and Dr. Griffith saw to it that I was going to play end, too, and I did.

So many memories of Ridley relate to the football field—the sights, the sounds and, yes, the smells. Leather, sweat, and socks in need of a wash. Scrimmaging against the first team, with Joe Mitchell calling signals; trying to stop Vic Francis, who had the effortless ease of the true athlete; the hollow thump as Pat Trench punted; the day Larry Redman went through on a line buck and when he'd broken through the secondary, he was so astonished he didn't know what to do, so he stopped.

With rugby, there were the A squad lectures. Gathering in a classroom in pajamas and bathrobe while Dr. Griffith, sitting on a table, swinging his legs, takes us back with words and gestures to the dawn of Ridley football and the legendary names: Casey Baldwin, Gord Slanker, Spark and Billy Bell, their strengths and, which was rare, their weaknesses. You could fantasize that in future lectures he might be talking about some of us: Francis, Mitchell, the McLachlan brothers, and perhaps even the Doherty brothers.

If you reminisce about your old school, you better say something about the academic endeavors as well. In my case, coming from an American high school into the top form in a Canadian public school was more than a shock, it was nearly a disaster. For one thing I did it backwards, taking the tougher 6A subjects the first year and struggling, taking the easier 6B subjects the second year, and coasting. I sure tried the instructor's patience in senior chemistry and physics. I did pass Canadian history the first year under Terry Cronyn's guidance and was quite surprised to learn that during the War of 1812 the British and the Canadians soundly whipped the Americans on several occasions, and even pushed them into the river at Queenston Heights. Dr. Griffith's son Adam was very long suffering in his nightly tutoring sessions. We had long discussions about the Canadian vs. the U.S. system. In the States the philosophy was to take a subject, pass it and forget it. I like the Canadian idea of taking a subject for several years and progressing with it.

Ridley kept calling us back, as an Old School will. In October, 1939, when the war that would affect both our lives was already raging in Europe, Boog and I were togged up in our lace-up canvas jackets, short pants and knee pads for that great Ridley tradition, the Old Boys Game. Boog and I had been playing rugby for several seasons and with quite good results. We were inter-school champions for four years out of five.

In September I'd had a call from a former teammate suggesting that Boog and I play in the Old Boys' game. We were now Old Boys ourselves. Well, why not?

Those games, I remembered, usually followed a pattern. The Old Boys would field a team that included a number of legendary players, including some who'd gone on from Ridley to play at their universities. The pattern was that during the first half we of the current teams were hard-pressed to hold the Old Boys, and sometimes we didn't. But slowly in the second period the tide would turn. We would not only be able to hold the All-Stars, we'd begin to score and we usually won. The answer was conditioning. The Old Boys just ran out of steam, and youth was served.

After I hung up the phone I began to have second thoughts. I hadn't played a game of rugby in four years and I was by no means in shape. I thought of the Old Boys running out of steam, and it was a fate I didn't want to share. But I still had two weeks, and I set up a program to help my legs and wind. I was staying at the cottage, which was a mile from the house in town. After supper at the house, I'd leave my car there and run the mile to the cottage. In the morning I'd take a brisk swim, and then run back to the house, have breakfast and go to work. I picked up the pace each day and was beginning to feel in pretty good shape.

I had a last pre-breakfast swim and then Boog and I drove to St. Kitts, as we called St. Catharine's, where Ridley was. We had lunch and grand meetings with old pals.

All of us on the Old Boy squad were really hoping we could beat the Ridley first team for once. I was playing in the backfield, where Dr. Griffith had never let me play, and I was hoping to complete a few passes, which he'd never let me try before.

The game followed the pattern of the previous Old Boy Games. We were ahead at the half, and with the help of some miraculous catches by the ends I even completed some passes. I don't remember exactly when my clock ran down. I may have dozed off sitting on the bench at half-time. But I did go back in the game, and I remember the big play quite clearly, up to a point. I was to fake a run around left end, pivot, and pass to Ping Snyder, who was going right. I got the pass away and then something rolled over my right ankle, and that was it.

They carried me off the field and left me to the tender mercies of Doc Chapman. The ankle hurt like hell, especially when Doc wiggled it around to determine that it wasn't broken, just some torn tendons. He strapped it up and gave me a shot, which helped a lot. Someone kindly stuck a cigarette in my mouth and I almost choked to death.

I hobbled to the shower and then to the post-game tea, looking for Boog. He and some cohorts had gone to the Falls for some night life. He left word that he would get back to Hammondsport on his own Great. I'd been hoping he would drive, because my injured right leg was the one that worked the brake and the accelerator.

My ankle pounding like a tom-tom, I went into town for dinner with a friend, Fred Wellington, who drove me back to school, where I'd decided to spend the night. The next morning I was in agony. The ankle resembled a balloon and felt as if it would burst at any minute. I'd spent the night in the infirmary and it was quite a chore limping down three flights of stairs and out to the car. Luckily the car had both a hand choke and throttle but the damned right leg did everything else, starter, brakes, everything.

It was a long trip back to Hammondsport. No four lanes and plenty of stop lights. I used the hand brake and the throttle and I got so I could shift without using the clutch. I looked for a hitchhiker who could drive, but no luck. And just outside Batavia I had a blowout. As I was coasting to a stop and rounding a curve, there was a gas station. That was my only happy break for the day.

I reached Hammondsport after what seemed an eternity and drove straight to the family doctor's house. Luckily, he was there and just sitting down to Sunday dinner. I hadn't been able to get a shoe on in the morning. He took off the sock and said, "My God," and then cut off Doc Chapman's wrapping, which was a blessed relief. I spent two weeks on crutches.

And I never played rugby again. When I did go back to Ridley once more, it was for that fiftieth reunion, where most of the time was spent sitting down, with a glass in your hand.

The Joys of Winter

The 30s

When Boog and I received those Flexible Flyer sleds for Christmas, a new winter world opened up for us. We were allowed to go off to Wheeler Avenue at the south end of town all by ourselves and go coasting with the other kids. But we soon graduated from Wheeler Avenue to Reservoir Hill, the steep dirt road that began not far from the mouth of the Glen and led up to the town reservoir itself and beyond to the farms on the hill.

Reservoir Hill had always been a favorite with the townsfolk. There used to be two large bobsleds, each carrying twenty people, including the driver. Being quite heavy, they were pulled up the hill by a team of horses, one of the same teams that pulled one or another of the fire wagons in emergencies. The bobsled driver was one of the firemen.

The starting point for the ride was the "Big Curve," where the road made a ninety-degree left turn before it plunged down into the village. It must have been a thrilling ride. The bobsled picked up considerable speed on the downhill run from the curve, then rocketed off Reservoir Hill and on to Pulteney Street, raced down past the village park and on down William Street to the lake—right on to the ice if the lake was frozen. At the lake it was retrieved by one of the teams and hauled back up the hill for another run. There was always a big bonfire blazing at the curve offering welcome warmth.

The big bobs were only a memory when we came along, but the tradition of the bonfire was still alive and we dragged along a small log or a packing crate as our contribution. We started our runs at the

Big Curve, but the big guys, who had small bobsleds, or dickies as they were called, would go all the way to the Quinns' house at the top of the hill. You had to be careful not to get run down by the dickies. We could hear them rumbling down the hill above us and we gave them lots of room.

Those were the days before sand and salt for the roads. The Hill was just hard-packed snow and we, too, would come rushing out onto Pulteney Street and down past the park until we began to slow down. There was no point in having to walk back any further than necessary.

When the sledding was good, we took our sleds to school so we could rush to the Hill when the bell rang and get in a ride or two before dark. We could almost always hitch a ride up. Very few of the farmers who did have cars drove them in the winter. They put them up on blocks and drained the radiators. They came to town on horse-drawn sleighs and, going back up the hill, would let us hitch our sleds at the back. If they had a heavy load, we'd have to walk alongside. Still it was a quicker way to the top, and it was to the top that we finally went.

Coasting was not entirely danger-free. It was risky shooting out onto Pulteney Street because adventurous villagers might be heading downtown for groceries and not see us in time. There were relatively few cuts and bruises at that, and I was probably the top scorer. I broke my wrist coming down Bully Hill, another steep and popular ride just north of town. I hit a sheet of ice and caromed into Otto Kohl's right front wheel. A more tranquil form of sledding was when Aunt Emily Howell would get out her Essex and, with a half-dozen sleds hooked on her bumper, tow us around town and once in a while around the whole valley.

Not long ago, watching my son, Traff, wend his way down a slope on his Space Age composition skis and fancy boots, I couldn't help thinking how far the sport had progressed in the nearly fifty years since I saw my first pair of skis.

That was the second or third winter after we left New Orleans. When the snow was right and we weren't sledding, we would walk across the valley and slide down the knoll at Uncle Charlie's farm. It was great sport and the bonus (unavailable on Reservoir Hill) was to go into his nice warm kitchen and be given mugs of hot cocoa and homemade cookies. Then one day Uncle Bob Howell showed up with a pair of skis and that changed the whole game.

Uncle Bob climbed to the top of the knoll where we'd been tobogganing, laid down the skis, put his boots in the single toe straps, gave a couple of sliding steps forward and gracefully went down the slope and on to the level field. We were absolutely enthralled. Actually skiing wasn't unheard of, and some of the guys had nailed straps onto barrel staves (very hard to steer). Store-bought skis were something else again, and that Christmas two pairs of Northland skis appeared beneath our tree.

Elaborate bindings were still well in our future. With our single toe straps the procedure was to ski along the level until you came to a hill. If it was down, you skied down it. With only a toe strap, there was no way of turning or checking, so it was straight down and out. If you had to stop, you tried to fall gracefully to the right or left. (We quickly learned that you didn't just sit down between your skis.)

When it came to making a run down a slope, the first person presumably chose the most challenging route and went straight down the hill. The next one put his skis in the same tracks and followed him. Each run made the track faster and the last one to go down it would slide well out into the field. Woe to him who tumbled and ruined the track.

Going uphill was boring. You had to take off your skis, put them on your shoulder and trudge up through the snow. But if you were lucky, the downhill run made it all worthwhile.

As our daring, if not our skill, increased. we began to add variations. We got hold of a door and made a ski jump. At first it was for the toboggans but we were soon trying it with skis. It was a challenge, and very exciting. The trouble was that with only the single toe straps the skis kept coming off, and you'd have to chase one or both skis down the hill and out into the meadow. And naturally you would have fallen in the snow. This resulted in frequent trips back to the farm's kitchen to dry off and have another warming mug of cocoa. The kitchen always had an interesting mix of aromas: cocoa and wet wool.

One Friday night not long after we'd had our Christmas skis, Boog and I made our regular pilgrimage to the movies at the Park Theater, sitting slouched down in the front row, as was the custom.

The feature was a western, but I remember nothing about who was riding the range that night. What I do remember was the short subject: a Pete Smith special called "Skiing in Europe."

What riveted my attention was what they could do on the skis. They were making abrupt turns between the poles on the run, and when they came to a bump they would sail through the air and when they landed their skis were still *on their feet.* A few scenes later skiers were shown starting from the top of a high tower, speeding down a ramp and sailing out over a valley. The majority of them landed safely and upright and then swung gracefully to a stop. Was this the same sport we'd been doing—sliding straight down a hill or jumping off a door with mixed results?

When I got home I was still bubbling with enthusiasm and curiosity. One of the wise family elders suggested I try the library for more information. I was waiting on the steps when Miss Laura Bailey opened the library at one o'clock that Saturday afternoon. I'm sure the library had a card index file, but I never used it and anyway Miss Bailey knew every book and where it was and whether it was in or out and if it was out, who had it.

But nothing about skiing. The closest she had was *The Bobbsey Twins at Snow Lodge.* She brought out some catalogues and asked me to choose a title from a list. I selected *Learning to Ski* by Proctor and Stephens. It arrived in an amazingly short time and it turned out to be a good choice.

The second chapter got down to the basics in a hurry. The most important items required to ski successfully, it said, were boots and bindings. We had neither! But the book had both illustrations and specifications, and where there is desire, there are solutions.

The boots were easiest to solve. I took a pair of Dad's Navy flying shoes, the type that were worn with putties, and the book along to Smitty's shoe shop. He added a square-toed sole nearly half an inch thick that extended out beyond the heel to create a lip that would hold the binding. Dad's boots were large enough so that I could wear several pairs of socks. They were also very stiff, as boots are today.

The harnesses, or bindings as they're called now, required a bit more ingenuity. Since there were metal brackets involved, my first stop was at Ned Hallenbeck's blacksmith shop, now located behind his house across the street from the town jail. He made a pair of non-adjustable steel plates that allowed the sole of the shoe to slide in under a lip that held the sides of the sole. There were slots for the heel harness. I went to Freidell and Lacher's for harness strap, copper rivets and buckles—and a fair amount of help. (It was about this time that whenever I went into the store, the clerk, Chub Benham, would say, "It won't work," before I'd opened my mouth. Sometimes he was right, but not about the ski harnesses.

They did work, but it was a long time, punctuated by a great many tumbles, before we gained any semblance of control. They did hold tight—very tight—and we were very lucky there were no broken ankles or other injuries, and that was due to luck and youthful suppleness rather than skill. Later, when the new self-releasing safety bindings came in, the non-releasing kind we were using were quite accurately described as "bear traps."

One thing we did discover was that because all our skiing was on loose, unpacked snow, the only turns we could manage were telemarks. Now, all these years later, with the popularity of cross-country skiing, the graceful, swooping telemark is *de rigueur.*

Introduction to the Bobsled

Lake Placid, December 1937

Everyone should have at least one fantasy come true. I know my cousin Harry (Champ) Howell and I did during Christmas vacation in 1927. We'd gone to a movie at the Babcock Theater in Bath, and the short subject was a travelogue about winter sports. One of the places it featured was the Mount Von Hovenberg Bobsled Run at Lake Placid. For one sequence, the filmmakers had mounted a camera on one of the sleds and filmed the run down the course. What a thrill.

On the way home I remarked that it would be great to take our skis and head for Lake Placid. Harry said, "Why not?" I didn't think for a minute that Aunt Emily would let her son make any such expedition, especially with me, whom she considered (unjustly, of course) quite irresponsible. But Harry called the next morning to say he was clear to go. So I faced the dilemma of broaching the subject with my family. I think they were so astonished that Emily gave Harry permission to go that they couldn't say no to me. Dad was a little concerned regarding our transportation. It was my pride and joy, a 1930 Packard roadster, a big, heavy car with a canvas top and Isinglass side curtains and a straight eight engine. I bragged that it could pass anything but a blonde or a gas station.

We left at seven in the morning. It was getting dark when we reached Saranac Lake and a little while later we pulled into Lake Placid. It exceeded our expectations: bright lights, decorations, sleighs, skiers on the street, an air of holiday festivity. In front of the Olympic Arena was a wall built of huge blocks of ice, lit from behind by colored lights for a spectacular effect. The tourist center gave us the name of a Mrs. Walton, who let rooms (a dollar a night). I stayed with her for a few days each of the next five winters.

We had dinner at a restaurant but were almost too excited to eat. We sat at the window, seeing dog teams as well as horse-drawn cutters go by. We walked past the outdoor skating rink and just beyond it was the high toboggan tower, steps up and a ramp on the other side leading to the frozen lake. That was for us. The temperature was near zero so we went back to Mrs. Walton's for suitable clothes. We returned and rented a toboggan and climbed to the top, which was about sixty feet above the surface of the lake. The ramp had been watered so the surface was clear ice. The ramp was pitched so steeply that as you took off you had the sensation of free fall. I had no idea how fast we were going, but the speed took us a long way out on the lake.

Fun; but we were cold and exhausted from the long drive. We stopped for a cup of hot chocolate to restore our circulation and went to bed.

The temperature dropped below zero the next morning, but miraculously the Packard groaned into life and we took off for the bobsled run a few miles down the road. We checked in and a teacher named Leonard, whom I got to know well over the next few years, outlined the course of instruction. First, you made a couple of passenger rides with one of the state's professional brakeman-driver teams. Next, you acted as brakeman with a state driver. Then, after several runs, you took the wheel yourself, with the pro braking for you. Starting from "Shady," where the course began, the brakeman held you in check for the first few runs. When (and if) your skill increased, so, with the brakeman's blessing, would your speed. Finally you were making the run with no braking at all, until the end, when the sled had to be braked hard to stop you before you came to the woods. There was, of course, more to braking than just stopping. With careful application of the brake you could correct a skid.

Harry had no interest in driving, but was willing to be qualified as a brakeman so we could rent a two-man sled and make some runs together.

Getting to Leonard's office, you crossed a bridge over the run, and as we arrived that first morning, we heard the rumble of a sled coming down the mountain. A moment later it came into view, really moving, then it swung into the last curve and roared under the bridge. We heard the driver shout "Brake!" A plume of snow and ice shot up behind the sled and it slowed to a stop. What a thrill that gave me.

But from my first familiarization ride until I checked out solo, it was one thrill after another. There were so many sensations to absorb—the speed (the more dramatic because you were only inches above the ice), the acceleration as you came out of the turns, the turns themselves. The turns were awesome just to look at, vertical walls of ice fifteen to twenty-five feet high, and you drove through them very near to the top. I don't know of any outdoor sport that was more exciting to learn, and it never lost its appeal to me. It was very gratifying to complete the course without a hitch and be given Bobsled Drivers License 199.

Since we'd had an early start, it was barely noon when Harry and I went to Leonard's office to rent a sled of our own. In those days they were pretty basic—four runners fastened to a heavy wooden base, a double-handled drag brake, steering wheel, and a one-inch-pipe guard rail along the sides and rounding in front to form a bumper. In no way did they resemble the streamlined, rocketing bobsleds of today. Two football helmets and two pairs of goggles completed our equipment.

We loaded the sled on the shuttle truck for the ride to Shady. We pushed off and whipped down to the bottom without incident, but when I yelled "Brake!" all hell broke loose. It felt as if a strong force had pushed the sled to the right and we went into a skid. I called for Harry to let up but still we skidded. The guard rails were coming up fast and the bumper hit a post, just off dead center. This kicked the sled to the left and me to the right and I ended up against the post. Harry piled up against me and then the end of the sled swatted him. It must have looked spectacular. I had the wind knocked out of me, but otherwise we were both all right. A lot of people gathered and were surprised when we both stood up and brushed the snow off. I had softened Harry's stop and the cushion on the sled had softened mine.

Several drivers were there and the consensus was that Harry had used only one hand to brake and that had thrown us into a skid. Since we weren't hurt, their advice was that we should go right back up and try it again. We did, and it went fine. We took one more run and called it a day because the place got very busy in the afternoon.

After lunch we found our way to Scotts Cobble Ski Center. By today's ski area standards. it would have been barely adequate for a beginner's slope. It was an open area about a quarter of a mile square. But it had a rope tow, the first we'd ever seen. The power unit was a new Ford tractor, with a grooved pulley attached to the differential which drove the rope. Between runs, we talked with the operator about increasing the rope's speed. He kept the tractor in low gear. He told us to come early the next morning and we could give it a try before the crowds got there. We did; we tried it first in second gear and then in third. By then we were going up hill as fast as we were going down. Approaching the top, we'd let go, make a climbing turn away from the rope, and zoom down. When we left, the operator was trying to explain to the other skiers that he couldn't legally run the rope that fast.

Late in the day we went to the Lake Placid Club for an apres-ski dance. The Club was a very venerable institution, the main building big and rustic, dating back to the late 1800s. It was made of logs, rough-hewn timbers, and massive stone work, including many large fireplaces, wonderful to stand in front of after a cold day skiing, with a mug of hot chocolate completing a pleasant experience.

We watched a collegiate hockey game in the Olympic arena that night, and thought of all the great skaters who had competed there, including Sonja Henie, who by then had become a film star.

There was another form of skiing that caught our eye: jumping. There was a ski-jump tower behind the high school and another at Intervales, on the way to the bob run. We watched several youngsters who didn't look to be much beyond kindergarten age going down the ramp and sailing through the air. It looked so easy and we gave it a try. It wasn't so easy, even off the fifteen meter ramp at the high school. The hardest part was the steepness of the landing area and the run out. That was where we came to grief. The sailing through the air was fun, but as hard as we tried to imitate the toddlers we had watched, spills were more frequent than successes.

We took bobsled runs every day. But they cost fifty cents each and our capital was running low. We ice-skated one night at the rink and tried again each day to master ski-jumping. One day we stopped the owner of a dog team (beautiful Siberian huskies) and asked if he had any puppies. He did. On our way home the last morning, we drove out a country road to his kennel. We walked through deep snow and the owner came out to greet us, along with several balls of fur, the cutest pups I'd ever seen. Harry made arrangements to buy one, but with a beagle and a cocker at home, I resisted. We named Harry's puppy "Ziggy," after Zig Zag, the famous double right-angle turns on the bob run.

"Just don't try to make that pup a house dog," the owner said as we left. "Kennel him outdoors regardless of the weather."

After the excitements of Lake Placid, the trip home was beautiful but anti-climactic. Ziggy slept all the way.

The Iceboat

Keuka Lake, January 1940

COUSIN JACK HORNE and I ran into Millard Babcock in White's Hardware Store in Bath. What we went in for is lost to memory, but after our meeting with Bab it didn't really matter. Jack and I mentioned that the lake was freezing and we were thinking about going in together on an iceboat, and that started it. Bab said he had an ice boat he wasn't using and why didn't we borrow it.

But first you have to know that Bab was a well-nigh legendary character around Bath. His father, or maybe his grandfather, started a company which manufactures wooden ladders in all sizes and shapes. Very successful and so far as I know still is. The stuff of legend is that when time came for Bab to enter the family firm, the family presumed he would start at the bottom and learn his way up. But Bab reportedly thought that the family connection enabled him to start at the top. The conflict was resolved, the legend continues, by an arrangement that paid Bab a goodly salary, said salary to cease the moment Bab set foot on Babcock Ladder property.

Whatever the facts, Bab had a lot of time for his hobbies. He was an excellent natural craftsman and became a skilled machinist, model maker, and gunsmith. And he had an iceboat.

We drove out to his house to look at the iceboat, which was stored in a barn. It was a big one. It was a rear-steering, Hudson River type, gaff-rigged, with a jib. It was built of oak and weighed more than a thousand pounds. Each runner was at least five feet long, with the runner shoes of inch-square steel bar. The wishbone or crossmember was solid oak, twelve inches thick where the mast was stepped, tapering down to five inches where the rudder brackets were attached. It was a big brute, all right, and our first problem was how to transport it to the Penn Yan end of the lake, where the ice was good and solid.

We accomplished it with the cooperation of Uncle Charlie, the Pleasant Valley winery truck, and a lot of back-breaking lifting. We arrived at the lake shore near Keuka College, but it was too dark, late, and cold to do anything that night. The next day was Saturday and we returned to the College to assemble our "monster." It took all our strength to line up the pieces and secure them with half-inch bolts and lag screws. The mast was like a medium-sized telephone pole and the stays were in comparable proportions. The boom was at least twenty-five feet long and the jib nearly ten. Unfortunately by the time we finished rigging it, there wasn't a breath of air.

There was no wind the next weekend either, but we consoled ourselves with hot chocolate and a pleasant evening at the Anchor Room in the Keuka Hotel. Since the lake was freezing over at the Hammondsport end we decided to move closer to home. One Saturday I hitched a ride to the College, set sail, and headed south, very slowly. There was a light west wind that would move the craft along—if I walked behind it, pushing the boom. Once in a great while I could even get on and ride.

About two miles north of Keuka I was running out of time and enthusiasm and was working my way toward the east shore when I was spotted by my friend Obie O'Brien and his pals, who had been escaping the cold in the Anchor Room. They all piled aboard the iceboat, and with the luck of the Irish, a very good wind came up and we made several trips back and forth across the lake. When the boat was moving fast it made a heavy rumbling sound, more like a train than the high-pitched whine of today's front-steering boats. At one point we nearly sailed into an area of open water. It was difficult to see because of the ice chips thrown back by the windward front runner.

After stowing the circus-tent-sized sails and putting the runners on blocks of wood so they wouldn't sink down and freeze in the ice, I hitched a ride back with Obie and his gang and we stopped at the Anchor Room to thaw out. Iceboating is a very cold sport and knowing the right spot to warm up is very important.

Having an iceboat is the opposite of putting a sailboat in the water early in the season. With an iceboat the weather invariably hits warm spells. So it did with us. Here we were at the widest part of the lake, ideal for long runs and speed. But those holes in the ice took a long time to freeze over again, and to be thick enough to support the monster. We did go down a couple of times after work for short sails with cousin Caroline.

At last the weather turned cold again, and we were able to sail across to the Keuka Hotel and park by the hotel's dance hall. We had some good runs but it did take a lot of wind to get the boat moving. Exasperatingly, there were good winds during the week but almost never on weekends. There had been heavy snowfalls and that didn't improve matters either.

In late February and early March the weather began to deteriorate (from our point of view). The snow was melting and the lake was rising and there was water on top of the ice, beneath the snow. There was also about fifteen feet of open water between the shore and the ice. At the hotel, we were able to get to the solid ice via the dance hall, which was on piles over the water.

Jack and I had no trouble agreeing to call it a season. The question now was how to get the monster ashore. Fifty-plus years of hindsight says the simplest thing to do would have been to get a long, heavy rope and attach it to a truck and just gently pull the monster off the ice and up on the shore. This would have involved a trip to town to get a rope, and the whole thing seemed not much of a challenge.

Ironically a strong wind was blowing and we decided on a last run. The boat moved but it sent up quite a bow wave (that windward runner again) but this time it wasn't ice chips but ice water and slush. But the ride gave us a brilliant idea (for which modesty prevented either of us from taking credit later). With the speed we were capable of, it would be simple to skim across the narrow strip of water and right up on shore. It was almost too simple.

There was really only one thing that concerned us. How much speed did we need? We wanted to clear the water, but we didn't want to cross the beach and climb the bank behind it. We made a couple of practice runs, primarily to get our nerve up. Then it was all or nothing. Well, it certainly wasn't nothing.

We went well out so we would get up to speed. Then in we came, slush flying, trying to see where we were going, holding our breath.

It didn't work.

I don't know how fast we were going when we came to the edge of the ice, but I was sure that we were going to clear that beach, climb the bank, and end up in the hotel garage. But we didn't. When the front runners ran out of ice, a great sheet of water rose in front of us and we just stopped. At least the boat stopped. Jack and I continued forward until we came in contact with something solid. For my part I think it was the mast. Jack bounced off the crossbar. We both ended up waist-deep in some very cold water.

A number of people had been watching this unorthodox procedure and we were able to enlist their help in beaching the monster. After lowering and securing the sails, we drove home and got into some warm, dry clothes.

We returned the next day to dismantle the monster for what turned out to be the last time. Derb Young of the hotel watched our efforts and asked if we'd like to store it in the hotel's garage. So we did. We called Bab and told him where we'd put the boat and whether he wanted it brought back to Bath. But he said he thought the garage was a great place, and if it was OK with the Youngs, it was okay with him.

Then along came the war, and away we went. During the war the hotel's garage was torn down. When I returned from four years in my country's service and ran into Bab for the first time, the first thing he said was, "Where's my iceboat?"

The Tragedy at Bohemian Lodge

1913

Just south along the lakeshore from the house where Mardo and I live stands what is now our guest cottage, a colorful place, now well over a century old, called Bohemian Lodge. It's a rambling, two-story wooden structure, with Victorian-era scroll work and gingerbread. In the style of the period, it has a wide "rocking chair" porch that runs across the front and along the sides of the house, with lovely views of Keuka Lake from every seat. In days past there were the lake steamers to watch; now it is sailboats and, in summer, the *Keuka Maid*, diesel-powered and a kind of floating restaurant.

Our guests, including Mardo's numerous family, are probably unaware how Bohemian Lodge relates to one of the first great tragedies of the aviation age.

For nearly eighty years the Lodge was owned by the Urbana Wine Company, which was just to the west across the highway. It was the guest house, the setting for meetings, outings, picnics and accommodation for company guests. From time to time it was also a summer residence for winery officials. So it was in the summer of 1913 that Walter Hildreth, the president of Urbana Wine, came from his residence in New York City to spend the summer at Bohemian Lodge with his wife and their two daughters, Ruth and Dorothy.

I often think now of Hammondsport and the lake as the girls and their parents must have experienced it in 1913.

Getting to the lake was itself a time-consuming adventure. It began with a train ride either to Bath or to Penn Yan to the north. Bath was usually favored, because visitors could then board the Bath &

Hammondsport Railroad for the eight-mile run down the valley to Hammondsport. There were six round-trips a day! At Hammondsport it was only a few steps to the steamer dock. The steamers carried grapes in season and still wines and champagne to be shipped on by rail. The steamers also stopped at the three main hotels on the lake—the Grove Springs and Keuka Hotels and the Gibson House—as well as at private residences like Bohemian Lodge, which had their own docks.

It's difficult to picture the lake as it was then. The vineyards began in Pleasant Valley and ran north beyond Pulteney. The rows of grapes often began at the lake and climbed the steep hillsides on terraces. There were fewer than a dozen summer residences between the village and the bluff.

The local wines and champagnes were winning national and international fame, and gold medals. Visiting the dozen or so local wineries and sampling their products was a very popular form of holidaying.

But during those first years of the new century, something else was bringing worldwide attention to Hammondsport. It was aviation and the dramatic achievements of Glenn H. Curtiss. From a bicycle repair shop on the village square, he had progressed to a chain of three, then to designing and manufacturing motorcycles and setting world speed records and then, fatefully, to aeroplanes (as they were then called). In 1908, as a member of the Aerial Experiment Association, Curtiss piloted the *June Bug,* which he had designed, on the world's first pre-announced flight of a kilometer. (In fact, the flight went further than that.) The achievement earned $10,000 and a trophy from *Scientific American Magazine.*

Its work presumably accomplished, the AEA disbanded, but Curtiss continued to design and manufacture aeroplanes. Since pilots were needed to fly them, Curtiss established a flying school, where the first U.S. Navy pilots and many others learned to fly those early, fragile, pioneering crafts.

They were glamorous figures, especially the Navy flyers, popular with local families and with the local belles particularly. The local lads were less enthused, and I've said elsewhere none of the pilots were ever asked to join Hammondsport's exclusive Glenwood Club.

Training flights required calm air, so they were often scheduled for daybreak or just before sunset when conditions were usually ideal. This meant the flyers had plenty of time during the middle of the day for the pleasures of the lake: sailing, swimming, and canoeing. It was probably inevitable that the flyers would discover Bohemian Lodge. Here was a place steeped in open-door hospitality, with the Hildreth daughters as hostesses, and with equally attractive feminine house guests or visiting friends.

The Lodge became a particularly favored visiting spot for the Naval officers, including Lt. Jack Towers, who was later to command the three N.C. planes on their historic transatlantic flight and still later to command Naval aviation in the South Pacific during World War II. Another was Lt. Holden C. Richardson and a third was Lt. Pat Bellinger, both of whom flew N.C's on the transatlantic flight. Bellinger also made admiral during World War II.

During that summer of 1913, the Curtiss flying boats were being tested and perfected, with daily flights from both land and lake, and they created wide and excited interest among the villagers and the visitors. That summer, too, Lincoln Beachey, probably the most famous of the world's first generation of stunt pilots, had come out of retirement and was in Hammondsport to take delivery of a plane specially designed for his stunt flying.

And so all the elements for tragedy were in place. We have to presume that Tuesday, October 7, 1913 was a nice fall day, not too windy. Lincoln Beachey was going to flight-test his new machine and a crowd had gathered at the field to watch him.

Among the early arrivals were the Hildreth daughters, Ruth and Dorothy. With their escorts, Navy lieutenants Richardson and Bellinger, they climbed atop the hangar and took seats as Beachey took off and began flying back and forth across the field.

In a special dispatch datelined Bath, New York, the *New York Herald* recounted what happened next:

> When Beachey recognized the party he dipped his wings in salute, and his act of courtesy was returned. He flew to the end of the field, turned and came back. When directly over the heads of the Hildreth party, Beach's machine was seen to

> dip dangerously. Immediately afterward the airplane hurled the girls and the lieutenants to the ground, a distance of ten feet. The airplane careened wildly and plunged thirty feet to the grass. Beachey was unseated and the machine was wrecked. Spectators rushed to the Misses Hildreth and their escorts. Miss Ruth Hildreth, one of the sisters, was insensible. Miss Dorothy Hildreth was also insensible. Lieutenant Bellinger and Lieutenant Richardson were able to arise when aided. Miss Ruth Hildreth was dead when a physician reached the spot.

Miss Ruth was twenty, her sister, who was badly injured but survived, was a year younger. A jury exonerated Beachey of any blame in the tragedy. He continued his stunt flying, specializing in continuous loopings of the loop. But in San Francisco in 1915 he was drowned when the wings of his plane collapsed during a steep dive, plunging him into the Bay.

The Hildreths never stayed at Bohemian Lodge again and Dorothy did not visit Hammondsport for several years. Ruth was apparently the first ground casualty of the age of aviation, a sad and ironic footnote to history. I can never walk over to the Lodge without thinking again about Ruth and that long-ago autumn afternoon.

Four of Tony's forebears gathered with friends for a portrait in about 1884. His grandmother (Nano) is seated at right in white. His great-grandmother, Emily Baker Champlin, is at the center in black. His great-aunts, Catherine (Kate) Champlin Bauder (top right), and Caroline Champlin Nichols (sitting on the grass at left), were Emily's daughters.

Tony's father, "Gink," flies the rebuilt plane of Prof. Langley off Keuka Lake in 1914. Curtiss and the Smithsonian hoped to establish that Langley's aerodynamic designs were valid.

W.E. Doherty, Sr. ("Gink")
Tony's dashing aviator father, probably in his thirties.

Tony at age four, 1921, playing in the Gulf of Mexico during the family's New Orleans days.

Tony the footballer played for the Ridley (Ontario) College varsity team. He graduated in 1936.

Tony at age twenty-three, having joined the Royal Canadian Air Force as an air cadet. The U.S. was not yet at war.

Tony in England, 1942. He had grown a moustache and become a sergeant-pilot attached to the RAF.

Bobsledding at Lake Placid in 1937. Tony steered; his cousin Harry (Champ) Howell braked.

Wilbur, the eagle Tony trained in the 1930s.

Above: Sailing on Keuka Lake in postwar days, Tony negotiated a nice breeze in a Hobey with his young cousin, Marge Chamberlain, as ballast.

Below: The Teal, a Schweizer seaplane with a top-mounted engine and propeller, was Tony's favorite airplane. Production was discontinued after another of the Teals crashed.

Tony sailing the Deltox, an A class scow originally owned by his uncles, Charlie and Malburn ("Kid") Champlin, but later owned by Tony. The class is no longer raced on Keuka.

Tony in a 1-26 sailplane.

Tony in the vaults at the Pleasant Valley Wine Company, with champagne fermenting in "tierage."

Left: Ice-boating on Keuka Lake. Tony was still at it into his seventies until a hard crash, a dunking and some broken bones slowed him down.

Below: Tony wind-surfing on the lake in his seventies.

The Doherty Brothers—Tony, Duane (or Boog), and Peter met again at the wedding of Peter's daughter Barbara in 1988.

Tony's house on Lake Street in Hammondsport.

This portrait of Tony hangs in the Glenn Curtiss Museum, of which he was director from 1987 to 1991 and a board member from 1966 until his death. The western hat he wears was given to members of a wedding party.

The War Years

Off to Enlist

1941

OUR WHOLE WORLD changed on that day in October 1939, when FDR reached down deep into that fish bowl, pulled out a capsule and announced, "One hundred fifty-eight!" Boog's draft number, the first one to be called.

From that day on, things moved in a blur. Boog and Edie Peden were married on December 26th and a week later he reported for induction. The finality of it really set me to thinking. Where do I go from here? Boog's letters home didn't help my dilemma a bit. The shortage of Army clothing, lousy food, going on maneuvers with trucks for tanks, and stove pipe cannons and such tidings did not whet my enthusiasm for military life. On the other hand, military life was going to be as inevitable as death and taxes. I'd have to do something about it.

So I joined the Royal Canadian Air Force. It was closer than Texas and a lot of my Ridley schoolmates were already in.

I signed up and exchanged my individuality for a number (R-131076) in Hamilton, Ontario, was herded on a train to Toronto, and then climbed aboard a crowded truck for a ride to the Exposition Grounds where we became just a few more bodies added to the 17,000 (yes, 17,000) recruits who were already there. We stood in queues to sign still more forms, were issued sheets, blankets, and a pillow, and assigned to the Sheep Pen.

Manning Pool, where we were billeted, had been the livestock facility, complete with a large show ring, where we now gathered for parades and lectures. The Sheep Pen was exactly that, an area of several hundred square feet covered with pipe-formed pens for sheep. Rather than tear down the pens, they were covered with a raised floor one plank thick. The floor was a wonderful sounding board, and five hundred double-bunks were placed on top of it.

Exhausted, I slept heavily until a noise like a thunder storm combined with a passing freight train brought me bolt awake. Nine hundred men were starting the day. I hadn't seen so many men in one place outside a football game. One of the recruits said the only way you could get any privacy was to put your fingers in your ears and shut your eyes. I realized the hard truth that you weren't an individual any more, you were a cipher.

It was my introduction to life in the service: parades, shots, lectures, more parades, lectures on careless sex and other items of hygiene. After a couple of days, I came up with the pip. Don't know if it was the shots, the food or the drastic change in lifestyle. I ended up in the sick bay for a couple of days and when I went back to the Sheep Pen, I was shocked to find it was empty except for a single bunk in the center. Mine. It was eerie being alone in the huge cavern. I went to the orderly room and was told my former companions had all been assigned to training flights and had left. Since I couldn't be found, I'd go out with the next assignments, just stand by.

The next two days I was in limbo, a man without a country or in this case a flight. My biggest problem was getting to sleep in that silent cavern. That all changed abruptly. One night after midnight all hell broke loose. Today it would be like ten jets taking off at once. The lights came on and a horde of blue-uniformed men stamped in. They were Royal Air Force cadets, nine hundred strong. They had arrived by ship at Halifax and entrained for Toronto. At that time, the British gave their servicemen steel heel plates to save leather, and with eighteen hundred feet banging on that sounding board floor, the din was unbelievable.

I was completely surrounded by Limeys, with all the different accents—Cockney, Midlands, Scottish, Lancastrian, Welsh. I was eventually able to distinguish one from another. They paid little attention to me except to ask basic questions about Canadian money and the availability of young ladies. I could help with the former but not with the latter, being a stranger in town myself.

The frustration they faced was that they were quarantined for ten days. But somehow one of the chaps snagged a pass into town and came back with a kind of pool report on Toronto.

Wizard city, he said. No bomb damage. Bags (British expression for lots) of pretty ladies on the streets and apparently they were very attracted to the RAF uniform. But there was a problem, he said. At the proper hour, he had popped in to a restaurant for a cup of tea, with a crumpet. Crumpet? Blank stare. He ordered biscuits and was asked if he wanted cookies. He settled for toast, a common ground. But the worst, he said dramatically, was that "They brought me a cup of lukewarm water and a muslin bag with a minute quantity of tea leaves. You were supposed to dip the bag in the water until it was stone cold and then drink the bally stuff!"

War is various kinds of hell, and we'd only begun.

Flight Training

St. Eugene, Ontario, March 1942

AS WE CLIMBED down from the truck that had brought us from the train depot to the Eugene Flight Training Station, we were exuberant. After six months of seemingly endless, mindless duties, we had been posted to a station with aircraft that we would fly.

We were awakened next day by the sound of the Fleet's Finches getting their morning run-ups. We were excited but subdued: from now on it was fly or fall.

En route to breakfast (very good it was), we saw the large wooden hangars and beyond them the flight line with the rows of the small, bright-yellow biplanes with their RCAF roundels. It was a sight to make the pulse quicken. The airport seemed to stretch to the horizon, an unbroken white waste. We could have been at an outpost on the Arctic Circle. I had thought that aircraft operations in winter took one of two forms: either the runways were kept clear of snow and ice and the aircraft used wheels, or they were equipped with skis and flew off snow. But at St. Eugene (Station 13), they used a third system. They packed the snow on the field. Whenever it snowed, out came big wooden rollers to compact the surface. The process was simple to maintain during the really cold months, but as the weather changed the runways became temperamental, as we were to learn.

The great day soon came when we went down to the flight line, met our instructors and took our indoctrination ride. My instructor was a former bush pilot, Hal McGuire. He was an easy-going, laid-back type who suited me just fine. It must have been mutual, because I was the first in the class to solo, and after just four hours.

As the days grew longer and warmer, the packed snow would thaw and then, in the colder nights, freeze. We were taxiing, taking off, and landing on ice. It was a real worry when the ground crews, standing on ice, spun the propellers to start the engines. The brakes were useless on ice and things got a bit hairy, especially if there was much wind. There were cases when a wing tip or tail feathers were chewed up by a propeller.

Afternoon landings to the west into the prevailing wind were another dicey business. The sun glared off the ice and visibility was marginal. I was lucky enough to obtain a pair of Rayban aviator glasses. They really worked, and I have them to this day.

There was another aspect of the "snow field" airport that could cause problems. Except for the hangars, the field was difficult to spot from any distance away when the weather was marginal. I learned this the hard way. I was scheduled for a cross-country solo—St. Eugene to Cornwall to Pendleton and back to St. Eugene. It was a marginal day at best: low clouds and about five miles visibility.

There was no problem finding Cornwall. Reach the St. Lawrence River and there it was. But when I turned back north I ran into snow, a lot of it. I realized later (about 8,000 hours later), I should have headed downwind for St. Hubert's, west of Montreal. But I opted to head for home. I did hold one ace in my hand: the Ottawa River just north of our field wasn't frozen over and was a good landmark. I headed north. The snow was quite heavy and the ceiling was lowering right along, forcing me to fly lower.

The river showed up through the thickening snow. I was quite certain I was to the west of the field, so I turned east. In a short time I was over the village of Hawksbury. It was on the river about four miles northeast of St. Eugene. I set a course, hopefully, for home. By now, with all the snow in the air, visibility was zilch. There weren't any familiar landmarks. After five minutes or so I knew we missed the field, so it was back to Hawksbury and the river for another go. The snow in the farm fields was so deep that a landing anywhere but the base would be my last choice.

I was at about two hundred feet, eyeballs uncaged, when off to the right I caught a glimpse of a red flare, then another. We were home! Two classmates weren't so lucky, they landed in deep snow and flipped over. But there were no injuries and no damage to the aircraft.

As the melt water got deeper, flying was stopped earlier each afternoon. We were finally grounded for two days while they dug out the runways. Then we had a new problem on our hands—drift. When we were operating off a smooth snow and ice surface, you didn't have to pay too much attention to crosswind landings and drift. But those macadam runways were something else again. We were all in for some special drill. Some learned more quickly than others and a few learned the hard way, in a snow bank on either side of the runway.

It was while I was at St. Eugene (lucky or unlucky Station 13) that I lost my uniform, and almost ended up in jail. The field was only thirty miles from Montreal, and Montreal a short train ride from the Laurentians—and skiing. In late March we were given a forty-eight-hour pass and some of us decided to ski at St. Sauveur. I had boots and ski clothes and was able to rent poles and skis at the Mt. Royal in Montreal, where I had a room. I changed and went down to the lobby to collect my skis and leave my room key. There was a long line at the desk, but I ran into Ed Brown, one of my St. Eugene classmates, and asked him to have the clerk drop the key in my mail box, and I headed for St. Sauveur.

I stayed with my friends from a 1939 visit, the Wilkensons. The snow was great and the skiing was fun. We watched the yellow Harvard aircraft from St. Hubert's fly over in the clear blue sky. The fun came to a sudden stop when I got back to the Mt. Royal. Some way or another my friend Brown had garbled his assignment (to turn in the key) and had taken another room in my name. There'd been a party in that room and it had really been trashed. When I showed up, the hotel welcomed me with open arms and presented me with a bill for the damage. There I was in the manager's office, dressed for twenty below and sweating blood. After a lot of explaining, and a call to my friends the Wilkensons, I was able to retrieve my uniform, change in a wash room and return to the restful routine of St. Eugene. With great self-restraint, I didn't punch Ed Brown in the nose. The following week he transferred to the United States Air Force and ended up as a glider pilot.

Americans in the RCAF

Ottawa, Summer 1942

Thousands of Americans crossed the border after September 1939 to join the Canadian armed forces. The motivations were various, I suppose—a sense of adventure, an idealistic wish to defend democracy against totalitarianism, maybe just to escape being passively drafted, or simply to learn to fly.

Then there were the All-Americans. The story as I got it was this. In the fall of 1941, the Ottawa Rough Riders won the Gray Cup, the equivalent of the Super Bowl in the Canadian Football Leagues. The day after the victory banquet, the team's star quarterback, Tony Golab, and a good number of his teammates marched off to the RCAF recruiting office in Ottawa. They were nearly all Americans who had played football at their universities and many had in fact been named All-Americans. They'd come north to play with the Rough Riders.

I met up with them the next May when we were all LAC's (Leading Air Craftsmen) at the Service Flight Training School at Uplands, near Ottawa. The occasion of the meeting was sad. One of their number, Bill Oquendo, had spun in through a low cloud, our first casualty. The class slow-marched his coffin to the railroad station.

One June afternoon, Tony Golab asked me if I'd ever played soccer. I said I'd played center and goal at Ridley. Tony had been asked to put together a pick-up team to play the station team. Tony said, "You play goal, I'll play center." The really unfortunate part of the scrimmage from our point of view was that the goalie on the station team was the Chief Ground Instructor (CGI) who was in charge of the Ground School and as such the man in immediate charge of our destinies.

He was a small man, about five feet five or six who'd been a school teacher in civilian life. He seemed a nice man and I developed a good rapport with him, although I detected a kind of cockiness that is often characteristic of small men.

The game was a rout. From my idle position at goal, I saw Tony score at least four times, and each time both the ball and the CGI ended up in the net together. The final score was umpteen to nothing. At school the next day, the CGI was very subdued, none of his usual good cheer. We learned later that the coach of the station team had decided to reformulate his squad, using Tony and his mates, filling in any open spots with players from the former station squad—not including the CGI. I played with the team that summer and we did well against an RAF team in Montreal. It was all very pleasant.

Not so the atmosphere at the Ground School. The CGI seemed to favor the newer classes. Our group got the tougher questions, tinged with sarcasm. At that time, the RCAF policy was only a quarter of a class received commissions. These were based on three factors: flying ability, Ground School grades, and—the real kicker—what was called Character and Leadership. Flying ability was judged by your instructor and the Wing Flight Examiner. The other two categories were in the hands of the Chief Ground Instructor, the CGI.

One night we were playing a crucial game with the Army and had a chance for the service championship. The CGI stopped me on the way to the game and said, "I wouldn't think you'd be playing on the night before the Ground School finals." I was taken aback, but said I was expected to play. He said the finals were important for my career and walked away.

We played well and won. On my way to the shower, the CGI stopped me again and said, "So you decided not to take my advice."

On the day of the Wings Parade, not a single member of the team received a commission. Only one American was commissioned, and he had been at the top of the class.

The following spring I was in London between assignments and ran into Bill Sandercock, who'd been a sergeant pilot but was now decked out in a new pilot officer's uniform. He told me the class lists were available at Canada House and I might want to check them out. I did, and found out what a thorough job the CGI had done on us.

Tony Golab and his teammates were clumped near the bottom of the list. I was next to the bottom.

For many of our group, the bad luck held. One died in a training flight, another lost a leg in a crash on a training flight in England, another transferred to the American Air Force and died in a crash. Tony Golab had his Spitfire mistaken for a German ME 109 and was shot down by an American. The American later visited him in the hospital and rumor had it that Tony straightened him out.

All these things happened a long time ago, but it is impossible to forget the indomitable Tony Golab and his Rough-Riders, nor do I want to.

A Helpful Spit

Bodney, England, November 1942

IT WAS A really good day for flying—about five-tenths cloud cover at 5,000 feet and eight-to-ten mile visibility. Norm Phibbs and I had been sent up to practice two-aircraft close formation maneuvers. We were operating out of Bodney, a satellite airdrome in Norfolk.

The drill was that one of us would lead and be responsible for the navigation, the other would concentrate on keeping his plane as close to the leader as possible, and staying there through tight turns and other maneuvers. We had recently been up with a couple of instructors who showed us the tightest formations I'd ever seen, the wingman's wingtips not more than six inches from the leader's fuselage. I wasn't tucking in quite that close to Norm, who was leading, but pretty close all the same and it took a lot of concentration.

We'd been up about twenty minutes when Norm held up his map and shook his head. We didn't have radio contact but the message was clear. He didn't know where we were. He throttled back a bit and swung under me and up on my wing—throwing the ball in my court.

England was a hard country to fly over. There were just too many landmarks and pinpoints. Through an opening in the clouds I spotted a good-sized village with distinctive features: a railroad intersection and a major road running east-west. It was about twenty miles southwest of our base, I figured, so I gave Norm a thumbs-up and swung northeast. There was fairly solid cloud below us, but I was checking the time and would let down when we were approaching the field.

Just as I was about to signal Norm to break off and let down through the clouds a Spitfire appeared on my left wing. The pilot made a circling motion with his hand and then an abrupt backward gesture with his thumb. At that moment there was a break in the clouds and below us there was nothing but water. The North Sea! Next stop, Norway.

I did a quick 180 turn and looked at the map again. I'd made a mistake. The village I had misidentified had a railroad on its north side, not its south side. Crossing the coast it was easy enough to pick a pinpoint and set a course for our base, which was about twenty minutes flying time away.

Shortly after passing north of Norwich, Norm pointed down and peeled off. We had been up nearly two hours and I'd been watching my fuel gauges very carefully to be sure I had a safe reserve to get home. When I'd realized we were lost, I thinned the fuel mixture until the engine began to run rough.

It wasn't long before I could see the distinctive pattern of woods and fields that was Bodney. After I'd landed and taxied to the dispersal area, I was met by the flight commander who wanted to know what the hell I was doing headed across the North Sea, and what I'd done with Phibbs. It turned out that Norm hadn't leaned his mixture and had had to put down near Norwich. But he made out very well since it was an American B-24 base and he enjoyed a warm welcome, including a steak dinner with ice cream for dessert.

The flight commander congratulated me on my decision to lean down the mixture to conserve fuel, and it may have been one of the reasons I received an "above average" rating for the course. I mentally thanked the Spitfire for correcting our navigational mistakes. It was a good lesson: not to think you're smarter than you are.

No Room at the Inn

Norwich, England, Christmas 1942

It would be our first Christmas in England, the first one I hadn't shared with my family. There were four of us, all sergeant-pilots who had earned our wings in Canada under the British Commonwealth Air Training Program. We were now attached to the RAF and based at an Operational Training Unit in Norfolk. We weren't far inland from the North Sea and it could be a very cold place at this time of year.

The two youngest of us were New Zealanders, Kevin and Don, scarcely in their twenties and from North Island, where their families ran sheep spreads. The other Yank was Red, who was large and heavy-set with a bushy red mustache. In civilian life he was a Cleveland, Ohio fireman. Our paths had crossed and re-crossed as we went from station to station. Now we were at Bodney, a satellite base for the RAF station at Watton. It was a dispersed base, meaning it was very spread out to minimize damage in the event of an air attack. It meant also that everything was to hell and gone from everything else, billets from mess, and mess from flightline.

We all had passes into Norwich, and given the icy nature of the base (and especially its sanitary facilities) we were all looking forward to warm bathrooms and a very long hot bath at the best hotel in town. So on Christmas Eve we rumbled through the countryside on a red double-decker bus, followed by a two-wheeled contrivance, a coke-fired generator that furnished the fuel for the bus. We rounded a hill on a curve and there was Norwich, and rising from the center of town was its famous cathedral, its spire glowing in the last rays of the sun. We drove down streets of identical row houses, drab from the outside but cheerful with glimpses of Christmas decorations.

It was blackout time when we reached the bus terminal. After a number of amiable instructions, we stumbled our way to the Armed Forces Center. The news that greeted us wasn't good. All the inns and hotels on the Center's list were full up. One of the women at the counter made some calls for us, but no luck. The only possibility, she said, was that we might be able to talk our way into the Royal Hotel. It seemed to be that, or back to forlorn and icy old Bodney. So we stumbled into the blackout again.

In a blackout, your other senses grow keen; you're aware of footsteps (British military footwear with its steel plates on the heels), the sudden scent of perfume or, more likely, the smell of cigarettes or of bodies long out of contact with soap. Losing our way and backtracking we did arrive at the Royal at last, and regal it was. Once past the blackout doors and curtain and in sight of its beautifully paneled lob by, there was no doubt it had to be the best hotel in town.

Standing behind the elegant reception desk was an individual in striped trousers and cutaway coat, who elevated his chin, sighted down his nose and said in an affected voice, "What is it you wish?" I said we wished two rooms with baths. Had we reservations? No, and before I could say we'd been sent by the Armed Forces Center, he sniffed that "There are no rooms available."

We were about to give up and head for the bus station when an American Air Force captain stepped up to the desk and said, "How about a room, Mac?"

"Yes, sir," said the clerk and turned the register around so the captain could sign it.

"Wait a minute," I said to my pals, "let's not be in a hurry. Let's see what's going on here." A few minutes later, two Yank Air Force lieutenants walked up to the desk and were immediately given rooms without benefit of reservations. At that point I was, as they said in the RAF, brassed off. The thought of going back into the blackout, dealing with bus or rail schedules—and, above all, missing out on those hot baths—was just too much.

I walked back to the desk, and the clerk quickly said, "There are no rooms available."

"I didn't ask you," I said. "I want to speak to the manager."

"He cawn't see you," the clerk said.

My first impulse was to grab this silly ass by the lapels and shake him thoroughly. Fortunately I swallowed that notion, but I slapped the desk loudly and said, "I want to see the manager. NOW."

At that moment, a door behind the desk opened and a pleasant-looking older man came out and asked the clerk what the problem was. Before the clerk could answer, I asked the manager if I might have a quiet word with him. He nodded and ushered me into his office.

With the passage of many years, I can't remember exactly what I said to him. But surely I fluttered the flag and murmured about being member of His Majesty's forces and this being our first Christmas away from home. It was all genuinely heartfelt, and might have wrung tears from a statue.

The manager led me back to the desk and said to our former nemesis, "Smythe" (or whatever his name was), "see that these gentlemen are given two rooms." With that the manager came out from behind the desk, shook our hands and wished us a merry Christmas.

After dropping our duffelbags and having a perfunctory wash (only a basin in the room; even at the Royal the baths were down the hall), we adjourned to the bar, to enjoy a moment of elegant warmth. God knows when we might enjoy such luxury again. The dining room was going to close early on Christmas Eve, so we headed for it. It was another great treat to sit down to linens, china, and crystal. Our elderly waiter wore World War I ribbons on his ancient tuxedo and was as elegant as the room. I've forgotten what we ordered, but it was wonderful. I do remember the plum pudding, but the really memorable moment of the evening was a half-bottle of Veuve-Cliquot champagne, compliments of the manager.

We inquired about midnight Mass, but there would be none because it was impossible to black out the cathedral. We retired to the rooms and Red headed for one of the baths, but rushed back and said it was nine o'clock and the porter was locking the baths. I said he might be working his way upstairs, why not run up a floor and beat him. Red won.

I'd been given a portable radio (the size of a carton of cigarettes) as a going in service present and found I could get Christmas Eve services in English, French—and German. Hatreds momentarily set aside in favor of the Prince of Peace, it seemed, and with that ironic thought in mind, I turned in. Clean sheets, soft pillows, and thick mattresses were irresistible.

I had my long soak in a tub the next morning. There was a black line five inches up from the bottom of the tub, marking the maximum depth you were allowed. Red argued that we should be exempt from the limit, being as far in arrears as we were in the matter of baths.

Even with wartime austerity, breakfast was a treat: scrambled eggs (from dried eggs), sausage (even though it contained so much cereal you didn't know whether mustard or marmalade was appropriate), pots of good strong tea, and plenty of toast in those metal racks the English use to be sure the toast is sufficiently cooled.

Kevin and Don went off to the Catholic church. Red and I opted for the Cathedral and stood in awe beneath its soaring vaulted ceiling and its fluted columns. You had to be amazed at the skill and knowledge of the medieval craftsmen who built such a magnificent structure.

When the processional started up the aisle, we noticed that beneath the red choir robes of many of the men, khaki battledress and service shoes could be glimpsed, and there was the occasional scrape of the metal heelplates on the stone floor.

As we watched the crowd leaving the Cathedral later, we were approached by a sergeant of the Royal Marines, who invited us to have tea with himself and his family later that afternoon. We accepted and agreed to meet in front of the Cathedral at three thirty.

Meantime we went back to the hotel for lunch and listened to King George's Christmas Day speech in the lounge. Then Red disappeared for another bath while the rest of us went into the lounge for a glass of sherry. I went up for a last bath myself and we gathered in the lobby to go and meet the sergeant, whose name was Fred. He was stationed in Cornwall and expected to be shipped out to North Africa or India.

He led us at a brisk pace to one of the row houses like those we'd passed on the way into town. Fred's mother and his two sisters greeted us. The father was in the Merchant Marine and they believed his ship was in a convoy in the North Atlantic.

We sat in the kitchen and watched the ritual of the tea (the scalding of the pot, the extra spoon of tea for the pot) and answered questions about America. The food was delicious—fresh scones with homemade jam, fresh baked bread, Christmas biscuits (cookies to us), and, the masterpiece, a fruit cake with golden frosting. Fred's mother had saved her butter ration for several weeks so she could make the fruitcake, and it was really delicious.

Then came a moment that very nearly ruined the whole generous, loving, and touching evening. His mother casually asked where we were staying, and just as casually we said the Royal. The effect of the statement was devastating and, to us, incomprehensible. It was if someone had loudly broken wind at the communion rail or done something equally distasteful. The atmosphere in the room changed completely and the warm camaraderie that had existed among us evaporated. I knew we'd made a dreadful *faux pas*, but at first I couldn't imagine what it had been.

Then I recalled the problem at the registration desk the night before, and the English sensitivity to social distinction—in our case, being enlisted men instead of officers. The fact that we were staying at the Royal, the poshest hotel in town, made us appear as swells and made them feel socially inferior, as if we were slumming. That was the last thing in the world we felt or would have them believe. We were so warmed and grateful to have been allowed to share their Christmas with them.

It was hard to know how to go about righting the situation. We told them about our frustration at the hotel, and how it had been either the Royal or a bus ride back to the base and the most cheerless Christmas imaginable. We also mentioned that the hotel was more than a little rich for our blood and that we'd be on short rations at the beer canteen until the next payday. What we said seemed to ease the tension somewhat, and by picking our conversational themes carefully we got things back to the comfortable level we'd enjoyed at first.

Then we had a bus to catch. Fred guided us back to the hotel and we begged him to have a last drink with us, but he refused on the reasonable grounds that it was the last night of his leave and he wanted to spend it with his family, especially since his father couldn't be there. We understood that all too well, and said we wished we could have been with our families and, for that reason, how deeply we appreciated their kindness and hospitality.

The four of us checked out of the hotel, found our way to the bus depot, and were soon rumbling through the English countryside again. It was our last outing together. By the end of January we had gone our separate ways. Kevin and Don went to a station in Wales to fly Spitfires. Red went to the Midlands to fly Typhoons, and I went to Lancashire to become a photo reconnaissance pilot-navigator.

Don was later posted to North Africa, but Red, Kevin, and I kept in touch and occasionally, more by luck than good planning, we met in London. Then, in November 1943, less than a year after our Christmas in Norwich, Red (Lieutenant Frank Gallion) was shot down over Holland in his P-47, while escorting bombers to Germany. (See "Red.")

A year later, flying a Spitfire Mark IX during the Battle of the Bulge, in marginal weather and amid heavy enemy fire, Kevin—Warrant Officer Kevin Loe of the Royal New Zealand Air force—was shot down.

After the war, Don returned to his family's sheep station on the North Island of New Zealand and I went back to the Finger Lakes and the wine business.

Collision Course

England, July 1943

WHEN OUR GROUP of American pilots serving in the RCAF and the RAF transferred to the US Army Air Force, it was with mixed emotions. Some of us hoped we would be allowed to remain with our original squadrons and finish our tour of operations. Others wanted to return to the States and join units there. But the Air Force had other plans. A few did go back to the States but most of us were transferred to a new squadron recently formed at Warton in Lancashire.

At the time we were transferred, the Eighth Air Force had begun its massive build-up. B-17s, B-24s and B-26s as well as P-47 fighters were rolling off the American production lines and the bombers were being assigned to crews who would fly them to the UK. Their ultimate destination would be a squadron at one of the bomber bases in East Anglia.

Difficulties developed. For pilots trained in America, flying in England presented a number of problems. Few pilots could appreciate just how small the country was. Visual navigation was difficult because, ironically, there were too many landmarks. There were no radio beacons as such, and the weather could be very sticky and unpredictable. The American crews had few problems flying the Atlantic and reaching the UK. It was then that the troubles began.

East Anglia had literally dozens of air bases, and from two thousand feet it was hard to tell one from another, particularly in bad weather and possibly with a mission returning to its home base. In one case, a B-24 en route from Prestwick to London was flying between layers of cloud. Nearing their estimated time of arrival, they started their descent and broke into the clear over a large island, which the navigator identified as the Isle of Wight. But anti-aircraft batteries began firing at them and knocked an engine off one wing. The plane reversed course and got the hell out of there, cursing British gunnery and frantically calling Darky, a ground listening watch that aided lost aircraft.

They were flying almost due north over a large body of water that turned out to be the English Channel. They landed at the first base they came to, safely but with the B-24 totaled. The next day the RAF notified the squadron that the RAF radar had tracked the B-24 from the time it crossed the coast until it began to set down at one of the Channel Islands, then occupied by the Germans and heavily fortified.

This and other such incidents resulted in changed duties for our group. We were assigned to the 87th Air Transport Squadron at Warton. We weren't thrilled about the change, but it was a chance to become familiar with American aircraft, which most of us weren't. We couldn't help remembering that Spitfires and Typhoons were being delivered to operational RAF bases by women pilots of the Auxiliary Transport Service. This was no help to our egos.

Another irritant was the attitude of the American pilots toward those of us who had trained in Canada and the UK. They questioned our ability as pilots, which was particularly insulting because some in our group had seen combat and none of them had.

There were two flights: fighters and bombers. I was assigned to fighters, but unfortunately there were no fighters coming through when I arrived. In time we did obtain a Hurricane from the RAF (delivered by a woman pilot) to help the pilots of the fighter wing keep current. Alas, our American flight leader, an overweight stuffed shirt, decided that he would make the acceptance flight. So he did, without even asking for a cockpit check from anyone who'd ever flown in a Hurricane. He stalled it in from about twenty feet and it had to be written off.

We managed to get in some flying time in L-4's, which we called Maytag Messerschmidts, mostly flying the brass so they could qualify for flight pay. That was the situation when the B-26 incident occurred which changed my career and might have ended my life.

There were literally hundreds of B-26 Marauders at bases in

southern East Anglia. It was a good aircraft, but the problem had become, what to use them for? Because of their high wing loading and short wingspan, they were nicknamed "the flying prostitute" (no visible means of support). They were virtually gunships, .50-caliber machine guns in the fuselage in addition to turret and nose guns. The first plan was to have them go in at low levels and blast everything in sight. The British warned them it was suicidal, and it was. On the first mission, twelve Marauders went in against defenses in Holland. One plane aborted with engine trouble and was the only one to survive. Many pilots were leery of the aircraft, which is one reason General Jimmy Doolittle flew a B-26 as his personal transport.

It was decided to modify the B-26's for medium altitude work. We were assigned to fly them to Northern Ireland for the modifications. I was assigned as co-pilot to a Lieutenant Smith, a high-strung and ambitious type who planned to fly for the airlines postwar and was piling up all the pilot hours he could. Some of the pilots swapped with their co-pilots so everyone got experience, but not Smitty.

It became one of life's ironies that I'd previously been assigned to a reconnaissance squadron at Squires Gate, near Warton, qualifying for a navigator's rating for photo reconnaissance work. I was very familiar with the area to the west, including the Isle of Man and Northern Ireland, having spent a lot of time over it.

The weather was marginal the day we were to fly a 26 from Warton to Green Castle in Northern Ireland. We pre-checked the aircraft and took off. Five miles north of the field was the resort city of Blackpool, famous for its 500-foot high replica of the Eiffel Tower, which we often used as a checkpoint when going out on patrol.

I suggested we fly over the tower, so I could use it as a check point this time to start plotting our course. It was a chance to practice my navigation, since I wasn't flying much. I calculated the wind's strength and direction and determined our ground speed and the correct course to steer. Douglas on the Isle of Man was the next check point, and it was easy to calculate the time en route and our ETA.

We'd been cruising a couple of hundred feet below the solid cloud cover, with visibility a hazy two miles. Smitty decided he should get some instrument time and he climbed to 1200 feet, into the heavy cloud. When I was navigating out of Squires Gate I was hitting my

ETAs plus or minus thirty seconds. I'd given Smitty our Douglas ETA, which he had acknowledged.

There was a range of hills 2500 feet high running down the center of the island. Two weeks earlier, a B-24 en route from Ireland to England had failed to clear the ridge and all aboard were killed. Looking at my watch, I said, "Five minutes to Douglas, Smitty." We flew on, Smitty's eyes glued to the gauges. Two more minutes and I said, "We need 3000 feet to clear the hills safely, or drop down so we can take a look." Still no acknowledgment.

I checked my watch again and we were at my ETA. I yelled, "I've got it," took the controls and put the ship in an almost vertical turn to the left. We shuddered around 180 degrees, losing some altitude in the process. We broke out of the cloud right over the center of Douglas. An airport loomed up in the mist, which Smitty claimed was the one in Ireland. By this time conditions had deteriorated so much I was able to convince Smitty we should pack it in and return to base.

Not much was said on the way back, but after we'd landed and shut down the aircraft, Smith started walking away, then turned and said, "I'm going to have you court-martialed."

When I got to Operations, the commanding officer motioned me in. He asked me what I thought I was doing by taking the controls away from the pilot. I tried to explain the situation and ending up by saying that I didn't want to be killed by someone else's stupidity, which it was.

I wasn't court-martialed. But as a result of the incident, a day or two later I found myself at the controls of a very ancient RAF Anson, flying east toward a base in East Anglia and a job flying bomb fuses and priority parts to B-17 bases throughout northeast England. And en route as well to a whole new adventurous life.

A Scottie Named Tat

Christchurch, England 1943

FOR FORTY YEARS, our family pets were an odd-couple mix of beagles and cocker spaniels. But I had also always admired Scottish terriers, those compact, perky little beasts.

The first Scottie I got to know was Duffy, who belonged to Aunt Eva and Uncle Harry Champlin. Duffy was quite feisty and had been known to nip those who got too rough with him. He was quite aggressive with other dogs but seldom got into fights because he usually bluffed the other dogs down. There was another Scottie in the village, a gentle female owned by a retired old gentleman who was an ardent fly fisherman. When he went to the post office, she waited patiently outside, willing to be petted but ignoring all other dogs. When her owner, flyrod in hand, started up the railroad tracks to Cold Brook, she would accompany him. He didn't carry a landing net and I have it on no better authority than the game warden, Toby Heffernan, who told me that when the man had hooked a trout and worked it into the shallows, the Scottie would jump in, grab the fish, and fetch it ashore.

The most famous Scottie of my early days was, of course, FDR's Fala. And in our Republican town, Fala was the most popular member of the Roosevelt household. A few years ago, driving south with our Scottie, Mandy, we made a visit to Warm Springs, Georgia and the FDR cottage and museum. As we were leaving the cottage, we saw a small white sign at floor level by the back door. An arrow pointed to scratches on the door and the sign said, "Made by Fala."

Nearly ten years passed since the days of the fish-retrieving Scottie before I became acquainted with another of the breed. It was 1943 in

England and I had transferred from the RCAF to the American Air Force. I was assigned to what I can only call miscellaneous flying. On a particular day I was flying to Land's End in Cornwall in a very tired old Anson Mark 1. The forecast was a bit iffy. A fairly strong cold front was due through the area, but the meteorology lads thought we should reach Land's End ahead of it. But, as was often the case, the front speeded up and the ceiling and visibility began to decrease as we were over Bournemouth. The Anson was old and tired and, remembering that adage about there being old pilots and bold pilots but no old bold pilots, I did a 180-degree turn.

The chart showed an airdrome at Christchurch, just east of Bournemouth. But in the lowering weather it was hard to spot. Being on the coast, it was very well camouflaged to begin with. We did spot a Whitley bomber parked near what looked like an abandoned warehouse beside what appeared to be a grass runway. We tightened our belts, cranked down the undercarriage, and committed ourselves.

There was actually more runway than appeared from the air as we taxied back to the dispersal area. But I was feeling a bit smug. We stopped to watch as a Spitfire floated in to a perfect landing. The pilot stood up in the cockpit, hit the release button on the parachute, and pulled off "his" helmet. A mass of auburn hair spilled on to her shoulders. She was a pilot with the ATA, the transport auxiliary. I quickly deflated.

A flight sergeant walked up and asked if we would move the Anson further up the field. The field was naturally camouflaged, with bushes and overgrown areas. As we turned the plane in one of those weed patches, we heard a splintering sound like someone crushing a dozen violins. The sergeant was waving his hands frantically, but too late. We had hit one of the large steel corkscrews the British use as tie-downs. It had completely demolished the underside of our wooden starboard horizontal stabilizer.

My crew chief, the sergeant, and I were looking at the remains of the stabilizer when a man in a business suit came up and said, "You couldn't have picked a better place for that to have happened." He led us to a big, rather dilapidated looking warehouse. Inside were jigs holding wooden wings in various stages of construction. There were a great many workmen, most of them elderly. They were building Horsa troop-carrying gliders. Watching the artisans work led me to believe that most of the prime cabinet makers and violin-makers in the British Isles had been recruited. We caught a bus into Bournemouth and stayed the night at the Red Cross Club.

We returned to the works the next morning and watched the craftsmen work on our wounded stabilizer. It was obvious they would have us airborne again soon. The big Horsas were fascinating to see. I think their wingspan was nearly ninety feet and the fuselage had a diameter of eight feet, all wood construction. They were works of art and it seemed a pity their lifespan was likely to be brief.

At noon I accompanied the works manager to lunch. Seated near me at the long table was a nice-looking young RAF flight lieutenant, wearing the ribbon of the Distinguished Flying Cross under his wings. His name was John and he was the pilot who made the test and the acceptance flights on the completed Horsa gliders. He answered my questions politely but coolly.

As we left the dining hall, there, sitting patiently on the stoop was a Scottish terrier. The flight lieutenant gave the dog a scrap he'd saved from lunch and patted his head. This was enthusiastically received. I said I was fond of Scotties and did it like to be petted. The lieutenant's reserve evaporated. "Name's Tat and he likes to have his ears scratched." After I'd given Tat a good scratch, John gave me a wave and went off to flight operations, Tat at his heels.

We met again at tea. John said he recently completed a tour of duty in Spitfires at Biggen Hill. He wasn't happy with his present work, which he considered civilian-type duty. He came from a small village in Yorkshire and his family raised Scotties. John also mentioned that he had a couple of gliders to test the next morning. I asked if I could go along. He said it was against regulations, but I could go along on one flight. I was then afraid the repairs on the Anson would be completed and I'd have to leave. But the plane wouldn't be ready until some time the next day.

In the morning John came out of the small shack that served as his office with a parachute slung over his shoulder. He went back in and got another for me. "Regulations," he said, smiling. He led the way to the huge wooden hulk parked beside the runway. We went aft to the large loading door. John tossed the parachutes inside and lifted

Tat in after them. We climbed up the ladder and he motioned me into the co-pilot's seat. Tat didn't seem to approve of this. I had taken his seat. After a very thorough cockpit check, John signaled the ground crew and the Whitley bomber we saw from the air moved up and the hawser tow-line was attached.

As I remember the Horsa did have brakes, activated by compressed air, as the flaps were. When the tow-line was taut, John released the brakes and we began to rumble down the field. I was surprised how slow our air speed was when we lifted off, although of course we weren't loaded.

Flying in the Horsa was a very pleasant sensation. Not exactly quiet, because of the sound of the air flowing over the wings and fuselage. But the only engine noise was of the Whitley up ahead and there was no vibration. The Horsa did have one unique feature: it creaked. As an aircraft, it was quite heavy on the controls and, due to the lack of slip stream, it was slow to answer rudder and elevator.

We climbed to about 5,000 feet, I judged, before we released. John did a series of easy turns in both directions. Then there was a gentle stall that was fairly noisy with the change in air speed. We were down to 1,000 feet when we lined up for final approach—a bit high, I thought, since the Horsa had a pretty fair glide angle. But no. "Hang on," John said, and hit the flap control, at the same time dumping the nose to what seemed to me to be past vertical. But our speed didn't increase appreciably. Looking back at the wings, I could see why. A huge "barn door" hung down—the biggest flap I'd ever seen. As we approached the end of the runway, John pulled back on the large wooden control and we flared and touched down and went rumbling down the tarmac. It was quite an experience.

I thanked John and said goodbye to him and Tat, went into the works office and signed some forms and gave my profound thanks to the works manager and his crew. We did a thorough walk-around of the Anson, hoping the old stabilizer would be as good as the repaired one. We took off and then swung back over the field, rocking our wings in salute. Below, walking from the little operations shack, was a figure in a blue uniform, followed by a small black dog. I remembered John's explanation of how the dog got his name. He'd arrived in a litter of nine puppies. He was the runt of the litter and consequently, the word was "No tit for Tat."

(Twenty-five years after that hair-raisingly steep landing approach, I would be giving prospective customers for Schweizer sailplanes what I called "the thrill of their lives" with a special high, steep approach in the SGS 2-32, with its terminal velocity dive brakes.)

An Evening Over Lake Windermere

England, July 1943

THERE ARE INTERLUDES in war as unforgettable in their way as times of mortal danger. Early one summer evening half a dozen of us were sprawled on the deck of an Anson Mark I. We were lumbering from Watton Air Force Base in Lancashire to Prestwick, just south of Glasgow. We were all brassed off, as the English say. We were all RCAF and RAF pilots who had recently transferred to the American Air Force. Now we had drawn duty as ferry pilots. Hell, the RAF had women who did that work.

We were scheduled to pick up a couple of B-17s and several P-47s. As the newest additions to the squadron, another fellow and I were at the bottom of the roster, and we were slated to bring back a pair of C-61s, Fairchild 24s in civilian life, a single-engine, four-place aircraft used mainly for executive transport. A nice little kite but not exactly awe-inspiring. We watched the others fire up their B-17s and P-47s and head south. Jim, who drew the other C-61, and I checked out our planes. His was fine and he had a date that night so he took off. Mine had a dead battery and that meant a new one and a considerable delay. It was already five in the afternoon, but British Double Summer Time and the fact that we were so far north (the same latitude, 55° 30', as the center of Hudson Bay) meant I had a lot of daylight left. (One night I'd had to pull the shade to keep the sun out of my eyes at 11:30 P.M.)

I was offered a ride to the mess, which was a large brick country house that had been requisitioned by the RAF for the duration. An assortment of yews in the huge yard had been sculpted into the shapes of birds and animals. With its paneled walls and numerous fireplaces, the manor was grand but the food was strictly GI fare. Still, there was plenty of it.

The engineers finally got everything buttoned up. I signed some forms and took off. I wanted a look at the seacoast town of Ayr, the birthplace of Robert Burns. It looked very picturesque and I added it to the mental list of interesting historic places I'd never get to see from ground level.

I'd drawn a track on my chart directly to the base at Watton and headed home. It was a beautiful evening and since I was in no hurry I eased the throttle back to a slow cruise at four or five hundred feet. I skirted the ridges and generally followed the valleys. I'd heard how beautiful the Lake District was and thought it might resemble our own Finger Lakes. Luckily my course ran almost down the middle of the area.

We crossed Solway Firth, a large bay, and headed a bit further inland, flying over a rolling highland that was covered with heather, which was reddish bronze in the setting sun. Ahead was a large, deep valley, and as we dropped into it we came to a sizable town. It was Ambleside, at the head of Lake Windermere, which was said to be the most beautiful lake of them all.

The ground was quite high north of the town, at least a thousand feet above the water, so I throttled back and began to descend. There was a slight haze in the valley and in the slanting sun the landscape had the luminous golden glow of a watercolor. I put on a notch of the flaps and we seemed to just float along. I could see many boats on the lake, rowboats, canoes, even a few sailboats. The surface of the lake was as still as a mirror.

It was a truly magical moment and it was over all too soon. I was tempted to reverse my course and make another run over the lake, but this didn't seem right. I was sure I wouldn't have been welcome a second time. So I increased the throttle, raised the flaps, and got back on track for Watton.

The rest of the trip was routine until we swung over the base a few minutes before midnight and set up the final approach, heading into the setting sun that was reflected on the clouds and sparkling off the Irish Sea. It was glorious. And unforgettable.

The Dominie

England, Fall 1943

I HAD BEEN a bad boy again.

I was transferred out of the Ferry Squadron at Warton Air Force Base on the coast of the Irish Sea near Blackpool, for taking over the controls of a B-26 because I didn't fancy slamming into a mountain on the Isle of Man (See "Collision Course"). I was assigned an Airspeed Oxford aircraft and sent to Honnington Air Force Base in East Anglia, just down the road a piece from Bodney, my first RAF station in England.

My duties were to fly bomb fuses and critical aircraft parts to the many Eighth Air Force bases in the area. My equipment was the Oxford and a very tired Anson Mark I, acquired from the RAF. Our main headquarters was at Hendon, in North London. I was kept very busy, flying more than a hundred hours a month with at least ten different landings a day at different fields.

One day at dinner I sat beside the officer in charge of the Transport Company on the base. He mentioned that he had a five-truck convoy headed for Burtonwood Air Force Base the next day to pick up some rebuilt engines. That same day I'd heard from our operations sergeant that two C-47s were due in the next day to pick up 10,000 pounds of aircraft batteries, destined for Burtonwood. I put two and two together, not always a keen idea. The convoy trucks would be going to Burtonwood empty, and I asked the transport officer if they could carry the batteries. No sweat; they'd be glad to do it. So I called the operations sergeant and scrubbed the C-47s.

I thought I'd struck a blow for the war effort. But next day there was a message ordering me to headquarters post haste, and I found myself standing before a very irate colonel. I tried to explain the rationale for my action: the savings in fuel and crew time. The colonel only became more irate. Wasn't I aware that the Group was judged by their monthly score of hours flown, personnel carried, tons airlifted? You wouldn't think that my "offense" would bear too close scrutiny, would you?

But that reckons not with the military mind. Within twenty-four hours orders had been cut, transferring me again, this time to the Headquarters Squadron at Hendon. I would still have the same duty, ferrying fuses and other parts. But Hendon was essentially a transport base and there was not likely to be a lot for me to do.

My first look at Hendon had been through the windshield of the Anson. I was en route to an airdrome on the Channel coast but had orders to drop off at Hendon a half-dozen officers who had forty-eight-hour passes to London. Until then I'd only flown the Anson for a total of five or six hours. No one had checked me out in it and the flight manual was probably in a military museum in London. I was significantly unaware just how slowly an Anson landed in comparison to B-26s, for example.

As I circled the Hendon field that first time, the tower gave me a green light (there was no radio contact). I set up an approach and headed in, noting what a short runway it was. We were landing to the south and on the north side was a high railroad embankment topped by telegraph lines. With flaps down and power off, we floated, and floated, and floated. With more than half the runway gone, we still hadn't touched down, so I flew around to try again. The next approach was lower and still slower. We touched down a third of the way along the runway. I touched the brakes and the plane started to skip. I raised the tail to put more weight on the wheels, but we were still moving right along, and the end of the runway was coming up fast.

At the end of the runway was a graveled area, which turned out to be the car park for the officer's mess. Thanks to gas rationing, there were only three or four vehicles in it, clustered at one side. I swung into the car park, locked the right wheel brake and gunned the left engine and around we went in a ground loop, and stopped.

Before the dust could settle (and there was a lot of it) my

passengers poured off the aircraft. The door of the mess flung open and out rushed a dozen or so RAF officers in their blue uniforms, inquiring "What the bloody 'ell's going on?"

The consensus was that no damage had been done to anything, but that my approach speed had been excessive. It was lunch time but I thought it wise not to loiter and I continued on my way. By the time I returned to base there was a message advising that I should be checked out in the Anson by a qualified pilot—a thoughtful but fairly tardy idea. But since I was the only one on the base who'd actually flown an Anson, other than the lady pilot who'd delivered it and then left, I was told to go out and do some circuits, touch-and-go landings and such to familiarize myself with the aircraft. I did and we had no more major problems.

I also occasionally flew a Miles Proctor, a sporty-looking little prewar kite the RAF used for personal transport. I was told that the RAF shops across the field were working on a De Havilland Dominie, and when it was finished it would be assigned to me. It was an unusual aircraft, a twin-engine biplane, whose wings were sharply tapered, almost diamond-shaped. The engines were sculpted into the lower wings (to reduce drag) and the wheels were as well. The engines were Gypsy Queens with fixed-pitch aluminum propellers.

The great day arrived when the Dominie was ready and delivered to our area. Needless to say, there was no instruction manual; it was probably in the museum with the Anson's. There was a six- or eight-place cabin and the pilot's office was a single seat in the very pointed nose. There were air brakes, a button for each wheel. It wasn't a complicated cockpit, just a bit different. At least the flight instruments were standard RAF.

It was a nice afternoon and seemed like a good time to become familiar with "my" aircraft. We called the tower for permission to take off. It was a delight to fly. It took off like a bird and the engines, below and behind the cockpit, were quiet and very smooth. I'd learned my lesson with the Anson, so after a fly-around I just retarded the throttles and let it glide down and land. It didn't need much help from me.

The next day we were sent out on our first mission, delivering aircraft parts to several bases, with an overnight stay at Grove. I decided to take the sergeant who ran the office along for the ride. I thought he'd enjoy seeing a little of the English countryside from the air. The sergeant had buddies at Grove and I ran into a friend, Jim Dwyer, from Bath, so we had a pleasant evening

The next morning the airfield was blanketed by a real English fog but we checked meteorology and found out that the fog was local. Hendon was clear. I finally persuaded the tower chief to give us clearance to take off. The sergeant wasn't too keen either on taking off into the foggy yonder. But we checked out the Dominie. Then the "Follow Me" Jeep led us out to the runway. We lined up on the white line on the center of the runway and I rechecked my compass and advanced the throttles. The white line was passing directly under our nose. Our air speed increased slowly, as I knew it would, but soon the tail came up and we got light on our feet.

I was sneaking another peak at the air speed indicator when we came to a runway intersection. There, directly in front of us on the intersecting runway and crossing our path from left to right was a 6x6 truck. I knew I didn't have enough speed to lift over the truck. I chopped the throttles and pushed the stick forward to put weight on the wheels and cut the switches. We couldn't miss it. The right wing caught the truck and spun the aircraft to the right and the nose entered the canvas-covered rear of the truck. There was then the damnedest banging imaginable. It was the props hitting the steel body of the truck. Then everything became very quiet. It was very dark under the canvas but there seemed to be six golf balls hanging in front of me.

The sergeant let out a yell and headed for the rear and only door. I wasn't far behind. When we hit the tarmac, we were just in time to see three black GIs, who'd been riding in the back of the truck, sprinting into the fog.

There appeared to be no danger of fire, so I climbed back into the aircraft and radioed the tower about our predicament. In a short time we were surrounded by fire trucks, crash crews, and ambulances. I think the medics were disappointed there were no casualties.

I walked around the wreckage and realized that my brief affair with the Dominie was over. I felt very badly because it was a delightful aircraft. I was held blameless, and I've often wondered what happened to the driver of the truck, who ill-advisedly took a shortcut across the aerodrome. Later that afternoon the sergeant and I were picked up by a C-47 and flown ingloriously back to Hendon.

The Camouflage Colonel

Hendon, England, May 1944

THE 86TH AIR Transport Squadron, to which I'd recently been assigned, was an all-purpose outfit. It was headed by Colonel Leslie Arnold, who in civilian life had been Eddie Rickenbacker's right hand man at Eastern Airlines. As a result we flew our C-47s as they flew commercial airliners—short, steep approaches and three-point landings.

Essentially we were based in London—at Hendon in North London when I first joined the outfit, then at Heston. We operated scheduled runs between London, Belfast, and Prestwick, near Glasgow. But we also logged many hours carrying out special assignments: transporting groups to a new base, carrying priority materials for a special project. Several of our planes took a long round-about route to Russia and back, and a half-dozen or so aircraft went on detached service in Sweden, under the command of Colonel Bernt Balchen, the well-known Polar expedition pilot.

Since I was a relative newcomer to the squadron, I was still checking out in the C-47s. My only flight assignments came up when a staff officer from the 8th Air Force would arrive at the base and announce that he wanted to inspect one of the bomber or fighter bases, usually in East Anglia. His flight time would be logged and go toward the monthly four hours he required to earn flight pay.

I got the nod on these flights not only because I was low man on the totem pole but because I'd acquired a wide knowledge of the English countryside. Our stable of executive aircraft reserved for this duty consisted of L-4s (Piper Cubs), C-61s (the Fairchild), UC-78s (Cessna Bamboo Bombers). I usually ended up with an L-4 and lousy weather. It wasn't difficult to fly out of Hendon, but feeling your way back wasn't much fun. I worked hard for *their* flying time.

I did come up with a winner in May of 1944. I was put on detached duty and assigned to Colonel Homer St. Gaudens. He was a striking individual, tall and slender with pure white hair and a generous mustache. He wore pince-nez glasses and his uniforms were beautifully tailored. At sixty-three he was the oldest and most senior colonel in the European Theater of Operations. He was the service's top camouflage expert, on loan from the Carnegie Institute of Technology in Pittsburgh, where he was the director. His father was the distinguished American sculptor, Augustus St. Gaudens.

During the interwar years, the colonel visited Europe frequently to see art exhibits and meet artists. But his itinerary was suggested, or augmented, by the War Department, and strangely enough many of his trips took him to sensitive areas in Germany. Villages in the vicinity of the Siegfried line evidently housed any number of budding artists.

As we began flying together, the build-up for D-Day was well under way—the invasion was hardly a month off—and the colonel's job was to make certain that the masses of men and material poised in England were being concealed from the Germans. They sent their high-flying Messerschmidt 88s, photo reconnaissance planes, over the coast every day to note movements and changes. There were literally thousands of men, and tanks, trucks, and other supplies crowded along the narrow lanes in southern England and hidden (hopefully) in wooded areas. I was told that one of the problems of concealment arose in the basic discipline of the different nationalities. Told to walk under the trees and around a field to the mess tent, the British and Canadian troops would. But the hungry Americans, knowing the shortest distance between two points was a straight line, would head right across a field. Several hundred feet crossing a hay field would blaze a path, which would show up in the aerial photos—a lush field one day, a well-traveled path the next. There would be nothing to do but plow the field and drag it.

Normally the colonel and I would be in the air five or six hours a day as we ranged from Lands End to Portsmouth. It was the loveliest time of year in that part of England. Often we would spot an irregularity from the air, land at the nearest airfield, round up whoever was responsible, take him up with us, and point out the trouble. You can be sure we checked it out again the next morning.

We put in a lot of air time but we also covered a lot of ground by road in a staff car. It was a rare treat, traveling the narrow, winding roads of Cornwall and Devon, crossing arched stone bridges built by the Romans and as sound today as they were a thousand years before. As a welcome break from K rations, we were sometimes able to stop at pubs for lunch. Despite shortages, it was always a good lunch.

The most interesting and pleasant time of the day came when we had tied down our bird and were transported to a country inn for the night. No Bachelor Officers Quarters (BOQ) and no RAF messes for the colonel. He had spent too much time in the area not to know who had the best cellar and spread the best board and was the most convivial host. It was over those dinners and a nightcap later that I really got to know the colonel. I consider him one of the most completely delightful men I ever met. I've never known anyone so interesting to listen to and talk with.

We spent one night at the best hotel in Torquay, where the colonel was greeted like a long-lost son. At breakfast the next morning, he told me he'd been honored with the bridal suite. What a waste, he said. He also told me that he had orders for us that would doubtless be a break from our normal routine (as if our routine was normal).

Twenty miles south of Torquay was a channel village called Slapton Sands. Its topography closely resembled one of the French beaches that would shortly be attacked by American forces. The town's populace had been evacuated and the Americans were going to mount a full-blown attack on Torquay as a kind of wet/dry run for the French beach—aircraft attacks with bombs and strafings and a naval bombardment followed by infantry and armored assaults.

The higher brass wanted Colonel St. Gaudens and two observers to fly over and check out several hush-hush pieces of equipment. We would have twenty minutes to get in, look around, and get out. We were told the time, the direction, and the altitude (400 feet) for our entry. There were two lieutenant colonels waiting at the field when we arrived and after a very thorough pre-flight check, we loaded up and took off.

Talk about realism. From the time we took off we could see columns of smoke and now and again the flash of an exploding shell. As we got closer, I saw something that the brass had forgotten about, or neglected to mention—a swarm of kite balloons hovering over the beach at six or seven hundred feet. A kite balloon was about a quarter the size of a barrage balloon, tethered on a relatively small diameter cable which was hard to see at most times. Their purpose was to prevent low flying planes from strafing troops on the beach.

We went in on time, the colonel in the right front seat and the two observers standing behind the front seats. I got only a brief impression of the goings-on below; I was too busy watching out for the balloon cables. We were flying a C-78 and they didn't call it a "Bamboo Bomber" for nothing. It had wood spars and fabric-covered wings.

The cables were relatively easy to spot going in to the west, but when we turned back to the Channel we were facing the sun. We were just leaving when I spotted a cable too close for comfort. I rolled up on one wing to miss it. As I rolled back level there was a loud WHOOMP and a rush of air. I turned around and the observer behind me was white as a sheet. I thought he'd been hit. When I rolled the ship up, he had been thrown down on the rear door—on the handle—and the door opened.

The other observer had his seat belt fastened and was able to grab his companion and haul him back in. The noise I heard was the door slamming shut. I'm sure it was a moment the colonel experienced as a nightmare many times in his later life.

During a television program commemorating the fiftieth anniversary of D-Day, an announcer referred to the exercise at Slapton Sands and said that a German submarine (or possibly E-boats) had made an attack on the force and caused 750 American casualties. It was hushed up at the time, but the toll was equal to a third of the American D-Day casualties.

The exercise had ended in tragedy, and we had come closer than I like to remember.

A Flight to Remember

England, October 1944

IT ALL STARTED with a search for my kid brother. I'd received a call from a small village north of Warminster. Peter, Boog's and my youngest brother, had arrived in the UK. He couldn't get leave but he hoped that perhaps I could get down to see him.

A day or two later, I arranged an afternoon off. Pete didn't have a phone number, of course, so it would be a question of searching and hoping. Not knowing where I might have to land, I took an L-4 (the civilian Piper Cub), the smallest and most basic plane the Air Force had to offer. I thought I'd be back before dark, but I left word with the operations officer to light a couple of flares if he heard me stooging around after dark.

The flight to Salisbury Plain went well. I circled Stonehenge for a quick look and flew on towards Warminster. Just east of the town a number of GIs were holding maneuvers on the Plain. I realized I was looking for a needle in a haystack, so I decided to land and ask for directions. The officer in charge said my best bet was to check headquarters at Warminster. I took off again and landed on the parade ground there. I figured I might lose a stripe for that, but nobody said a word. I was told that Pete's regiment, the Umpty-umpth Infantry, was six miles north, just south of a small village.

A short time later I was circling a cluster of tents and wondering where to land. A field alongside the camp had cattle grazing in it but looked to be the smoothest spot around. The cattle scattered when I landed and taxied up to the fence. A captain walked over and asked if he could be of any help. Yes, he said, this was Pete's outfit, but he was off on a route march. They were due back in a half-hour and why didn't I have a cup of coffee while I waited.

I said I was delighted, but also concerned that the cattle might start nibbling on my aircraft. Ever since barnstorming days, cattle have been attracted to dope and fabric airplane surfaces, sometimes with dire consequences. No problem, he said, and in a minute a half-dozen GIs with fixed bayonets were guarding the L-4. Over coffee in the mess tent, I learned that the outfit was composed of infantry replacements, due to head for Germany or Italy.

The marchers returned a little before five. Peter spotted me and came over as soon as they'd fallen out. We sat on a nearby bench and pumped each other for news. We hadn't seen each other in two years. I wanted news from home. He wondered what Duane and I were up to. Duane had arrived in the ETO a year earlier and we'd been able to get together several times, but now he was thrusting into Germany with the Third Armored Division. I told Pete I was flying C-47s to a variety of destinations in Europe.

There was more to talk about, but I had a two-hour flight back to base and would need gas to get there. A crowd had gathered watching the GIs fend off the cattle. They herded the critters out of the way and I took off.

I realized that the timing on the re-fill would be close. I had to skirt the Plain because it was a restricted bombing and gunnery area, but there was an RAF emergency field on my course and I headed for it. It was spartan, a tower and a couple of hangars, not a plane in sight. The fuel, delivered by a farm tractor, came with frustrating slowness. Heading due east, my first checkpoint was Andover, where I could pick up the rail lines as landmarks. The weather was suddenly unpromising. A cold front was due to pass through London around midnight, and a heavy overcast and lowering visibility were already announcing its coming. I had no radio and my only navigation aids were a chart and a small computer (calculator, actually).

After Andover, I followed the rail tracks until they swung south to Guildford. I turned northeast on a compass course for my base at Heston, on the western outskirts of London. The visibility was poorer than ever. It was down to a half mile when I spotted a landmark, the old Brooklands Race Track. Only ten miles to go. Once I saw the large reservoirs at Staines, it would only be a couple of city blocks to the field. But I could hardly relax: with a cluster of barrage balloons west of Staines, and the main London balloons a few miles to my right, I couldn't afford to stray off course.

I could no longer read the unlighted compass. The rapidly decreasing visibility should have made me realize I was flying myself into a corner. Not only was it getting darker, the northeast wind was moving London's industrial haze into the area, as predicted. Within minutes, I would be flying in instrument conditions—with no instruments. I expected to sight the reservoirs at any moment, so I held to my course as best I could. I flipped on my Zippo lighter, trying to see the compass, but I only flew further into the murk. A moment later I couldn't make out the ground.

I stumbled my way around 180 degrees and headed back out. The lighter burned out and I was having difficulty maintaining level flight. I wanted to climb but the only reference I had was the sound of the engine and the feeling of the controls. One last flicker of the lighter showed I was at five hundred feet on a southwestern heading. At least I was headed away from London.

Wobbling along in that noisy, dark void, I cursed my stupidity. How does one get in a spot like this—no instruments, no radio, no parachute, and over a completely blacked-out countryside?

I expected to run out of the fog momentarily, but there was still the problem of finding a place to land before it became totally dark. It was well after sunset and it was increasingly difficult to control the plane. The engine would wind up as the plane started to dive and then begin to labor as I eased back the stick and started to climb.

After an eternity the fog thinned a bit and I could just make out the ground, but it was only a darker mass without any distinguishing features. As I struggled to keep the plane under control, I was more angry than scared, but I had no doubt I was heading for a crash landing. There were no airports in the immediate area, but since I had no way of identifying myself they wouldn't have been any help anyway. I decided to circle and postpone the inevitable. My fear was that I might be over a blacked-out village.

Then I saw a vertical slit of light. It remained steady while I continued to circle, trying to figure out what it was. Letting down as I flew toward the light, the leafy top of a tree suddenly loomed in front of me, hiding the light. The light reappeared as I pulled up and I continued flying toward it. I could finally see that it came from a gap in the blackout curtains of a house.

I made a careful 180-degree turn and flew back until I was sure I was beyond the tree. I turned again and began descending. I pulled up just enough to clear the tree and cut the switches. I braced my arm on the back of the forward seat, eased back on the stick and waited for the crash.

We bounced and hit again. I pumped the brakes as hard as I dared. Bouncing along we literally slid to a stop. We hadn't hit a thing. Providentially the light had been aligned between two rows of large oak trees stretching down the lawn of a large country manor house. I climbed out of the cockpit, and stood there, thankful, humble—and very lucky.

The beam of a flashlight hit my face and a voice demanded "Who are you? Advance and be recognized." Below the flashlight, I saw the gleam of a double-barreled shotgun. I said I was an American pilot who'd been forced down by darkness, and I pulled out my identity card. I added that I needed to make a phone call without delay. My captor looked at my ID and told me to follow him. I took a couple of steps and walked into a waist-high iron fence. The tip of my right wing extended over it.

I followed him up stone steps and into an elegant paneled hall. My captor was a stocky, middle-aged man in tweeds. He seemed quite excited and called out, "Mother, can you come here a minute, please?" He said he was a member of the Home Guard, but things had been pretty quiet up to now; they hadn't even been bombed. Tonight he'd been alerted the first time I'd flown over.

Soon a dignified and attractive lady in her early seventies appeared. "Mother," the man said, "this man is an American pilot; he landed on our back lawn." She said her name was Mrs. Stuart-Sandeman. I said I must call my base before I was reported overdue. As I was placing the call, I saw the son asking his mother a question that displeased her. The son, whose name was Edward, asked if I would stay to tea.

He said in some embarrassment that his mother had certain

reservations about Americans. I thought to myself, "Now here's a nice challenge to improve British–American relations."

We were served tea in a small sitting room by an elderly maid who stared at me as if I were a visitor from outer space, which I suppose I was. Mrs. Stuart-Sandeman said there was a nice inn just down the road where I could spend the night. But I had told myself I wanted to spend it under the roof of the manor house. Crossing my fingers under my napkin, I told her that U.S. regulations stipulated any plane not on a base must be guarded at all times. If I could borrow a blanket or two, I said, I would sleep in the plane.

There was silence, and then Edward asked what I did before the war. I said I worked in the family winery, which produced champagne. What a coincidence, their family had been in the wine business for years. Of course! Sandeman Port.

Edward disappeared for a few minutes, returned and said, "My, you certainly came close to that tractor and plow." "What tractor, what plow?" I asked. We went to the fence and by flashlight I saw that indeed a Ford-Ferguson tractor and a gang plow were nestled under the left wing. Their estate, like many, was being used for food production. "Marvelous flying," Edward said. I only shook my head in disbelief.

Edward and I had a whiskey in the impressive library and he asked if I would stay to dinner. There were four of us at a table for twenty (Edward's aunt had joined us) and we had a very British meal—joint, roast potatoes, Brussels sprouts and a fine claret, and a trifle for dessert.

After dinner and over coffee in the library, I learned why Edward's mother had, to say the least, mixed emotions about Yanks. Shortly after the Americans had arrived in England, she had invited an Air Force finance officer to tea and he had been a classic patronizing boor and braggart. I prayed I had done a little better.

I think I had. Edward's mother asked me without preamble if Air Force regulations would allow me to sleep in a bedroom above and within sight of the aircraft. Keeping a straight face as best I could, I said that would be allowable. She fetched me a dressing gown and pajamas she said had been her late husband's. I felt very humble and hoped that my thanks conveyed my genuine gratitude.

The morning brought a shock. I looked out the window and saw that the L-4 was really boxed in, the iron fence on the right, the tractor on the left and just in front of the plane great, deep furrows. If I'd rolled another ten feet, the plane would've been kindling.

After a fine breakfast (fresh eggs!), Edward went out to help me pull the plane out of its cul-de-sac and aim it in the clear, unplowed area between the oaks. I checked it out and then went back inside to give my hostess my heartfelt thanks for their hospitality.

Standing behind the propeller, I started the engine and then climbed in and let it warm up. There was a row of trees at the end of the lawn too tall for me to fly over. I'd have to turn before I reached them. It was a strange feeling, taking off with the oak branches so close on both sides, but I had good air speed when it was time to turn at the trees. Heading back toward the house I throttled down and leveled off. Mrs. Stuart-Sandeman and Edward were standing on the steps waving. I rocked my wings and headed for the base.

The Air Chief Marshal

London, 1944

FROM THE POINT of view of Air Chief Marshal Sir Trafford Leigh-Mallory, KCB, DSO, our first meeting was quite unofficial. But from mine, it was all spit, polish, and nervousness. I was a dinner guest at his official residence at Stanmore, just north of London. I had met the Leigh-Mallorys' daughter, Jacqueline, a month or so before at a dance at the officers mess at the RAF station at Hendon. We had both been transferred to the station that very day. Jacqueline had come from a station in Wales to take command of the base's WAAF contingent. I had come from a base in East Anglia to the USAAF 86th Air Transport Squadron. Although it was an RAF station, the two services actually got along rather well.

Since the officers shared the mess and various other facilities, Jacqueline's path and mine crossed fairly often. Eventually after a number of in-town dinners and a couple of shows, she took pity on the wayward Yank and invited me to the family home for dinner.

At that time her father's name and photograph were in the news quite often. The Allies were implementing Operation Overlord, the planned invasion of Europe. As commander of the Twelfth Group of the RAF Fighter Command, Leigh-Mallory was the front-runner to head the Allied air force for the invasion (as indeed he did). I was very much aware of his rank and position, and not at all sure how I would measure up.

When the day arrived, I met Jacqueline at the Hendon tube station and we traveled by tube, train, and bus; Stanmore was not easy to reach from the base. I worried all during the trip about whether or not to salute. Americans salute with or without a hat on, but the RAF salutes only when hats are worn, and I was meeting the Air Chief Marshal indoors. No hats.

When we got off the last bus, it was still a good walk to the house, a stately and substantial country home with a very impressive entrance. The heavy oak door was opened by a houseman and we entered a high-ceilinged and paneled hall. I surrendered my hat, which was placed on a table alongside a blue one covered with gold braid.

Jacqueline led the way from the hall to a handsomely furnished drawing room where the Leigh-Mallorys were waiting for us. As it turned out, I had nothing to worry about in the matter of saluting. Jacqueline's father solved the problem very nicely by stepping forward, grasping my hand and giving me a warm greeting. His eyes had a twinkle that was both friendly and probing. Lady Leigh-Mallory (Doris) was extremely cordial and gracious.

She said with a delightful grin that her husband had spent the day stooging around in that aircraft of his (a Hurricane), supposedly inspecting bases in the Midlands.

I was to learn that light banter was very much a feature of their family life. As time passed and I became a more frequent visitor (and during the buzz bombs a regular resident), I also learned that when the Air Chief Marshal came home from his headquarters at Bentley Priory, walked through the door, and put his hat on the table, he became a father and husband, taking his ease. They were a close, warm family, and if they had their differences, I never knew of them.

First impressions are usually lasting. I know that the one I formed of Trafford Leigh-Mallory that first night was right on track, and my impression only became stronger as time went on. What I felt most strongly was a relaxed informality between us and, despite the differences in our status, a mutual admiration and respect. I was to learn that while he was a very warm person he was also strong-willed. He did not suffer fools and had a reputation in the service for posting those who had incurred his wrath to such outposts as the Hebrides or Burma. Physically he was rugged, just under six feet tall and an excellent athlete. Before the war he had played rugby and in the days when I knew him played excellent golf and tennis. He was an experienced sailor and in prewar days took cruising vacations on his leaves.

The dinner conversation was wide-ranging that night, and everyone took part. After the passage of years I can't remember all the details of the talk, but I do remember that I was spared the stereotyped question, "How do you like England?" The Air Chief Marshal quizzed me about my training and what I'd been doing since I arrived in the UK. He was also interested in where I lived in the States and what I'd been doing before I went in service. He was fascinated that I'd been with a winery that produced champagne and every other kind of still wine, including vermouths.

Leigh-Mallory himself was well grounded in wines and belonged to a society that before the war had commissioned agents who traveled the wine districts buying wines for the society according to the tastes of the members. He lamented that the war had stopped all that, and that current pickings were pretty slim. As a matter of fact, he said, at dinner we were going to have an Algerian red of dubious lineage, and it was currently resting on a radiator because it had to be above room temperature to be at all palatable.

Our dinner took place not long after the Quebec Conference, when Roosevelt and Churchill met in company with the ranking officers of the American and British services, including Leigh-Mallory. I asked him a leading question: What were his impressions of the American officers? He did not seem put out, and fielded the question very adroitly. His comments were pleasant and rather neutral until he mentioned General George C. Marshall. Then he became quite effusive. He said he considered Marshall one of the finest men he had ever met, and an officer without peer. He was very much looking forward to working with him on the upcoming "show." I regarded this as privileged information and didn't repeat it until after Leigh-Mallory was dead.

The evening was the highlight of my wartime experiences to that moment. I must have passed muster because I was to be invited back on many occasions, and eventually to become a member of the family.

The next time I went for dinner, I met Jay (as the family, and therefore I, called Jacqueline) at the house, as she had had the day off. It wasn't easy, but with only a few wrong turns I reached the house and was admitted by Chandler, the butler. The family was again waiting in the drawing room and I felt very much at home.

A few days before, I'd spent a day off wandering the interesting little side streets midtown London is famous for. I stopped in front of a small wine shop, my eye caught by a magnificently designed and wax-sealed bottle of Napoleon brandy displayed in the window. A wonderful gift to take to Stanmore, I thought, and it really would have been, except that it cost fifty guineas, or three hundred U.S. dollars, a bit stiff for a second lieutenant's purse. I was looking at some splendid Bordeaux when I spotted a bottle of the legendary 1921 Chateau d'Yquem. I bought it for ten guineas (about forty-four dollars).

In the drawing room I presented it to Leigh-Mallory. He looked at the label and gave a low whistle. "Not a dinner wine," I said, "but it should go well with the sweet." "I should think so," he said, and so it did.

After dinner we sat in the drawing room enjoying his cigars (Egyptian?) and talking Air Force shop in generalities. At that point, I was a more or less permanent co-pilot on C-47s but still hoping to be posted to single-engine fighters. It wasn't intended as a hint, and the Air Chief Marshal obviously didn't take it as such.

I remarked that a newspaper article predicted that General Eisenhower was a leading candidate to head Operation Overlord, the invasion of Europe. He admitted that this seemed to be a possibility. He didn't say so, but remembering his admiration for General Marshall, I sensed he was to be deeply disappointed if Marshall were not to be the Supreme Commander. Months later, shortly before his posting to the Southeast Asia Command, I asked him directly why Eisenhower had gotten the nod instead of Marshall. He said that it was Churchill's doing. The Prime Minister didn't believe he would be able to influence Marshall in matters of high strategy or political considerations. History seems to agree that that was the case.

After Jacqueline and I announced our engagement and wedding preparations were going forward, Leigh-Mallory was deeply immersed in plans for the invasion. I was getting checked out on C-47s and was also on detached service with Colonel St. Gaudens in Cornwall and Devon. There was almost no time for relaxation. Some time before D-Day, Leigh-Mallory acquired a Dakota (the British tag for the C-47). His personal pilot had recently completed a tour on Mosquito bombers and the ACM suggested that perhaps I could be assigned to his crew because of my experience with C-47s (although at that moment I'd had very little). But Lady Leigh-Mallory sternly put the kibosh on that idea; she wasn't about to have both her eggs in one crate, so to speak. That settled the matter although I did go across the field at Hendon, and did some circuits and bumps in a C-47. After the wedding and a one-day honeymoon, we didn't visit Stanmore for some time. Jacqueline had miraculously managed to locate a flat. It was in Chelsea, about equidistant from Hendon, where she was, and Heston, where I now was. The flat was in Chelsea Cloisters, a quite modern nine-story building. We had what was called a bed-sitting room or studio flat. The building had a lounge and a dining room, and it was all very pleasant when I was able to get into town.

I was in residence one night when about midnight the air raid sirens went, and to the south the ack-ack guns began to cut loose. We were less than a mile north of Battersea Power Station which, with its towering stacks, was a favorite target of the Germans. It looked as if tonight would be no exception. It was getting quite noisy out when a low-flying plane roared directly over our heads. I told Jay the pilot had some guts to fly that low, and how had he managed to get through the barrage balloons? There were a few explosions north of us and then the all-clear sounded and we went to sleep.

The next day Jay called me at the field and said, "You were talking about the brave pilot who flew so low? Well, there wasn't any pilot. The Germans have a new robot bomb!"

A few evenings later I was back at the Cloisters and by then everyone in London was aware of Hitler's inhuman new weapon, targeted as it was not at strategic sites but randomly aimed at civilian centers. We'd eaten supper and were back in the flat when the sirens began to wail and the guns banged and we could hear the soon-to-be-familiar blam, blam, blam of the V-1s. We looked out the window at the people in the street. When a buzz-bomb was coming, they would duck into a shop. When they could hear it pass over, they started walking again. It was when their motor went off and they went silent that terror set in because they were about to drop. After the third bomb went over we beat a hasty retreat. Our flat was on the top floor with only a few inches of roofing between them and us.

We didn't head for a bomb shelter but for a flat on the north side of the building inhabited by a man named Garrity, a yeoman in Lanny Callan's office at the Embassy. He had a well-stocked larder, I knew, and we introduced Jacqueline to the calming effects of good old U.S. bourbon.

A day or so later Jay notified me that, on the orders of Lady Leigh-Mallory, we would be taking up residence at Stanmore. Move we did and it was a most interesting and enjoyable period. It was a long haul from Heston, involving a six-mile ride on a wonderful steam train. One afternoon I got away early and was standing on the platform admiring the little engine. I struck up a conversation with the engineer. He explained the various controls and when it was time to leave he invited me to join him in the cab. The line ended at Stanmore and as luck would have it Jay and her mother walked to the station to meet me. I can still see the look on Lady Leigh-Mallory's face when she saw me in the cab and at the controls.

That same night Jay and I walked to the highest point of a golf course that abutted the house. It was a beautiful night and there was a spectacular view of London. It was briefly hard to remember there was a war on, until you saw a column of smoke, followed in a few seconds by a dull boom. I think we counted seventeen buzz-bomb hits on Greater London that night, even after they had set up the belt of barrage balloons and had a strong line of interceptor fighters on the southern coast. It was a suffering time for London.

It was a time of almost unreal contrasts. We were living in a beautiful country house with a warm and delightful family. Yet we were in the midst of a cruel and devastating war (whose effects would outlive the war by several years). But of course if it hadn't been for the war, I wouldn't have been there and wouldn't have met and married Jacqueline.

They were difficult times for all of us. The Air Chief Marshal was experiencing his most critical period. The Allies were breaking out of Normandy and the aircraft were flying around the clock. Our squadron had been flying into France from shortly after D-Day, landing on those pierced-metal landing strips that were often not airfields as such but labeled A-1, B-2 and so on. We were bringing in vital supplies and flying out the wounded.

Henson had taken a couple of buzz-bomb hits and Jay had the sad duty of arranging the funerals for several of her airwomen who were killed. We had also taken some hits at Heston, and there were casualties among the ground personnel.

Stanmore was the oasis for all of us. Leigh-Mallory set the pattern. I think his many years in service, especially during the difficult days of the Battle of Britain, gave him the resilience and the common sense to shift gears and let down. He never let the conversation get too heavy. His only reference to his day's work was likely to be a funny incident. He needed to unwind and saw to it that we unwound, too.

There was one exception that I remember. There had been a high level meeting shortly before the invasion of Southern France. He mentioned that most of those present were out of sorts with the Prime Minister. "He was being very tiresome," Leigh-Mallory said, "pushing for his favorite maneuver, invading the soft underbelly of Europe—the Balkans." I gathered the P.M. was very much in the minority.

I remember on another evening a discussion of Field Marshal Bernard Montgomery, one of the most widely publicized of the English military men. I'd read a folksy story in one of the British papers about Monty at his HQ after a day of strenuous battle. A large photograph showed Monty sitting in an easy chair outside his caravan and being served tea. On either side of him were cages containing canaries. The story quoted him as saying that after a day of planning his offensive and setting up his troop movements, nothing bucked him up more than having a cup of tea and listening to his canaries sing.

I couldn't wait to get to Stanmore and discuss the article with the ACM. There'd been several veiled comments earlier when Monty's name had come up in conversation. I described the hearts and flowers piece. There was what I would call a pregnant silence, followed by a dry comment that it was too bad that Monty's war staff wasn't as efficient as his PR staff.

In time it came out that the Imperial General Staff felt that Field Marshal Alexander, who really masterminded the victory in Africa, should have been appointed to represent Britain on the SHAEF command staff, and Monty relegated to the Italian campaign. But Monty was Churchill's choice for SHAEF, and that was that.

November 12, 1944 became our last family night at Stanmore and it is forever burned into my memory. Late that afternoon eight of our squadron's C-47s took off from Le Bourget, the airfield northeast of Paris, for Burtonwood Air Force Base near Liverpool. It was a marginal day, the beginning of a siege of atrocious weather that covered the European theater for the next several days. Visibility was low and there was some icing. We contacted British Air Defense as we approached Chester, were advised that the field was socked in and that we were diverted to Valley on the Wales coast. By now it was dark and the idea of muddling around in this muck over the Welsh hills did not appeal to me one bit, especially since there were eight of us doing the same thing. I took a direct reading fix and reversed course for Northolt Air Base, northeast of London. We contacted the base; they were just above the minimum and we could land.

The crew weren't heartbroken that we would be remaining overnight in London. It was their old stamping ground. I wasn't heartbroken either; it wasn't far from Stanmore. I arrived at the house in something less than a Class A uniform—GI combat boots, RAF battledress, and a .45 in a holster which I parked on the hall table. As luck would have it, I got there just in time for dinner. Jay was there, having taken a few days leave to be with her parents and see them off before they left two days later for the ACM's new posting as chief of the Southeast Asia Command Air Force, working closely with his old friend, Lord Mountbatten.

The evening was quite different from our previous dinners. The atmosphere was subdued, a mixture of excitement and expectation, mixed I'm sure with sadness about all they would be leaving behind. Lady Leigh-Mallory had been busy sorting and packing (deciding what had to be left, since there was only so much room even in a large aircraft.)

After dinner we went upstairs for a last game of snooker. Lady L-M sat on the couch where Sam, their ancient Airedale, usually sat to watch us play. She patted Sam's pillow sadly. He was too old to leave with friends, and had to be put to sleep.

The ACM dismissed the ladies and said that he and Anthony (!) were going to smoke their pipes and have a nightcap, Scotch and water, no ice. As a last question, I asked him confidentially what he thought of the American generals he'd been working with. "Confidentially?" he asked with a smile. I nodded.

"Well," he said, "they were an interesting group. Van [Hoyt Vandenberg, the ACM's deputy] has an excellent tactical mind, but I don't think we gave him enough to do and he ended up in the social whirl. I believe he'll head the Ninth Air Force before long." The ACM sometimes flew with Lieutenant-General Elmwood (Pete) Quesada in his two-seat P-51 to make sweeps inspecting the battle fronts. This was against Lady L-M's wishes, but the ACM liked Quesada.

"Now Tooey [Lieutenant-General Carl Spaatz, then the commanding general of the Ninth Air Force] could be difficult," the ACM said. "We would set up an important mission, needing his support, and at the last minute he would send a signal to the effect that other priorities prevented their participation, even if there was nothing more important scheduled." (I wondered if it was possible General Spaatz was still a bit miffed that the ACM got the post as Allied Air Force Commander, and not Spaatz.)

"Jimmy," said the ACM (Lieutenant-General James H. Doolittle, the commanding general of the 8th Air Force), "was one of the finest people I've ever known. If Jimmy told you he would do something, you could consider it done."

As we were going upstairs to bed, the ACM asked me the nearest airport to Hammondsport where his York aircraft could land. I thought Elmira but needed to know how much runway the York required. He suggested I stop in the hangar at Northholt and ask Squadron Leader Lancaster, his pilot. At his bedroom door, he took my hand and put his other hand on my shoulder. "Take care of yourself and Jay," he said, "and we'll see you in Hammondsport. We're looking forward to it."

Early the next morning at Northolt I met Lancaster, who gave me a tour of the York. It was very cavernous inside, as the ACM intended to have it fitted in India. I wasn't impressed with the cabin. It had a standard RAF instrument flying panel, but the rest seemed cluttered. The windscreen was divided into quite small panels and there didn't seem to be a windshield wiper.

I said thanks, and left with a small feeling of uneasiness.

[The Leigh-Mallorys and their staff took off from Northolt airbase at nine in the morning on November 14, 1944 on a 5,000-mile journey to Kandy, Ceylon, with a first refueling stop scheduled at Pomigliano, near Naples, Italy. The plane never reached Pomigliano and a massive air-search was launched, but had to be abandoned after two weeks. Seven months later, on June 4, 1945, a French electrical worker who lived nearby discovered the wreckage in a steep and almost inaccessible crevasse some 7,000 feet up in the French Alps east of Grenoble, France. The York, 250 miles off course, had evidently crashed in a zero-visibility snowstorm. Tony, still stationed at Amiens, reached the site a week later, and passed to RAF and French officials Jacqueline's wish that her parents be buried near the site, as they were, rather than in a military cemetery.

Tony attended the burial service on June 15 at tiny Rivier d'Allemont, and he and Jacqueline were present at the memorial service in Westminster Abbey on June 28, 1945.]

The Kid Gets a Bath

France, 1944

IT WAS A DULL morning. They usually were when you were on standby. It was nearly noon and I was reading an old copy of "Yank" when Linville, one of my pals in the 52nd Troop Carrier Squadron, came in from the flight. "Hey, doc," says Linville, "you got a brother in the infantry?"

"I do," I answer.

"Well," says Linville, "I am about to take off from Cherbourg when this dogface runs up in front of the airplane and flags me down. So I set the brakes and go back to see what the problem is.

"The GI tells me he recognizes the 'Sad Sack' emblem on the aircraft and wants to know if I know his brother, Lieutenant Doherty, who flies for the same outfit. I say that I do and I promise to tell you I saw your brother Peter at Cherbourg."

The last time I'd seen Pete was a couple of months earlier in England, when he was in training. He had obviously reached France.

I checked the operations board and saw that Burns, another of my pals, was scheduled to take the one o'clock to Cherbourg and on to Burtonwood, in England. I contacted Burns and found that he was most agreeable to changing with me, as he would rather fly to Paris that evening and continue the French lessons he was taking from a Russian girl.

So I took off at one. I made a wide circuit of the field when I reached Cherbourg to check the layout. At the eastern end of the runway was a cluster of tents, back of the apron where the aircraft revved their engines before takeoff.

After our cargo was offloaded, I taxied back to the apron, keeping well clear of the runway. As I climbed down from the plane, a sergeant approached and saluted. He said they'd been there for several weeks and wondered if I was their transport out of there. I hated to disappoint him, but I said I was looking for Pfc. Doherty, my youngest brother. I said I thought he'd been in the area recently. The sergeant said he knew him and would locate him for me.

The sergeant returned in a few minutes, but I thought he'd made a mistake. The soldier with him appeared to be colored. But when he came closer and stuck out his hand, I could see through a heavy coat of grime that it really was Peter. It turned out that the GIs thought the Air Force had a grudge against the Army. Every aircraft that took off swung its tail toward them blasted all the crap and corruption on the field right into their tent area. I tried to explain that it was standard and necessary procedure to rev up the engines and check the mags before takeoff. The look the sergeant gave me made it clear he hardly believed a word of it.

I suddenly had an idea. Drawing the sergeant aside, I asked if it would be possible to take Peter with me. I'd have him back early the next morning, I said. The sergeant said that the way things were going we could keep him a week and no one would notice. So Peter climbed aboard, I filed a clearance and took off for England. It was all strictly against regs of course, but how often does a chance like that arise?

Pete was standing between the pilots' seats and it was soon evident that he was pretty gamy. An occasional shower was possible, he said, but there were no facilities for washing your clothes.

The flight to the airbase near Liverpool was routine. The co-pilot moved out of his seat so Pete could drive for a bit, and he did a pretty fair job. After we landed, the crew chief volunteered to take Pete to the enlisted men's mess. But I said we were going to the PX and then see if we could broach the Officer's Club.

We had no problems at the PX, where we bought Pete several pairs of socks and longjohns plus a tooth brush and a lot of soap.

At the officers' billet there was a temporary problem. The sergeant in charge started to give us an argument, but I explained the situation. He could see or scent what I meant, grinned and gave us a room with two beds. Gathering up our purchases, we headed for the showers. I told Pete to take off his combat boots and his jacket, leave everything else on, get under the showers and lather up good. After he gave his shirt and trousers a good scrubbing, he soaped his long-johns. He handed the clothes out of the shower and I soaked them in basins of hot water. Pete finally got down to his bare essentials and he actually looked familiar.

He put on his new underwear and socks. I always carried an extra pair of GI trousers and a shirt, and I donated them to the cause. We wrung out his washed clothes and hung them in the boiler room, hoping they'd be dry by morning.

We went to the mess and had a good meal (superb, according to Peter, with real feeling). We sat in the lounge and brought each other up to date on family doings, and swapping a few memories of better times in a nicer place, until we could hardly keep our eyes open.

After breakfast we went out to the field, where they were finishing loading our cargo. The weather was good. I filed a clearance, and we flew back to Cherbourg. As we taxied onto the ramp, the sergeant was there, waiting nervously. "Holy Toledo," he said, "I thought you'd never get here. We're moving out!"

Peter jumped out the rear door before we could put the steps down and we said a quick goodbye. It was a short get-together, but we had struck a blow for cleanliness.

Brothers in Arms

E.T.O. 1943–1945

FOR ME THE big news in the fall of 1943 was that I'd been transferred to the RAF station at Hendon, not far from London. The other big news was word from brother Boog. He had arrived in the E.T.O. and was stationed near Salisbury. We were able to meet in London and have dinner with an old Hammondsport friend, Captain J. Lansing (Lanny) Callan, USN, now a Naval attaché at the American Embassy, doing liaison with Governments in Exile. That was the first time Boog and I had seen each other in a year, and despite our tight schedules we were able to get together fairly often, either at his camp or in London. In spite of the severe restrictions imposed by the approach of D-Day, he was able to get into London to be my best man when Jackie and I were married on May 20, 1944.

I hadn't heard much from Pete after I urged him to join the Air Force. Then I had a letter from Mother telling me that he'd been drafted—and didn't like it.

Needless to say, the summer of 1944 was busy and momentous. Boog, now a tank commander with George Patton's Third Army, had hit the Normandy beaches on D-Day Plus 2. Only a day or two later we (of the 52nd Troop Carrier squadron) were landing at forward airfields in France. By late September and early October, the 52nd was in the process of moving to France and I got to London very infrequently, but the buzz bombs had stopped and Jackie had moved back from Stanmore to our apartment in Chelsea.

One evening Jackie informed me that Peter had arrived in the E.T.O. I asked her how she knew and she said her father had told her.

Peter had gone right to the top to get our number. He called that night to say he was stationed near Warminster and please could I come see him; it was important.

A week or so later I wangled a day off and flew down to see him in an L-4 (a wartime Piper Cub), as I wrote in "A Flight to Remember." What he hoped was that I could ask the Air Chief Marshal to intercede on his behalf and wangle a transfer for him out of the Infantry and into the Air Force. That was about the last chore in the world I wanted to lay on the ACM, who had a full plate those days, to say the very least. But I said I would do what I could.

I had dinner at Stanmore not long after, and the ACM kindly asked if I'd been able to locate Pete and how he was. That was as good an opening as I could have asked for and I mentioned Pete's request. It was obvious the ACM was not enthusiastic about passing along the request but he promised he would touch base with General Carl (Tooey) Spaatz, his American counterpart in the European command. But the transfer never materialized.

I had a couple letters from Pete, who was still in the Infantry and not liking it any more than he did before. His letters were censored and his return address was an APO number so I had no idea where he was. Then one day in November 1944, I got word he was living in a tent at the Cherbourg airfield, awaiting shipment to Italy. I was able to sneak him away to Liverpool for a hot shower, a change of clothes, and a decent meal ("The Kid Gets a Bath").

I next heard that he was in a rear area in Italy. He was in a group of GIs who had been moving to the front lines as Infantry replacements and had come under heavy mortar attack. A near miss had damaged his hearing and he was out of combat. He remained in Italy until the end of the war, was then sent to the Caribbean, and finally to a base near Miami.

Like millions of other servicemen, Pete took advantage of the GI Bill and graduated from Syracuse. As it happened, I was discharged before he was and by the time he got home I was converting Grandmother's barn into an apartment for Jackie and me.

Boog survived in good health, no thanks to the Germans. He became a major in the Tank Corps and was photographed by one of the wire services standing in the turret of his tank and looking every inch the fighting commander, which gave the home folks a thrill. After the war, he and his wife, Edie, rather idealistically and unrealistically, went into farming near Geneva, and then proceeded from bad to worse by getting into chicken-raising. I sometimes found myself lending Boog a hand by helping to shovel what seemed like tons of his poultry's principal by-product. Pete never caught the excitement of this activity, and anyway he had his homework.

A Walk Through Yesterday's Hell and a Visit to Mecca

Reims, Fall 1944

IT WAS TO be a short flight, a special load carried to a flight strip just south of Reims, the heart of the Champagne district of France. The field was also on the edge of still scarred lands in northeastern France that had never healed from the terrible trench warfare battles of the First World War.

Flying over the area you could see the patterns of furrows and fields where farmers were returning the devastated land to production. Obviously the layer of dark top soil was relatively thin; below it was the chalky white of the limestone undersoil (ideal for growing champagne grapes). The fields south of the old battlegrounds were relatively dark. The fields that had been churned up by the cannonading were a light gray. You could still make out the light gray zigzag traces where the communications trenches had run, and even the star-shaped splotches where a large artillery shell had hit. We never flew over the area without experiencing a deep sadness, moved by events that had taken place only a quarter-century before.

On this particular day the weather was marginal, with fairly low cloud cover and a hint of rain, so when we took off from Le Bourget we "motored" northeast at about five hundred feet. As we approached the field at Reims we could make out the classic towers of the cathedral in the misty distance. We landed on pierced-steel matting that gave out its characteristic rumbling clatter. As we turned off onto a taxi strip at the end of the runway, the plane gave a lurch to the left and began to list. We'd blown a tire; a piece of the matting had broken loose and pierced it.

We were well off the single runway, so we left the plane as it was. I sent the crew chief to the operations office to get repairs going. He reported back that they would get right on it, so I went to the office to file our flight plan for the return to Le Bourget.

As I walked along the taxi way, I saw piles of what appeared to be artillery shells, rusty and caked with mud. A passing sergeant told me they were supposedly duds from World War I. They had starting using bulldozers but after a couple of the "duds" had exploded, they switched to "tankdozers"—tanks with dozer blades that had been used to bust through the hedgerows of Normandy. I asked the sergeant where exactly the shells had been. He gave me an odd look and told me to walk east beyond a line of tents, and I'd find my answer.

I walked from the air strip fifty feet into another world. Behind the line of tents was a monochromatic landscape you might then have envisioned as resembling the surface of the moon. There wasn't a living thing to be seen, not a bush, a tree, or a blade of grass. Nor was there any sound, only an eerie silence. I was walking through the untouched expanse of a 1918 battlefield. The misting rain was falling and seemed to shroud the horizon and blend with the ground itself. I had to look back at the tents to be sure of my bearings.

As I walked around, it became obvious that this had been a defensive trench. There were still scraps of burlap from the sand bag fortifications. Looking more closely, I saw other relics of battle, rifle cartridges, some empty, some unfired and presumably still live, a rusted-out canteen, and webbing with buckles. I saw a round white object the size of a golf ball protruding from the earth and I picked it up. It was an upper fragment of a human thigh bone. A few feet further there was a French helmet (amazing that it had escaped the scavengers) and inside it was a large fragment of skull bone.

I felt suddenly that I was desecrating a piece of sacred ground and I turned and retraced my steps. (That might explain why the relics were still there.) I experienced feelings of great sympathy, but also of deep sadness and a sense of futility. The Frenchmen who had fought and died here were trying to make the world a better, safer place. Here we were, only twenty-five years later, trying to do the same thing.

I went back to Reims again, in happier circumstances. It was late in an afternoon in the fall of 1944 and my co-pilot, Woody, and I were en route back to the UK, with a stop at Reims. (Woody had been with me when we tried to get Spike Jones to his meeting with Ike on time.) We were slow getting off-loaded which meant an even later arrival back at Burtonwood air base in England, and all the problems of late meals and arranging billets for our non-Burtonwood crew.

I decided that remaining overnight at Reims would not hold up the war very much. I told the crew that I didn't much like the sound of the starboard engine, which was true but not central to my private dilemma, which was this: Before the war I'd worked for a winery in Hammondsport that produced champagne and was so French in spirit its post office was Rheims (pronounced Reems rather than the French *ranz,* expressed through the nasal passages). Here we were hardly a mile from where it all began. How could I not have a look? The crew had no problems with the decision, so we secured the plane and hitched a ride into Reims.

The billeting office found rooms for Woody and me at the Lion d'Or. After dinner we window-shopped both sides of the main street. Across from the hotel we came to a very large and opulent cafe, called, if I remember correctly, La Maison de Champagne. A string orchestra was playing quietly in the background. The maitre d' showed us to a table and in my best high school French I ordered *une bouteille de champagne.* He returned with a bottle in the classic napkin. I held up my hand for him to stop and I examined the bottle. The label looked to have been printed on a piece of old wallpaper and the wine itself had a slightly orange cast through the green bottle. I tried to say no way in French and asked for a better bottle. As the waiter left, I glanced at a middle-aged couple at the next table. *"Non bon,"* the man said, holding his nose; *"pour les Boches."*

The waiter returned with another bottle, with a slightly better-looking label, but one I'd never heard of. I couldn't believe the Boche had drunk or stolen all the good champagne, and I said, *"Mais non! Un bon champagne—Mumms, Cliquot, Lanson!"*

I knew the names but doubt if I'd ever tasted one of them, but I obviously sounded authoritative.

The waiter returned with a bottle in a bucket of ice. He drew it proudly: a Lanson '37! I ordered extra glasses for the couple at the next table, and we drank toasts, *"Vive la France, vive America."*

The champagne was superb, the company marvelous, and we communicated easily despite the language barrier. I had visited Mecca and sampled the competition. It made a very early takeoff the next morning a very small price to pay.

Fire in the Hold

Le Bourget, Paris, January 1945

IT WAS EVIDENT when we came out of our quarters that it was going to be a lousy day to fly. As we walked over to Operations, we debated whether what we had was a very heavy mist or light rain. The ceiling was very low and visibility, as we used to say, was zilch.

But fly we would. We could see the ambulances backing up to the C-47s on the flight line and the stretchers being loaded aboard. One very important question was, what was the icing level, and how severe would it be?

At Operations we were assigned aircraft and crews. Then we checked Meteorology. There was practically no ceiling (it was at ground level, in other words). The cloud tops were at 10,000 feet; there was mild icing between 4,000 and 5,000 feet. The weather in the south of England, partial cloud cover at 2,000 to 3,000 feet. Not bad by normal (English) standards.

We made our way to the aircraft and did our walk-around inspection while the last of the stretchers were being loaded and secured. We would be carrying twenty-seven stretchers and a flight nurse. We felt a tremendous responsibility on every flight when we were evacuating the wounded. Our passengers had been through the hell of ground combat, been wounded, and were entitled to be delivered safely to the hospitals in England where they would get the treatment they required. On this flight we had several men with head wounds, which meant that we couldn't fly above five thousand feet. Our destination was Membury.

The crew and I boarded and walked up the narrow aisle between the stretchers. The nurse reminded us of the head wounds and the altitude restriction. We went in the "office" as we called the cockpit and began our check list and start-up procedures. All in order. We fired up the engines and taxied up to the active runway (there was only one at Le Bourget). We called the tower for permission to take off.

As we swung out on the runway and lined up on the center stripe, we paused to check our gyroscopes and do a final instrument check. The far end of the runway was barely visible as I advanced the throttles. As speed increased and the tail lifted, your eyes would flick from the line on the runway to the directional gyro to make sure it was operating correctly.

With the copilot calling out the airspeed and the runway blurring beneath us, we approached the end of the runway and lifted off. Within seconds the ground disappeared and we were on the gauges. The landing gear came up and I pulled back the throttles to give us climb power.

Then all hell broke loose.

The cockpit filled with acrid black smoke. Many of our planes were equipped with oxygen masks, and I fumbled for a mask but it wasn't there. Our plane didn't carry them. I slid open the side window. At the same time the crew chief, who was standing between the pilot seats, reached forward and closed the master switch, shutting down our electrical system. That meant that all of our systems were out, including the radio. We did have our gyroscopic instruments that were vacuum driven, including the artificial horizon and the bank-and-turn indicators. So we were back to the basics: needle ball and air speed.

The crew chief determined that the inverter had caught fire. I'm still not clear what its actual function was but it was mounted under the floor on top of the two-hundred-and-fifty-gallon fuselage fuel tank. It wouldn't have to get too hot before the fuel expanded and BOOM! The chief unlimbered the CO2 fire extinguisher and gave the area under the floor a healthy blast. It quelled the fire but now the cockpit was filled with both smoke and carbon dioxide, a nice combination.

After we were fairly well stabilized, my concern was our load of wounded. I told the chief to keep the door to the cabin closed. I couldn't think of anything worse than being strapped to a stretcher in a burning aircraft. There was no way they could get out until we were on the ground.

We didn't know what did it, shutting down the electrical system or the blast from the fire extinguisher, but the fire was out. Now it was a matter of going back to flying the gauges and dead reckoning navigation.

We were lucky in that we broke out between layers of cloud at about 4,000 feet. We had a fairly accurate check on our position from timing our climb-out speed. With fair visibility between the clouds we could get out our charts and plotter and lay out a course. Since I was familiar with East Anglia, we laid out a course for the area, for Honnington to be exact.

Since Meteorology had forecast eight-tenths visibility over England (eighty percent of the sky cloud-covered), we hoped to be able to pinpoint a familiar landmark and make a let-down through a gap in the clouds. When our ETA (Estimated Time of Arrival) over the coast arrived, the cloud cover was 10/10 (total cover) so we continued northeast toward East Anglia. Our normal procedure was to refuel in England and I was concerned about how much time we had to spend looking around, given our fuel supply.

The cloud cover didn't appear to be thinning, so I called Darky. Darky was an emergency system to aid lost aircraft. It consisted of a number of ground observers who manned posts throughout the country. An aircraft not sure of its position would call Darky on its radio transmitter, identify itself, state the problem, and Darky would give it the course to steer to an airbase. They had a safety check so the Germans couldn't take advantage of the system, but I confess I've forgotten what it was.

Darky had a drill for aircraft in our predicament, and we followed it. You would fly an equilateral triangle, three miles on each leg. The ground observers would report the passage of the aircraft to their control center who would in turn notify an aircraft which would be standing by in the area.

We had made about three or four circuits of the triangle when an RAF Hurricane popped up through the cloud deck, a half-mile off our port wing. He made a swing around us (we were flying slowly under reduced power to conserve fuel) and formed up on our wing. I took a pair of ear phones and tossed them out the side window. He got the message and motioned us to form up on his wing, which we did. We didn't have to pay attention to the instruments now, just hold our position on his wing.

After the smoke had cleared out of the cockpit, the chief went back and explained the situation to the flight nurse. Luckily very little smoke had penetrated the cabin. The chief told the nurse about Darky and our escort, so she could reassure her patients.

It was a bit tricky holding the position when we were letting down through the clouds but luckily they weren't too thick and we broke out over a fair-sized city I recognized as Cambridge.

There were several airdromes nearby, but there would be the problem of transportation of our wounded. They had been through enough already without having to face the possibility of a long bumpy ride in an ambulance. We checked our fuel and decided we had enough, with our reserves, to make Membury. The visibility was now several miles and this was familiar territory. So we set course for Membury and took off. In a very short time we were over the field, rocked our wings, got a green light to land, and were quickly on the ground. Despite the fire, we had reached our destination.

It had not exactly been a routine flight, but it had a very happy ending.

Linkup

April 1945

THE DUTIES of a Troop Carrier Command are varied. Its primary mission is to airlift troops into combat, which means carrying paratroopers to their drop zones behind enemy lines. In fact there were only five airborne assaults mounted by the Allies in Europe during the war. But Troop Carrier aircraft were kept busy evacuating the wounded from front-line aid stations and carrying them to hospitals in France and the UK, returning to the battle zones with replacement personnel, fuel, ammunition, and other supplies.

I was assigned to the 52nd Wing of the Troop Carrier Command, based at Amiens, France, early in 1945. In late April, I was assigned to a high priority and exciting mission: to locate and evaluate forward German airfields as to their suitability for evacuating wounded as well as for re-supply. The organizers of the mission also saw it as an opportunity for a close look at the forward battle areas.

We were a well-equipped expedition. In addition to the standard C-47 crew of crew chief/ engineer, radio operator, and myself as both pilot and navigator, there were the mission leader, my mentor, Lieutenant-Colonel John M. Brodie, Major Eugene Glass, the Wing's ordnance officer, and Captain John Conquest, who came along for the ride (as an observer, to put it more tactfully).

Our specific target was to survey the field at Leipzig. Flying low and keeping a careful watch for enemy activity (the area was very fluid and Operations had had no fresh data to give us), we reached Leipzig without incident. But the field had been heavily bombed and was badly cratered. Some repairs had been attempted but I concluded it was a bad risk: a questionable landing surface with the possibility of mines.

The nearest field was Merseburg, about twenty miles west. It turned out to be a very interesting place. On the east side of the field was Junkers Flugzeug und Motorenwerke. This factory produced the well-known JU-88 and there were a number of them visible in front of the factory. There were also a dozen or so Focke-Wulf 190s, considered by many American fighter pilots to be the best of the German fighters.

What had been taking place here was the production of one of Germany's "last-gasp" weapons. The 190s were being mounted piggyback on top of the 88s. The 88 was stripped of all unnecessary weight and loaded with high explosives. The 190 was mounted on a stilt-like frame, and the appearance very much resembled the Space Shuttle returned from its mission and being shipped back to Canaveral atop a 747.

The pilot controlled both planes from the 190. The pilot would navigate to the target, separate his 190 from the drone 88 and direct it to the target by radio. It was a devastating weapon and the allies were fortunate it hadn't gone into operation a year or more earlier.

The factory had obviously been evacuated before the advancing Americans. There didn't seem to be any Americans or anyone else around so we landed on a clear area on the south side of the field and offloaded the Jeep. We left the crew chief and the radio operator in charge of the plane, with orders that one of them had to be with it at all times. There were stretchers that would serve as bunks, plenty of C and K rations, and a .45-caliber Tommy gun. They were better equipped than we were.

We climbed into the Jeep and with Gene Glass driving and me map-reading from the back seat, set out for Leipzig. The Americans had liberated it only two days earlier and the going in the city was difficult. We found an Army field headquarters and were briefed on the do's and don't's of the situation. There was a strict curfew thirty minutes before dark; a German underground movement was developing that planned to prowl at night and "scragg" every American they could. We learned where the billeting office was and where we could get something to eat.

On the way into the city, I was told that in addition to checking out airfields, a little souvenir hunting was on the agenda, and that General Mark Clark himself had advised Colonel Brodie that he expected some interesting Kraut souvenirs.

After supper we drove around the city and found ourselves, tourist-like, at the Leipzig Zoo, which must have ranked with one of the best in the world and which still looked in surprisingly good shape. We saw a magnificent peacock striding across a wide expanse of lawn. "Hey," cried Brodie, "just the thing to take to the General," and he took off in pursuit. But the wily old bird had no intention of being caught. When Brodie ran, the peacock lengthened its stride; when Brodie slowed to catch his breath, so did the bird. They did three laps and the bird won handily; meanwhile the rest of us were falling about with laughter.

We pushed on. The animals were in habitats designed to resemble natural surroundings, sometimes isolated by water, or barricades and bars. I found a cage with two of the most beautiful huskies I'd ever seen, possibly donated by an explorer back from Greenland, which a sign gave as their origin. I wanted to see them close-up. One at least seemed very friendly when I called, "Here, boy!" I found the entrance to the tunnel that ran behind the cages for feeding and access. There was a series of small steel doors with mesh openings. I put my nose to one opening and realized I was nose-to-nose with a Siberian brown bear. I don't know who was more surprised and I didn't wait to see.

I located the huskies and cautiously opened the door. I've always loved dogs but also have great respect for them. I let the friendlier dog sniff and lick my hat and then my hand. Encouraged, I opened the door further and stepped inside and petted the friendly dog, who responded with whines of delight.

Out of the corner of my eye, I caught a flash of movement. In one bound, the other dog came after me. I just had time to spring back and throw out my right leg while I reached for my .45. The mouthful of teeth that had aimed for my face clamped down on my lower calf. I was wearing combat boots which took the brunt of the attack, but one incisor went through the leather.

Before I could draw the .45, the other dog whirled and took the attacker by the throat. He drove the attacker to the other side of the enclosure where he stayed. Then my friend came back to me. He was limping and one ear was bloody but he was wagging his tail and obviously glad I was still there. I had a K ration in my jacket and gave him the meat and cheese (he waited until I'd dropped it on the floor before he gobbled it up). The chocolate disappeared as well. After a final couple of pats I left the enclosure and re-bolted the gate, only wishing there were some way we could return and liberate the husky.

I went to the Jeep, got the first aid kit, broke an iodine capsule, and with a cotton swab pushed the iodine into the puncture, which was bleeding and thus cleansing itself. The iodine stung enough to convince me it was doing a lot of good. Major Glass, when he heard my tale and saw the toothmarks on my boot, said, "You were bitten by a German dog; we'll get you a Purple Heart." I modestly declined the offer.

As we walked on, we met an elderly zoo attendant who was in tears and said a drunken GI had just shot Katrina, one of the zoo's elephants. The soldier said he'd always wanted to shoot an elephant and this was the first chance he'd had. Now he was after a lion and tiger as well. The attendant begged us to stop him. The idea of confronting an armed and drunken GI who probably hated officers and Air Force officers in particular was not thrilling. But two MPs who'd heard the rifle firing appeared and dashed off with the keeper to find the shooter.

A large building behind us was the cat house, and in a large cage was a magnificent Bengal tiger with two cubs asleep in one corner. The mother was at the other side. Brodie reached through to stroke one of the cubs. He damned near lost his arm. It was amazing how fast that big cat moved. Not as fast as Brodie, lucky for him.

It was near curfew time, so we returned to the Jeep, which was being checked over by the MPs who had chased the elephant-shooter. They demanded our papers, which were luckily in order. They said the shooting of Katrina was a blessing. There was a critical shortage of food for the animals, and Katrina would supply the carnivores for a good two weeks.

We went back to the city, checked in at our billet, and sacked out. It had been a long day. The next morning I hitched a ride to check out the plane. The engineers reported that it would be three days at least before the field would be serviceable—assuming the Germans hadn't had time to set many mines before they left.

Back in town I met Major Glass, who led me to the council chambers at City Hall. The military government had ordered all citizens to turn in all their firearms and cameras. And here they were, everything from flintlocks to automatics and from Brownie-type box cameras to big studio jobs. (The Leicas and Contaxes, if any, had already disappeared.) The colonel picked up a pair of dueling pistols—for the general, he said. The major liberated a beautiful Mauser sporting rifle with an eight-power scope. I confess I found a muzzle-loading military issue pistol which is now transformed into a lamp decorating my den.

But now came the central event of our saga. We found Captain Conquest at the Jeep, talking with two other officers. They were telling John that American troops were about to link up with the Russians at a town called Torgau on the Elbe, only a few miles east of Leipzig. If we got our act together, we could eye-witness this historic occasion.

We re-mobilized our Jeep. (Jeeps were a very popular item and it was prudent to remove one or two vital parts if you were leaving it unattended.) The major drove, I navigated, and the colonel rode shotgun with his Mauser, for which we unfortunately had no ammunition. A few miles down the road we came to Ellenburg, a fair-sized town which had just been liberated. There were buildings still burning and wrecked vehicles along the main street. We picked our way through the debris, and an MP at an intersection gave us directions for Torgau and waved us on.

Just outside town we crossed a river and came to another intersection. There was a lot of activity, troops, trucks, and armored vehicles, the troops hot and dusty and most of them resting and smoking. We asked a lieutenant leaning against a tank for directions to Torgau. He noted the Air Force insignia and looked at us strangely, but waved us down the road that ran east.

We rounded a curve a mile down the road and met a column of German prisoners being escorted by GIs in a Jeep with a .50-caliber machine gun mounted on it. They were neither kids nor old men, as the last defenders were said to be, but fine-looking men, and about the first of the enemy we'd seen. We made some smart-aleck remarks, along the lines of "You don't look like supermen now."

A mile or so further on, we came to another German column and started to make the same smart-aleck remarks, until we notice something different. There was no armed Jeep with them and they were still carrying their rifles, muzzle down on their shoulders. This gave us a jolt and we couldn't explain the situation, so we carried on.

We soon saw buildings on the horizon and assumed it was Torgau. As we drew nearer, we saw a substantial barricade across the highway. Glass said, "Looks like we'll have to detour." He swung off the road, down in the ditch, up out of it and around the barricade. We found our way to the town center and pulled up in front of the three- or four-story hotel at one corner of the square. What was weird is that Torgau was a city of six or seven thousand people, but we hadn't seen a single soul. The center of the village was undamaged, although we could see smoke on the outskirts. It was very strange.

We walked into the hotel. The lobby was empty but we heard voices and walked toward them. It sounded like German, interspersed with laughter. The room off the lobby turned out to be the bar. Seated at a table was large, blond, very handsome man in a light blue uniform I couldn't identify. But we were drawn to his companion, a very striking woman, also tall, also blond.

The man stood up, saluted, and said, "Ah, Americans. We've been expecting you." He spoke excellent English with only a slight accent. He said he was Colonel Hendrick Something-or-Other of Her Majesty's Royal Netherlands Forces, and that he had been a prisoner since the fall of Holland. None of us thought to ask for identification papers and I did wonder how he kept his uniform in such immaculate condition. The girl, we learned later, was on the staff of a prisoner-of-war camp on the outskirts of town. They'd become friends through her official duties, and it was said she was a member of the anti-Nazi underground.

The colonel and his lady were finishing a bottle of schnapps. When the hotel staff exited, they went by way of the bar, leaving its shelves bare, but there was a well-stocked cellar, the colonel said. The reason the town was deserted, he explained, was that the word was out the Russians were coming, and the populace wanted to be as far away as possible.

We went to the cellar and encountered a very substantial door. But where there's a will there's a way. Several sore shoulders and feet later, we were gazing upon gorgeous bins and cases of wine, spirits, and beer. There were no lights, so we made our selections and were starting upstairs when a commanding voice barked, "*Stoie!*" Someone said, "What the hell! That means 'Stop' in Russian." And indeed the very large person pointing a submachine gun at us was our very first Russian. Not a very auspicious start to the linkup.

We couldn't raise our arms without dropping our loot, although if he'd given another gruff command in Russian, you'd have heard a terrible crashing of bottles. We called out, "Tovarich! Friends! Americanisch!" He stepped back and with a sweep of his weapon waved us up. I don't remember who was in the lead, but when the Russian saw what was being carried, he shouted, "Ah! Vodka!" and swept the four of us into the bar, where two more Russians were regarding the colonel and his lady with great interest.

Our first Russian acquaintance took one of the bottles from Brodie's arms, held it with one hand, and gave the bottom a smack with his other hand. Out flew the cork. He clicked his heels, said something in Russian, and took a long pull. He passed it to his friend, who repeated the ritual. We had no idea what was being said but we figured it had to be a toast, so we followed the drill and made some inane remarks about victory, cooperation, and postwar friendship.

Our new allies were very interesting individuals. The one we met at gunpoint was a major, built like a tank and I suspect just as tough. One of his comrades was smaller but looked like a steel spring with a tanned leather exterior. The third was halfway between the other two. None was anybody you'd choose to pick a serious argument with.

Another bottle was popped and the ritual continued, with a new trick. When you made a toast and downed a slug, they roared with pleasure and slapped you on the back. The first time I thought my shoulder was dislocated. But we returned the favor and gave slap for slap. We changed our toast to something along the lines of, "You're the toughest bastards we ever saw and thank God you're on our side."

We were starting the third bottle when a British sergeant appeared, came to attention, and asked to speak to the officer in charge. No one was eager to claim the honor, since our situation seemed vaguely disreputable. But since I don't like vodka, especially bad vodka, and had been only tonguing the bottles, I was in relatively good condition and I asked the sergeant if I could help him.

He said he was from the prisoner of war camp and there was an American soldier who needed medical attention. I retrieved the Jeep key and rotor from the major, and the sergeant and I headed for the camp. We rounded a corner and encountered a sight I still find hard to believe—a column of Russian Cavalry. They rode past us with no more than a casual glance. If we thought our Russian pals at the hotel were tough, they were choir boys compared to the cavalrymen. They were sitting at a trot and when the men came down the horses winced.

At the P.O.W. compound a group of soldiers were gathered just inside the gate. They surrounded the Jeep. Where were all the American troops? All we could tell them was that they were coming. Meantime we needed to know about the injured soldier.

The man had been a rebel, constantly baiting and insulting the guards. He'd been in solitary more often than anyone could remember. Just before noon the guards had heard that the Russians were crossing the river and they decided to split. One of the guards had a concussion grenade and as he passed the rebel's cell, he pulled the pin and tossed it in. One of the prisoners, who was a medic, had examined the man, concluded he had internal injuries and needed attention urgently.

The senior officer at the camp asked if I could possibly locate a medical officer and an ambulance. The rebel's courage had made him a hero in the camp. I said I'd do the best I could. The sergeant decided he'd best stay in the camp until it was officially liberated, so I took off alone.

I retraced our steps through the town, in and out of the ditch around the barricade until I finally met the American column—armored personnel carriers and trucks led by a tank. I held up my arm and the tank clanked to a stop. A helmeted head appeared and demanded to know what the blanking hell I wanted. My report on the injured soldier did not arouse much sympathy. The nearest ambulance was ten miles back, I was told. And anyway, where in hell had I come from? Torgau, I said. That was their objective, the tankman said. They were on their way to take it. Speaking with a great boldness I didn't really feel, I said, "We've already taken it." He asked me who the hell we were, and I said, "The 52nd Troop Carrier Wing." That remark obviously didn't go over well with him. But he said he would radio back and have an ambulance and medic hurry to the P.O.W. camp.

As I turned the Jeep around, he gave a helpful parting shout: "Keep out of the ditches, they're probably mined." That made me feel really good, especially as I approached the barricade through the ditch. But I eased along our previous tracks. I made it back to the hotel without incident, but discovered that what I might call the battle of Torgau was over and lost. The toasts were continuing, but there were fresh Russian replacements and our forces were pretty much out of it. The bottles were coming up from the cellar in a steady stream and being distributed to the Russian troops.

Leaving Brodie and Glass in our "command post," Conquest and I took off to watch the Russians cross the Elbe. As we were about to take off, a young Russian officer and a non-com (tough-looking, but, hell, they all were) demanded a ride to the river. Neither Conquest nor I were happy with our arrogant new friends, but each was carrying a submachine gun, and who were we to argue.

We started toward the river, when the officer tapped me on the shoulder with his machine gun and pointed to a narrow alley. We'd been told that next to women, the Russians were most keen to liberate Jeeps and not squeamish about how they were obtained. I wasn't eager to drive down a narrow, deserted alley with these two Ivans.

I went straight down the street toward the alley then, without slowing down, I cut the wheel sharply to the right onto the next street. Anyone who's driven a Jeep knows that when you turn the wheel sharply, that's the kind of turn you're going to get, and you'd better hang on for dear life. I was expecting it but the others weren't and we damned near threw them out. Even Conquest was taken by surprise and almost ended up in my lap. The two in back were so busy trying to hang on that by the time they recovered their equilibrium we were back on a street with a number of other Russian soldiers around. I glanced at our passengers and received a pair of very dirty looks.

We got to the bank of the Elbe with no more back seat commands and parked to watch the spectacle. There'd been several bridges across the river but the allies had knocked them out. The Russians were crossing in boats and lend-lease Duks. I still wonder how they managed to get the Cavalry across.

The Russian strength was increasing and we still hadn't seen any Americans. We took some pictures, got slapped on the back when some of the officers recognized us for whom we were. Then we drove back to the hotel, to be met by an interesting sight.

Brodie and Glass, assisted by the Dutch colonel, had carried several easy chairs from the lobby and, bottles in hand, were watching the activity along the main street. In the window behind them was a hand-lettered sign, "HQ 52ND TROOP CARRIER WING."

They told us to grab a couple of chairs and sit down, because we were in for a treat. A couple of GIs had come by a bit earlier and said that the Umpty-umpth Infantry would be arriving for the official link-up with the Russians. I wondered where the column I'd met just outside town had got to. We still hadn't seen any tanks or other American vehicles.

The cellar had been stripped of all the spirits, but there was still some good Rhine wine, which was fine with me. We located a cork-screw behind the bar and were enjoying a nice Hock when the first Jeep came into view.

It was all very impressive. There was a colonel riding in the lead Jeep, followed by a couple of armored vehicles and then more Jeeps and troops. The colonel did a double take when he spotted all of us, and our sign. We stood up and saluted as he passed and Brodie in his best Yale accent yelled, "Welcome! We've been waiting for you." The salute was returned, but not with much grace, I thought.

When the unit had passed, we got in the Jeep and made our way to the riverbank to observe the ceremonies. By this time there were quite a number of troops gathered, many more Ivans than Yanks, but everyone seemed to be in a good mood—lots of saluting, heel-clicking, and bear hugs. Many flashes as this momentous occasion was photographed.

We returned to the hotel, where the Dutch colonel and his lady were waiting. He told us he'd been ordered back to the P.O.W. camp for the night. The Americans would be providing transportation for the prisoners the next day. He wanted us to be sure we would look after his friend. From the gleam in one of my companion's eyes, I felt sure she would be looked after. (There was, of course, a strict no-fraternization order in effect.)

There were a number of Russian women about, and we were told that they were for the most part slave laborers who had been sent to Germany when their region was overrun early in the German invasion. We noticed that there seemed to be any number of enthusiastic link-ups upstairs in the hotel between some of these displaced women and the Russian soldiers. In the circumstances, I wouldn't have wanted to say who was leading and who was following as the giggling couples thundered up the stairs.

An American sergeant came by early in the evening and said his commanding officer wanted us to know that the American troops were being pulled back about five miles to avoid any possible troubles between the Yanks and the Ivans. I wasn't sure where that left us.

There was onc sad incident. A young German girl with a Red Cross armband rode up on her bicycle. Glass said he had a headache and asked if she knew where he could find some aspirin. She volunteered to find some. Conquest and I thought it was a bad idea, but off she went. A few minutes later she was back, crying. She'd been accosted by two Russian soldiers. One wanted the bicycle, the other wanted her. They must have been pretty drunk because she'd been able to break away from them and ride off, but not before they'd stolen her watch. I was all for loading her and the bike in the Jeep and driving her out beyond the town limits and heading her toward the American lines. But I was outranked, and one of my companions volunteered to look after her.

Amazingly enough, the pantry was still well stocked. Our English-speaking Russian friend said that that was probably because his compatriots were more interested in booze and women and hadn't gotten around to food yet. He added that because the Russians had been told there would be no Americans in the area, we would be wise not to venture out after dark. We were only too glad to take the advice. We cobbled up a fair dinner of ham and boiled potatoes, found some rooms where the beds were made up, and we retired.

We scrounged a pretty skimpy breakfast the next morning—no coffee, not even ersatz. The English-speaking major announced that the hotel had been commandeered as Russian regional HQ. It was nice to have met their valiant American allies, and goodbye.

We spent the day looking around, picking up a few souvenirs and exploring the house of a colonel in the Wehrmacht, some of his uniforms still hanging in a closet. It became too late return to Leipzig, so we stayed the night in the house. We slept poorly, despite a bottle of brandy we discovered. The night was punctuated with short bursts of machine gun fire, the Ivans opening doors with what we already called "Russian keys." The next morning we headed back to our C-47. We were low on gas but the driver of an American armored reconnaissance vehicle kindly gave us some.

We drove straight through Leipzig to the field at Merseburg. I had wanted to stop at the zoo and liberate that wonderful husky, but it was impossible and impractical anyway. The crew were relieved to see us; we'd been gone three days and they had no idea what might have happened to us.

The crew had had their own excitement. I mentioned that there were a number of Focke-Wulf 190s parked on the field, waiting to be mated with the JU-88s. Just after we'd landed, I had climbed into one of the 190s and remove a unique blind-flying instrument which combined an artificial horizon and a bank and turn indicator. I took it home and years later gave it to a friend as part of the price I paid for a sailplane I bought from him. Now the 190s all had white stripes on the ground around them, meaning Off Limits. An American soldier had been sitting in the cockpit of one of the 190s. No one knows what he did, pulled a lever, flipped a switch, but the plane had been booby-trapped and it blew up, killing the soldier.

We loaded the Jeep back aboard the C-47. Once we were airborne I asked the radio operator to check the base at Amiens for a weather report. It was fine where we were, but we didn't have reserve fuel to go very far to an alternate field if the weather was a problem. But the operator couldn't raise Amiens. Our set was out, although we had VHF tower communications and could hear other aircraft transmitting.

The adventure obviously wasn't over yet. As we flew west, the cloud cover began to build. At three thousand feet we encountered a snow squall. Conquest grew agitated, and Brodie, always a joker, quietly indicated we should go higher so we would stay in the snow squall and upset Conquest some more. We didn't have to; the snow stayed with us as we descended. Luckily, the temperature was above freezing so we didn't have to worry about wing ice. It was a storm front; we couldn't tell how extensive.

With visibility down, there would be no more "tourist" navigation, reading landmarks, rivers, and towns. It was dead reckoning, and without radio for position fixes, out came the Weems computer and scale with which I worked as a navigator.

Our track would put us directly over Liege, Belgium, on the Meuse River. We'd been flying two hours when I started calling the Liege tower. The weather there was a 500-foot ceiling and three mile visibility. The problem was that the ceiling was too low for us to let down in that area without knowing exactly where we were. I'd flown in and out of the airport several times, and there were tall piles of coal or slag, and many cables on the airport's fringes.

We decided the best bet was to fly into Holland, which was low and flat. We broke into the clear at 400 feet and were able to position ourselves as near Maastricht, which was also on the Meuse. So it became a matter of following the river back to Liege. The river is east of the field and the first time we overshot and didn't turn west in time. There was simply no margin for abrupt maneuvering, and conditions were deteriorating, so we poured on the coal and returned to Holland for another shot at Liege. That time we were successful. We were perfectly aligned. The tower started firing flares as we came up the river and our turn on the approach was just right. The only person who didn't enjoy this magnificent display of airmanship was Conquest, who had retired from the front cabin.

We stretched our legs while the crew chief supervised the refueling. I went up to Meteorology to check the weather. The front had passed through and Amiens was clear. How nice to have known sooner.

There was to be one last mini-exicitement. As we were about to reboard, Colonel Brodie sauntered up with a very attractive young woman in an American nurse's uniform. She was a New Zealander married to an Air Force colonel at SHAEF headquarters in Paris and hoping to join him. Brodie had gallantly offered her a lift. I hated to be a wet blanket, but by the time we got to Amiens, I'd have had enough flying for the day, even without making a detour to Paris. Brodie didn't give me an argument. He had a better plan. At Amiens he would clean up, change into his Class A uniform, have cocktails with the nurse at the Officers Club, and then drive her to Paris so she could rejoin her husband and he could have a night on the town. Inspired! What a guy.

And so it was, with a pretty lady in tow, that "The Rover Boys"—as we soon began to be called when the details of our participation in the historic linkup became known—returned to Amiens after one of the war's more bizarre missions.

Vermouth, Champagne, and Generals

Amiens, May 1945

HOSTILITIES HAD COME to an end, and more than ever the 52nd Troop Carrier Wing was a very civilized organization. The headquarters contingent was billeted in two small hotels on thc town square in Amiens. One of the hotels included a well-stocked Officer's Club, and now that official duties had lessened, the cocktail hour began at 1600 hours (four in the afternoon). But a crisis developed. There was no more vermouth for the dry martinis.

But the executive officer of the Wing was Lieutenant-Colonel John Brodie, who had been the leader of our mission to the Russian-American linkup at Torgau on the Elbe. The colonel's feats of acquisition were legendary. In Africa he actually located an electric refrigerator to provide ice cubes for the mess. At Amiens his first coup had been to obtain two cases of Beefeaters gin from a nearby British outfit in exchange for a case of bourbon. Acquiring some vermouth was not about to stymie Brodie, and it didn't.

He learned that vermouth was available at the source, so to speak, at the Noilly Prat company in Marseilles. In no time at all I found myself with C-47, a French liaison officer, a Jeep, and a document authorizing the company to provide the bearer with three cases of their best vermouth.

We onloaded the Jeep and were completing the walk-around inspection of the aircraft when the line chief told me to wait for the general. The general? Moments later, a staff car, with a red-starred flag fluttering on the front fender, drew up in front of the aircraft and two men emerged. One was General Mark Clark, the other a civilian whom General Clark introduced as Emanuel Lemette. They were old friends. Monsieur had been a French ace in World War I. After the war he had been assigned as an instructor in advanced tactics at Randolph Field, Texas, where Lieutenant Clark, as he was then, was stationed, and the two became close friends.

Monsieur Lemette now lived in Epernay and the general asked if I would drop Lemette off on our way to Marseilles. When we boarded the plane, I invited M. Lemette to sit in the right hand seat since we didn't have a co-pilot. He was delighted and after we were airborne, I offered him the controls. He beamed from ear to ear and had a great time as we meandered all over the sky.

As we were approaching the airdrome at Reims, M. Lemette asked me what I did before the war. I told him guardedly that I worked for a company that made wine. He said that he, too, had a company that made wine, and what type of wine did we produce? That was a tricky question to answer because the French believe that only the wine produced in the Champagne district of France can rightly be called champagne. I told him that we were the largest producers of American champagne. I didn't mention our Rhine wine, Claret, Port, Sherry or French and Italian vermouth. "Why," said M. Lemette. "I make champagne, too. Our firm is called Champagne Mercier, and it is the second largest cellar in France. It is in Epernay."

After we landed, there was a car waiting for him and as I escorted him to it, he asked if I would like to see his cellar. If so, he would speak to the general, who was planning to spend the following weekend with the Lemettes. He would have him bring me along.

We took off from Reims and flew south. It was a beautiful day in May and the weather was visibility unlimited. The fresh green countryside passed under our wings, and as we flew down the Rhone Valley we could see snow-capped mountains to the east—the French Alps in the foreground, the Swiss Alps on the distant horizon. It was all quite spectacular. Before long we could see the Mediterranean, brilliantly blue, and we were soon circling the busy port of Marseilles.

We landed and unloaded the Jeep and, with the French liaison consulting a map and asking directions, we found our way to Noilly Prat. We produced our cachet and were warmly received, given an interesting tour of the establishment and samples of their vermouths.

Back in Hammondsport before the war, we'd been attempting to duplicate their taste and aroma, without much success. I thought perhaps I could pick up a secret or two, but even with a good interpreter I didn't get so much as a hint.

We did a quick bit of sightseeing, but I kept an eye on my watch. We were under orders to have the vermouth at the club by 1600 hours. We did, and there was great rejoicing, from the general on down.

On the following Wednesday, the adjutant told me to appear at the airfield at 1500 hours Friday in Class A uniform, equipped for a weekend at Epernay. M. Lemette had made good his invitation. I had the unique experience of sitting in the cabin with a general and being chauffeured to our destination. Heady stuff for a lieutenant.

M. Lemette was at the airfield with his car and we drove country roads through miles and miles of beautiful vineyards. He identified the varieties and told us which of the great champagne houses the grapes would go to. Entering Epernay, we passed the huge stone house of Moet et Chandon, the world's largest champagne producer, and directly across the street was its nearest rival, Champagne Mercier. We turned off the road and through an imposing gateway and up a long driveway to the Lemettes' large, turreted stone chateau. Madame Lemette greeted us in the entrance hall. She spoke little English but made us feel immediately at home. In short order we were seated in a drawing room, sipping some of the local product, and delicious it was, too.

During the flight down, General Clark had told me more about M. Lemette. He had been a regional leader of the French Resistance. Yet many of the local people considered him a collaborator because he associated with the Germans and even entertained them. He walked a dangerous tightrope.

At dinner, which needless to say was elegant, M. Lemette's nephew, Jacques Mercier, persuaded his uncle to tell some of the incidents involving his work with the Resistance. I remember in particular an evening when M. Lemette was driving the road that led south out of the town. Hidden in the trunk of his car were two RAF pilots he was taking to the next station on the underground escape route.

As he rounded a curve, he had to brake hard to avoid hitting a

German patrol that was undoubtedly looking for his passengers. He was very worried until the officer in charge approached the car and saluted. M. Lemette breathed again. The officer was a frequent dinner guest at the chateau where, after several glasses of champagne, he was a fertile source of information about the Wehrmacht. As he and the officer were exchanging pleasantries, M. Lemette caught his breath again; he had become aware of a strong odor. He looked at the officer's expression, but it didn't change. M. Lemette gave the officer an invitation to dinner and a quick *au revoir* and drove off. As soon as the Germans were out of sight, he pulled off the road into a lane, opened up the trunk and said, "You very nearly got us all shot!" The pilots were smoking, and M. Lemette recognized the smoke as being from English cigarettes.

The next morning Jacques gave me a tour of Champagne Mercier. The main vault was a half-mile long and connected by a secret passageway to the chateau itself. The vaults, or caves, were dug out of the chalk that underlies the area, and the natural temperature year-round is fifty-five degrees.

After lunch, M. Lemette drove General Clark and me around the champagne region and into Reims, where we stood in awe in the great Cathedral. He introduced us to some of his friends in the well-known champagne houses of Henri Lanson and Veuve Cliquot. To be polite we sampled the various vintages, which were each marvelous, and we returned to the chateau for tea with Madame Lemette in an extremely jolly mood. A grand day, but there was more to come.

M. Lemette had a message from General Matthew Ridgeway's headquarters at Reims, inviting him and his guests to his billet for cocktails at 1700 hours. (General Ridgeway would later replace General MacArthur in charge of the United Nations forces during the Korean War.)

After a quick wash, we got back in the car and drove to another imposing chateau. When we entered the main salon, there was a lot of merry noise and a fine display of brass. General Ridgeway came over and warmly greeted M. Lemette, General Clark, and Lieutenant Doherty. He also asked his aide, a captain, to look after me, which I thought was very kind. As a matter of fact, the captain later gave me a German aircraft clock, which I still have.

There was a very well-stocked bar, but being a firm believer that discretion is the better part of valor, I decided to pass on the martinis and stay with champagne. I think this was wise.

I was standing to one side watching the other guests when a brigadier-general approached me. He was quite tall, his bearing erect, and his expression serious. As he came up, I hit a brace and we saluted. And then this exchange took place.

General: "Where are you from, Lieutenant?"

Me (standing even straighter): "New York State, sir."

General: "Where in New York State?"

Me: "Central New York State, sir." (Who had ever heard of Hammondsport?)

General (fixing me with a stern look): "What *town?*"

Me: "Hammondsport, sir."

General: "Hell, I'm Lem Mathewson from Bath. D'you know Sam Balcom?"

Well, I did know Sam Balcom, an old and dear friend of the family, and I realized I knew a lot about General Mathewson, too. His brothers were Dallas and Dr. Joe. Dr. Joe was Uncle Kid's doctor and Dallas was a chemist at the Urbana Wine Company at Hammondsport. The general himself went on to command the American troops in Berlin during the Blockade in 1945.

And so, on a home town note, ended the wonderful saga of vermouth, champagne, a story good enough for the movies, and an armory's worth of brass.

Friends of High Rank

1939–1954

UNLIKELY AS IT is for lowly lieutenants in any war, I became friends with two of the highest-ranking officers in World War II. My military bearing or prowess had nothing to do with it. It was just that in one case I was and in the other case I had been a suitor for their daughter's hand, not at the same time, needless to say.

I had courted Admiral John H. Towers' daughter Marjorie one summer in Hammondsport, and perhaps the way to describe it was as a summer romance, as lovely and fleeting as most of them are.

I had met Jacqueline, the daughter of Air Chief Marshal Sir Trafford Leigh-Mallory, when she and I were both stationed at the RAF airfield at Hendon in North London. For something over a half-year he became in fact my father-in-law, until he and Jackie's mother were killed in a tragic plane crash in the Alps on their way to a new assignment in India. In the several months altogether that I knew him, I found him one of the wisest, kindest, and most perceptive men I'd ever known.

My parents' friendship with Jack Towers began in 1911 when he was a young Naval lieutenant who arrived in Hammondsport to study at the Curtiss Flying School, where my father was also learning to fly. Their friendship continued through their lives. During the early years of World War I, my father commanded the Anacostia Naval Air Station, and he shared a house in Washington with the Towerses.

In the spring of 1939, Jack Horne, Toby Champlin, and I drove to Washington for a weekend, and at Dad's suggestion we called on Admiral Towers (two stars then) at the Bureau of Naval Aviation, which he headed. He gave us a letter of introduction that enabled us to visit Anacostia, where Dad had served. At the time, the admiral said he was considering taking a vacation in Hammmondsport with his family, and asked if he knew a cottage that might be available. I said we'd check it out and that Dad would let him know.

Admiral Jack took a cottage Lad Seely had, and he and his wife Pierre, their daughter Marjorie, and their son Charles arrived for the month of August at the lake. It was the momentous August when the war broke out in Europe, the last peacetime August. But for the moment there was still a chance to seize a vacation, and there were a number of parties that often included both the older and younger generations, so Marjorie and I saw a lot of each other.

People who notice such things noticed that when the admiral and his lady arrived at the party or dinner, they were quite reserved and dignified, even stiff, at first. One of my friends said, "He acts as though he was still on his quarterdeck." But when the admiral had had a second very dry martini (Noilly-Prat vermouth specified), he eased out the main sheet and became charming and conversational, if still several nautical miles short of back-slapping.

The fact was that the admiral's climb up the command ladder had not been easy. As Naval Aviator No. 3 and a fierce advocate of air power, he confronted the battleship admirals who had all the high seats, or the high cards. It took a great deal of determination and finesse to win his point, ultimately, about the effectiveness of naval air power. Meantime, he was a very serious man, and not even two martinis could conceal the fact.

The admiral remained "Admiral," but his vivacious wife became "Pierre" instead of "Mrs. Towers" and there was an appreciable easing of the formalities. One night at a dinner at Uncle Charlie's, Pierre arrived in a gown that could only be compared with a Roman toga. Our ever-irrepressible family friend, Sam Balcom, took one look and cried, "By damn, you're all ready for bed!"

Admiral Towers was an ardent small-boat sailor, dating from his days at Annapolis, and often borrowed our Barnegat Sneakbox that summer. Boog and I were sailing the Mystery, a forty-foot A class scow, and he expressed a desire to go out with us. One afternoon the time seemed right. There was a steady south wind and it was a lovely, sunny day. As we approached the Seely cottage we could see that canvas screens had been put up on the sides and the back of the dock. We were about to give hail when we quickly decided not to. The Towerses were stretched out on the dock—in their birthday suits. As we'd neared the shore, the wind slackened and we had almost lost steerage way. But we just managed to put the helm over and do the sailing equivalent of tiptoeing away before they saw us.

One Friday afternoon we were sitting on the winery's porch, which commanded a fine view of the valley and the local grassy landing strip. The admiral had been in Washington and was expected back about five. We heard the drone of an engine and a cabin biplane appeared over the hills to the south. It was a "staggerwing" Beechcraft, a hot little ship with retractable landing gear, used by the Navy for transporting personnel.

As the pilot lined up for the final approach, Dad remarked that he looked to be coming in a bit high and fast. The plane touched down on the short strip and carried on to the adjoining potato field, where it came to an abrupt halt in a large cloud of dust. We hopped into our cars and hurried down to the field, where we found one very irate admiral chewing out a very unhappy pilot, an ensign. As we came up to them, the admiral said to no one in particular, "I told him he was coming in high and hot." Dad said, kiddingly, "Jack, you should be glad you weren't landing on a carrier."

We were starting to man-handle the aircraft back onto the grassy strip when another car drove up and the admiral's son Charlie popped out. He said, "What happened, Dad, run out of runway?" "Shut up and push," the admiral said in quarter-deck tones.

Admiral Towers' final command was as Chief of Pacific Operations, and he retired as a full admiral. He became a vice-president of Pan American Airways and lived in New York. I met the Towerses in New York several times for drinks, and we talked about Hammondsport and the wine industry, but we never spoke of the landing in the potato field. The admiral died in the mid-1950s. When Jacqueline was being treated at Sloan-Kettering Hospital, she stayed with Pierre Towers for a month and they became close friends. Later we visited the admiral's son Charles and his wife, Lois, in Beaufort, South Carolina, when Pierre was living with them. The younger Towerses have returned to Hammondsport several times for events at the Curtiss Museum, extending a fine friendship through another generation.

Red

Hammondsport, February 1995

I HAD THOUGHT the vicissitudes of my past year would be sufficient: a six-month session of treatments for prostate cancer, followed by the pain and discomfort of a slow-healing knee replacement. Then an Associated Press dispatch datelined Millersburg, Ohio, brought the war and its friendships and its casualties rushing back at me. Red Gallion, the burly Cleveland fireman who had shared a memorable Christmas in Norwich, England, with me and a young pair of New Zealand fliers was, in a sense, coming home after fifty-two years.

Friendships are an important factor in most people's lives, but they are particularly important in wartime. You meet any number of individuals with whom you could develop a lifetime friendship. But life in the military in wartime is transient and unpredictable. Finish a course of duty and inevitably you are sent in one direction, your friends in another. So it was with Red Gallion and myself.

We first met at the Manning Pool in Toronto when we enlisted in the RCAF in 1941. We got acquainted while standing guard duty at an airfield on the shores of Lake Erie. With his burly build and his full mustache, he would have looked completely at home in a football uniform posing on one of Walter Camp's All-American team photographs in the 1880s. But contrary to his size and looks he was a gentle man and his strongest expletive was "Carn sarn it!"

Red and I didn't train together in Canada, but after we'd received our wings we met again in Halifax and sailed to England on the *Queen Elizabeth.* We were both posted to an RAF base in East Anglia and it was there we celebrated our first Christmas in England. Before long came the inevitable splitting, Red to fly Typhoons, me to do photo reconnaissance in Spitfires.

We did meet again in London a number of times, and picked up where we'd left off. The last time, as I'll never forget, was in October of 1943. I was in town for the day and had stopped by the American Embassy to see an old family friend, Captain J. Lansing (Lanny) Callan, who was posted there. Lanny asked if I would take his car and driver and pick up some things for him at the PX. I'd just completed my purchases when I spotted Red Gallion and we quickly agreed to have lunch.

Red was, as I mentioned, a gentle man, easygoing and trusting, and so a perfect foil for practical jokes, which he enjoyed more than anybody, especially when they were on him. As we left the PX, I saw the car and driver and saw a chance for a "leg pull."

"Hey," I said, "let's see if we can hitch a ride to the Red Cross Club on Charles Street."

"Shucks, no," said Red, "she's probably waiting for an admiral."

I opened the door and said to Lynn, the driver, "Miss, could you run us over to the Red Cross Club?"

"Certainly, sir," she said, and I pushed Red into the car. She and I started laughing, and I introduced her to Red.

"Carn sarn you, doc, you've done it again," Red said, joining the laughter.

Then that December I ran into a mutual friend at a bar in London and he told me that Red had "bought the farm"—been shot down escorting bombers on a mission to Germany. That was all I knew for fifty-two years, until the brief AP dispatch appeared in the papers.

The story said that Frank Gallion, twenty-four, had been shot down in his P-47 Delta Thunderbolt by Messerschmitt 109 fighters while he was escorting B-17 bombers on a mission to an attack on a German naval base at Wilhelmshaven, German. He was declared missing in action after his plane was seen going down over the Isselmeer Inland sea. The plane had first been spotted in October 1993 during a survey of the sea, about fifty miles north of Amsterdam. The body was found in the cockpit, along with Red's boots and part of a jacket—and his dog tags. When the identification was definite, a military escort brought Red's relics home to Millersburg, Ohio, a community of some 3,200 people about sixty miles northeast of Cleveland.

Death was a part of life in those days. You knew it could happen at any moment but you taught yourself not to expect it but at the same time to accept it stoically when you lost friends like Red. The impersonal lines of the news story hurt a lot, but to ease the sting a little I found myself thinking, "Carn sarn it, Red, we never knew where you went." It was some small consolation that after half a century, Red's story was closed at last.

The Postwar Years

Osceola

The 30s and beyond

IT'S ONLY A fly speck on a New York State map, printed in the smallest type, to indicate the smallest population. It's Osceola, fifty-five miles north-northeast of Syracuse and located at the western edge of one of the largest areas of unoccupied land in the state. If you squinted hard at the map, you could see that Osceola was located on a tributary called Salmon River.

I first came to know of Osceola in the early Thirties. I had become an enthusiastic stream fisherman under the tutelage of Uncle Charlie. He was an absolute master of stream fishing with both wet and dry flies. My introduction to stream fishing for trout had been on Cold Brook, the inlet to Keuka Lake from the southern end of Pleasant Valley. It was an excellent natural stream, winding and twisting with numerous deep, still holes. This was long before the state took it over and turned it into several miles of holeless ripples.

It was while I was fishing Cold Brook alongside Uncle Charlie that he would mention that this or that hole resembled one on Salmon River and that he had found the best way to work it. Setting action to his words, he was usually successful in hooking a trout. But his references to Salmon River and the place called Osceola piqued my curiosity. I asked questions and Uncle Charlie's answers gave me a mental picture of a fly fisher's paradise.

It seemed that a small group of men had formed a fishing club in the foothills of the Adirondacks on what seemed a legendary trout stream called Salmon River. The club had a lease on eight miles of the stream and employed two private wardens to patrol and oversee the stream. Fish could only be taken with flies, wet or dry, no spinners allowed, and keepers had to be longer than seven inches. There was a strict daily limit and members were allowed very few guest days per season. Uncle Charlie and two of his friends were partners, Bob Cole, a lawyer from Bath, and Harry Botchford, the sales manager for the Pleasant Valley winery. They were all excellent fly fishermen and close friends.

Listening to Uncle Charlie's descriptions of the place and of their adventures on the stream, I put together a mental picture, like assembling a jigsaw puzzle. I finally visualized a perfect calendar illustration of the stream, boulder-lined, with deep, dark pools shaded by large evergreens, with their camp itself nestled in the woods just back from the bank of the stream.

My moment of truth, a chance to compare my imagination with the reality, came in late July in 1935, a few days after Hammondsport's devastating flood. Uncle Charlie called and asked if I'd like to go up to the camp for a couple days of fishing. Would I! Valhalla at last. He would pick me up early the next morning. He always drove a Chevy business coupe, always equipped with an ice chest on the shelf behind the seat. On this trip it was stocked with tomato juice and a special elixir of his concocting that consisted of horseradish, Worcestershire sauce, and Tabasco. My job was to open the tomato juice and add the elixir.

At the first stop he opened the trunk and I noticed a large iron casting. It was a "water front" that was going to be installed in the fire place to provide hot water. It looked pretty heavy and I asked how far we would have to carry it back to the camp. He said we could drive right up to the back door. Hm. So much for having to pack in. He said we would need some milk, but we could walk over to the store after we got there. Another wilderness illusion shot down.

It was a nice four-hour drive up and the time passed all too quickly, with Uncle Charlie's stories of hunting, fishing, and family history. His interests were endless, and all fascinating. We left the main highways and were driving along smaller country roads, although they were still paved. There were fewer and fewer farms and more land covered with woods and brush. Finally, the road wound down into a valley. As it leveled out we came to an old girdered bridge that crossed a stream only slightly wider than Cold Brook. "Salmon River," Uncle Charlie said. Another illusion gone. We came to a four corners with a hotel on the left and diagonally opposite a general store. "This," said Charlie, "is Osceola."

We turned right at the corner and drove up the street two hundred feet or so and came to a pair of cobblestone gate posts. We turned in to a large open field. There were two one-story cottages about a hundred feet apart without a vestige of shade, although some small pines and spruces had been planted around the cottages. We did drive right up to the back door, as my uncle predicted, and began unloading our duffel, including the heavy iron waterfront for the fireplace.

The camp was very nicely laid out, with an adequate kitchen with a kerosene stove, a large living room with a big fireplace, a bathroom with a shower, and two bedrooms, each with two double beds. There was a front porch facing the main street, with a swing. All very neat and tidy.

It was midday and there was no point in going to the stream. On a sunny day the water was so clear nothing would rise. We walked back to the store, where I was introduced to Ken Quinn, who was the proprietor and the village's mayor in fact if not in law. If Ken hadn't heard about something, it just hadn't happened. He brought Uncle Charlie up to date about all the latest events—the stream conditions, what was being caught, who had been in town, who was coming.

There were about six camps in the cluster which comprised the syndicate which leased the fishing rights: Dr. Prince, a surgeon from Rochester; the Hardens, who made beautiful cherry furniture in McConnellsville, New York; Dick Reynolds from Elmira; and a couple I never got to meet. Next door to the store and across the street from our camp was a very attractive house, obviously built during Osceola's boom years as a lumber town in the 1890's. It was American Victorian in style and was owned by the Drakes, Glen and Kay, who operated of all things a voice school, which was a place of considerable interest to the locals and the club members alike.

During the summer there were always a number of aspiring actors and actresses in residence at the school. Glen was the instructor and Kay handled the tuition, rooms, and meals. Nearly all the students aspired to be in Broadway musicals. The males tended to be dark and handsome and the girls were all very pretty, long-stemmed American beauties. Their dress style was quite casual, the girls favoring halters and shorts. The Drakes had set up a croquet lawn as well as a badminton court for off-hours relaxation. It's easy to imagine the local interest in the long-legged beauties playing badminton or, as they did, volleyball. I did notice a pair of binoculars on the mantel in the camp.

The fishing schedule began before dawn. It took a while to reach the stream, and the idea was to reach the best pools just as the first hatch was rising. There were a number of very fine holes that would produce at least one keeper. The best lure was a Number 14 nymph or an equally small Coachman on a four-pound leader.

It was important to remember a hole's configuration, which I found out the hard way. The fish would be rising and all of a sudden the action stopped. The sun rose higher and the rise ended. We would return to the camp for a late breakfast and relax or do whatever chores needed to be done. An afternoon nap was routine, although I skipped it only to regret it later in the evening or the next day. The cocktail hour was a definite ritual, hosted in turn around the camps, depending who was in residence. Supper was the main meal of the day, and the heart of the feast was of course the day's keepers. They were rolled in corn meal and sautéed in butter. You picked them up in your fingers and ate them like corn on the cob. There were usually pan-fried potatoes and a cucumber and vinegar salad. Unfancy fare, because the gents, of course, did the cooking.

After finishing the dishes we would start for the river just as it was getting dusk. By the time we got to the water it would be a pretty dark dusk, and this was when it became very important to have memorized the stream and where the holes were. We didn't use waders; you felt the bottom through light sneakers. I went in over my head twice before my first evening was over. Where we had used very small flies in the morning, we were using bass flies at night. I had tied on a number 8 coachman and Montreal, and it was the Montreal that did the trick: a fourteen-inch native brown trout.

When I rolled out of bed just after dawn the next day, I could see the wisdom of the mid-day nap, and I didn't pass it up that afternoon or thereafter.

The two wardens who watched the property were Stanley and Lee. Lee raised mink as a sideline. I went out with Lee the next morning and learned about how to fish Salmon River. I also heard a lot about the locals, and I got the impression that Osceola had the makings of a very good soap opera. Such goings-on.

Lee was a very nice fellow and obviously very fond of Uncle Charlie. The owners had things mapped out well. Bob Cole took care of all the legal matters concerning the camp. Harry made sure there was an adequate supply of wood (Harry was the only one who came up in the fall, for the grouse-hunting). Charlie took care of the other incidentals, like taxes and insurance.

That first trip to Osceola was more than a chance to fish a first-class stream. There was something about that little valley and its inhabitants that grew on me every time I turned in at those cobblestone posts.

World War II was a time of change for Osceola. Lee went into service and we heard that Stanley was working in a war plant in Rome or Syracuse. Somewhere along the line the lease on the Salmon River fishing did not get renewed and the state took over the stream. From a first-class fishing preserve it became just another trout stream. Yet something did remain, and I think of it as "The Osceola Factor."

It's almost impossible to put into words the quiet charm and the tranquillity you felt in this tiny hamlet. I had returned twice with Uncle Charlie before the war. I enjoyed the finest fishing I'd ever known. It wasn't easy and you often got skunked, but as you became familiar with the stream and could read its changing conditions, there was great satisfaction when you were successful.

Yet it wasn't just the fishing that was enjoyable. It was Osceola's people, and the surrounding countryside.

My first visit to Osceola after the war was with George Lawrence, a boyhood pal who was with Taylor Wine. We did a little fishing and some walking—up to the big falls in Fall Brook. Later we went over to the hotel and joined Ken, now back from service himself, for a couple of drinks before dinner. As much as I like to fish, our very low-key weekend was very close to perfect.

The following fall, four of us—Greyton (Spink) Taylor, Zeke Mendel, George Lawrence, and I left after dinner at the Glenwood Club on Keuka and headed north for Osceola and some partridge shooting. Someone coined the phrase that getting there is half the fun, and so it was, what with stops for refreshments and getting lost a couple of times. When we finally arrived we had to jimmy a window because it was too late to get the key from Ken. The camp was stone cold but it was too late to build a fire.

We were quite successful the next day; each of us got at least two birds. That night George and I introduced Greyton and Zeke to the hotel, now named Finlay's Salmon River Inn. The next morning Zeke picked an old canasta score sheet out of a waste basket and presented it to Greyton, saying it was his bill for the rounds of drinks he'd bought the night before.

The following fall—1950 now—the camp came under new ownership. Uncle Charlie had passed on suddenly that summer. Bob Cole wanted out, but Harry wanted to stay, so it became a four-way partnership: George, Zeke, Harry, and I. We decided we would split the expenses evenly, including the wood.

We made some improvements. We installed a wood stove in the kitchen and then a bottled gas stove. An electric hot water heater was donated and installed the next summer. We were really getting civilized.

Zeke and I went up that first fall for more partridge shooting. As we drove down the hill into the village we noticed that every house had a TV antenna. This was in the early days of television and Hammondsport didn't have it because it sits in a valley and couldn't receive the signals. How come Osceola had it? We stopped at the inn and asked Finlay. He said that because of some electrical phenomenon Osceola receive four channels very clearly. So we had a TV set at the camp before we did at home. That same weekend the Drakes invited us over to watch the fights on television, and we sadly viewed the spectacle of Joe Louis being knocked out by Rocky Marciano.

While the stream and the woods were Osceola's initial attractions, getting to know the local people made the picture complete. We saw most of Ken Quinn and his wife, Anne. As I said, they ran the general store, the real backcountry kind with a pot-bellied stove in the center of the floor, groceries on one side, clothes, hardware, and other sundries on the other. Ken was a frequent visitor to the camp at cocktail time. He and Anne had a winter apartment over the store but for the good weather they had a fine camp a couple of miles up the road on a little feeder stream.

Without doubt, the area's best known and most colorful character was Leo Fox. You could say without fear of contradiction that he lived off the land. He was probably best known as a guide for hunters seeking grouse and bear. It was never our luck to enjoy the benefit of those skills. The State Conservation Commission reserved Leo for several sessions each fall. But we were able to have him take us out on a number of occasions—frog-hunting with .22 rifles. Leo supplied a number of restaurants with frog legs.

It was only natural that when we returned from an expedition to Osceola we regaled our friends with tales of our experiences. This was usually at the Glenwood Club over dinner or games of pitch on Thursday nights. But it was difficult if not impossible to put into words the true mystique that was Osceola. The only path to enlightenment was for them to experience it for themselves. Two of our friends had shown particular interest—Joe Meade of Mercury Aircraft and John O'Neal, our Irish dentist. So we set a date for a long weekend in July.

We were in a festive mood when we started out. There were five of us: George Lawrence, Zeke Mendel, Joe Meade, Doc O'Neal, and me. We arrived at the camp in time to make a quick visit to the hotel and meet Ken. When we arrived early enough, dinner was steaks from Richards in Hammondsport, and that night we were in good time. After dinner, George and Zeke went up to Leo Fox's place on "Poverty Knob" to see if Leo could go out with us the next day. Luckily he could. We were all equipped with .22s but Leo was carrying a Colt Woodsman in a holster.

We drove down winding back roads (there not being many front roads in that country) until we reached one of the small feeder streams to the Salmon. We got out of the car and Leo warned us to walk quietly and slowly. Just as he finished his briefing he quickly drew the Colt and fired. He went over and picked up a huge bullfrog. The hunt was on. As we walked downstream it sounded like the last day of the Alamo. We soon had a good bag and we bragged a little about our shooting. But the good dentist topped us all; he claimed that a specially ferocious bullfrog had charged him but he'd shot it between the eyes.

Leo sat down beside the stream and demonstrated his skill with a knife. We were amazed how quickly he could remove the hind quarters of the frogs and keep a conversation going about fishing, hunting and national politics. He was slender and wiry and gave the impression of immense nervous energy. His glasses did not hide a pair of sharp and perceptive gray eyes. His interests were boundless, and Uncle Charlie used to save and send him the stamps from all his foreign mail.

That night we all ate too much—the frog legs, home fries, and a blueberry pie Leo's daughter-in-law had baked. Unfortunately overeating was dangerous for Zeke, who'd had part of his stomach removed earlier in the year and was supposed to have several small meals a day and no big ones. He began to feel real pain and distress. We went to a pay phone and called his doctor, who just said, "He should have known better. What you guys need is a camp physician and I volunteer." Time was what Zeke required. We all had a couple of nightcaps to ease our minds and in the end we all slept well, Zeke included.

The next day the water was clear and low and nothing was biting, so we adjourned for a morning of tennis. After some doubles in which we managed to exhaust Doc O'Neal pretty thoroughly—he looked like a boiled lobster—Joe Meade and I played singles. At one point I served to him, then went to the net and bashed his return away from him. He lunged for the ball and then went down like a stunned ox. "What did you hit me with?" he said. Joe had severed an Achilles tendon. We helped Joe to the camp, put ice on the ankle and located a doctor in Camden, the nearest village of any size. He confirmed our diagnosis and said that Joe would need surgery when he got home. He strapped the ankle and gave him a supply of pain pills, which saw Joe through the rest of the weekend, augmented by the occasional stiff drink.

It was a hot day and I proposed a trip to a swimming hole below a log dam in the river. En route across a field we encountered what we first thought was a large and unfriendly bull. Against advice, the good doctor picked up his pace. As we got nearer, we saw that the "bull" was equipped with a full set of large udders, about which O'Neal razzed us unmercifully.

Seeking revenge, I told Zeke, now recovered, that we should go in the water first and pretend it was wonderfully warm. It was in fact bitterly cold. But I got in and lay on my back, making sounds of great enjoyment. John leaped in and then leaped out again, calling Zeke and me every name he could think of. We laughed so hard we almost froze to death before we could get out. But the dentist's anger was short-lived and we were all laughing when we got back to camp.

But maybe the best of our boys'-night-out escapades began on another typical Thursday night at Glenwood in February, 1954. During a lull in the card action, Zeke said he'd had a letter from Osceola. Previous owners of the camp had made an arrangement with a man to sweep the snow off the roofs for a fee of twenty-five dollars for the season. We had inherited the arrangement and the man said please remit. Well, the winter had so far been mild, with very little snow. The man obviously had a good thing going. It began to seem like an interesting idea to visit the camp unannounced and assess the situation.

George couldn't go, but Zeke Mendel, Joe Meade, John O'Neal, and I took off that weekend. We made a couple of refreshment stops, one at a favorite watering hole called Jack's Reef and another in Pulaski, where we paused to watch the TV fights in a bar. We pushed on toward Redfield, where we had hotel reservations, not wishing to arrive at a cold camp in the middle of the night. We hadn't gone far when we hit snow, lots of snow. The ground became white and then there were drifts at the side of the road left by plows.

Crossing the railroad tracks in one village the car skewed to the left, raising an alarmed cry from John in the back seat. Coming next to a sharp right, I thought I'd give John another thrill. I turned the wheel and hit the accelerator, but the wheels didn't turn and we slid to a halt in an open area in the center of town, the car refusing to move forward or backward.

We got out of the car and sank in snow above our knees. We'd made a lot of noise getting out of the car. Lights in nearby houses went on and people began to gather. John explained in a voice audible throughout the county that I had tried to kill them all. I opened the trunk to get a shovel, John spied a bottle of Joe's gin and began passing it around the crowd as a kind of good will gesture. It worked and the townspeople came to our aid. Some ripped boards off a nearby fence and put them under the wheel. I replaced the shovel in the trunk and John slammed it shut. With most of the people pushing we regained the road. We thanked everybody, John distributed the last of the gin and we pushed on to Redfield through that snow drifts that became ever higher. The snow in the parking lot at the hotel was piled six to eight feet high. We were in the snow belt, all right.

Our entry into the hotel was worthy of the Marx Brothers. When we opened the trunk it smelled strongly of gin. John, slamming the trunk lid, had driven the shovel into Joe's sleeping bag and smashed his reserve bottle of gin, giving all our luggage the unmistakable aroma of juniper berries.

(While we were checking in, John wandered into the bar and got into a conversation with a huge fellow who turned out to be the driver of the huge snow plow we'd parked beside. "I've never seen so much damned snow in my life," he said, and he was a native.)

What the hotel made of our gin-smelling little troupe is not recorded. Joe had brought his sleeping bag inside to dry out. As Zeke opened the door of his room and fumbled for the light switch, a woman screamed for him to get out. He'd been given an occupied room. When Joe finally hit the sack, the bed collapsed with a loud crash. After that, things settled down and we had a good night's sleep.

When we finally hit Osceola the next morning it looked like a Christmas card. Ken Quinn, enjoying the pot-bellied stove in the store with some of his buddies, fell out of his chair when he finally recognized us in our winter togs. One of the cronies asked if we hadn't got lost on the way to Syracuse. We borrowed extra shovels and it took us an hour to clear a space so we could park the car at the camp. We got the fireplace going and Ken came over late in the afternoon for a seasonal toddy.

Soon it was time to bed down and so began a comical adventure within the adventure. Zeke and I shared one room, Joe and John the other. I sleepily heard Zeke get out of bed and then a muffled click, but thought nothing of it. It seemed possible he was taking a squirt off the back porch because we had no running water. I had my old GI-issue down sleeping bag. It was warm and comfortable and I was quickly sound asleep.

The next thing I knew I was awakened by a loud banging. Looking into the living room in the faint light of dawn, I saw John, wrapped in a blanket, splitting kindling and trying to start a fire in the stove. The power had gone off in the night and John, who had an electric blanket, was suddenly very chilly.

Sleep was over for everyone. We got the fires going and made coffee. Zeke tried one of the lamps, and it lit; the power was back on. Zeke said we needed something from the store and I volunteered to walk with him. On the way over he told me that the click I heard in the night was him turning off the main power switch. He'd intended to wait until John started to complain and then turn it back on, but he fell asleep instead. Now Zeke wanted to get to Ken at the store and prime him to say the power had been off in the night, and he played his part when John went in the store later.

The epilogue to the story was that I was certain that John knew the true story about the power "failure." A month or so later I was in his dental chair and he told me an amusing incident. I said, "That's the funniest thing I've heard about since Zeke turned the power off on you when we were up in Osceola." John said, "Zeke did what?" He hadn't known after all.

A few days later Zeke had an appointment with John for a filling. As he settled in the chair, John produced his household tool kit, took out his quarter-inch electric drill and said, "Now I'm going to get even with you for cutting the power up in Osceola."

I don't remember what we concluded about the man who swept snow off the roofs.

I make it sound as if Osceola were exclusively a stag affair. It wasn't, although it is true that we were apt to experience unusual situations when our wives and families weren't with us.

From what George Lawrence's wife, Mary, had heard about the camp she expected the most primitive conditions. George fed her illusions on their first trip to Osceola by stopping at an extremely dilapidated farmhouse and saying, "As you see, we've still got a lot of work to do." I'm sure she was pleasantly surprised when they got to the actual camp—with electricity and running water!

Our frog-hunting guide Leo Fox had a pet crow he named Harry, after President Truman. Harry the crow did not like women, for reasons that are not clear. Once when his wife, Rosalie, came up with

Zeke, they went up to Poverty Knob to visit the Foxes and Harry spotted Rosalie, literally and copiously. On another occasion when Jackie and I were visiting the Foxes, Harry was flying around scolding everyone. Then he landed on Jackie's head, sat there for a moment, still talking, then pecked the top of Jackie's head hard enough to draw blood. There were two squawks, one from Jackie and the other from Harry as he took off for the tall pines.

When I left Hammondsport and moved to Horseheads for a new career, and George was no longer well enough to go up to Osceola, we decided to sell the camp. Rip Lowman was a dedicated fly fisherman and we hoped to sell it to Rip and a couple of his friends. But somehow Ken became involved in the transaction and it ended up in the hands of a Rochester physician. I didn't have a chance to clear out any of my gear, which included an ancient pair of Iroquois snowshoes.

In the late 70s, Mardo and I decided to visit Osceola. We stopped at the Salmon River Inn and there at the bar enjoying a cold beer was Leo Fox's son Duane. He told us the store was closed and that Ken was in a Rome nursing home in poor health. We drove slowly past the camp, and the pine trees now towered well above the roof. We went on and came to Fish Creek, where we had all fished at different times. It had been a beautiful stream, but a few years before a large dam had been built to supply Rome with clear spring water. From the bridge we could see the new lake stretching to the east. I remembered a time Joe and I had fished that lovely stream, now fifty feet below the surface of the lake.

We went on to West Leyden and turned north to Constableville. On the outskirts we turned into the long driveway that led to Constable Hall, the manor house. It was a very gracious building dating from 1810 and had been carefully restored a few years before. It was completely furnished with period pieces. The English-style flower beds and the herb and vegetable gardens were handsomely laid out and beautifully tended.

We'd reserved a room at the Hotel Parquet. John Parquet, whom I had known, had died several years before, but the young couple operating the hotel now were doing a fine job. In some ways, nothing had changed in the nature of that Adirondacks foothill country I had come to love so much, and yet so much had.

I took another nostalgic trip to Osceola with Zeke, one of the old gang, in the late Eighties. We started from Hammondsport very early in the morning and we reached the village just before noon. We stopped at the top of the hill and looked down at the cluster of buildings in the valley. I don't think it looked much different from the village I saw when I first caught sight of it with Uncle Charlie fifty years before. But there was one significant change. When we came to the Salmon River, the old truss bridge had been replaced by a fine and much larger new one, which somehow seemed to make the river look very insignificant.

We turned in at the cobblestone gates and found a man working in the side yard of what had been Duane Fox's house. We stopped and talked with him and it turned out he owned both the Salmon River Inn and the hotel at Redfield where we'd stayed that blizzardy night years ago. The man said he didn't know what had become of Duane.

We left the car and walked to the camp. Zeke said, "Hey, look!" And there on the porch were my Iroquois snowshoes. Without hesitation I went back for the car, backed it up to the porch and threw the snowshoes in the trunk. We asked the man about lunch and he recommended his hotel at Redfield. But instead we went west out of the village and up the hill past Poverty Knob, where Leo Fox's home had been.

We had learned that Leo had not been feeling well and his doctor at Camden and then a specialist in Syracuse confirmed that he had cancer in an advanced state. He went home, wrote some notes, and shot himself with his shotgun. He left instructions that he was to be buried in a clump of evergreens near his house, and that his headstone would feature, in addition to his name and dates, a grouse on the left and a leaping trout on the right, and that he was to be buried with his shotgun at his side. We wanted to stop but there were no cars in sight at the house, so we drove on to lunch at the hotel in Redfield and the drive back to Hammondsport, not saying much but both of us reliving our memories of Osceola and the camp that was.

The Gas Station

1930–1968

The double whammy of Prohibition and the shut-down of the Curtiss plant had just about paralyzed the Hammondsport economy in the 1920s, and once the national Depression got going, the village's situation grew even grimmer. A man did what he could to stay afloat.

Leo Hemmer was a house painter by profession, and a very good one. But what good were references when few if any buildings in the area were getting painted. So Leo became the proprietor of the Sinclair gas station at the corner of Lake and Main streets, directly across from Grandmother's.

It was a thin livelihood at best, but it was also a roof over their heads for Leo and his wife, Ethel, at a time when, as Leo said in later years, they badly needed one. The station was a rudimentary structure, a small, white clapboard affair about twenty by thirty feet. There was a salesroom which contained the basic supplies of the trade—oil, antifreeze, wiper blades, and so on. There was also a counter stocked with a mixture of candy and school supplies, the local school being just across Main Street. Opposite the counter was a cooler for soft drinks and a freezer for ice cream. There was a unisex bathroom that served both the customers and the residents.

The living quarters were minuscule, to put it kindly. Opening off the salesroom was a living room about fifteen feet square. Across the back was a tiny kitchen and opening off of that a small bedroom. It was crowded enough for them, but darned if they didn't hold a kind of perpetual open house. For a lot of us teenagers, it became our favorite hangout.

Leo and Ethel had no children of their own, but they had no more moved in than they acquired a large family. It could have gotten out of hand. But one of the Hemmers' close friends was Arnie Paulson, the coach at the high school and unmarried at the time. He became our "proctor" and established some strict house rules. No profanity. One slip and you could be ejected, two slips and you could be banned for a week. No smoking (for everybody except Leo, who liked a cigar now and again).

There were no other rules or regulations, but there was a ritual. A number of us would try to be excused from dinner to get to the "club" at 6:45 to listen to the radio. That meant getting there in time to hear Lowell Thomas say, "Good evening, everybody." At seven, all conversation ceased as "Amos and Andy" began. It was Leo's favorite show, and part of our enjoyment was hearing Leo chuckle. After that a young crooner named Bing Crosby came on singing his theme song, "When the Blue of the Night Meets the Gold of the Day."

Card-playing was our most popular activity. Five Hundred was the favorite game, with occasional hands of rummy or euchre. Except when the radio was on, the place was a constant bull session, and since most of the regulars were high school athletes, games were replayed again and again, with Coach Paulson's critical comments.

The coach was a strict disciplinarian, as witness his treatment of Eldon Burns. Eldon was the star forward on the basketball team. But he had been caught "sneaking a butt" behind the station. His punishment, said the coach, was to run around the valley, a five-mile jog. It was a second offense for Eldon, whom we now called "Smoky." The first time he'd pulled a fast one. He'd started down Main Street but instead of continuing across the Valley, he swung into Davis Avenue, then went up Wheeler to the Thomas's tiny general store. He spent forty-five minutes chatting with the Thomas daughters, then dashed down Lake Street, arriving at the station convincingly out of breath.

This time Smoky started out the door toward Main Street when the coach called him back. "Oh, by the way," Coach Paulson said, "when you get to Pleasant Valley, stop in at Longwell's General Store and call me here at the station. I'll want to speak with either Charlie or Mrs. Longwell."

There were two exceptions to the "No Gambling" rule: the movie lottery and "Break and Takes." The Hemmers were great movie fans, and went to Bath every Sunday night to see whatever was playing at the Babcock. They would take three passengers along, but there were always more hopefuls than seats. Leo solved this by having the hopefuls write their names on slips of paper, which were put in a bowl and the winners drawn by one of the Hemmers. The ride was free, but you needed thirty-five cents for admission and another nickel if you wanted a bag of popcorn.

Break and Takes was an elaborate display of candy, with chocolate-covered mints in a center compartment, costing a penny apiece. If the mint had a white center, you had a mint and that's all. But if it had a green center, you got a chocolate bar, and a yellow center earned (as I remember) a larger chocolate bar. The display featured a whole box of candy, which went to whomever bought the last mint. As the mints ran low, the suspense (and the calculating of the money you had in hand) got very tense.

A lot of us received early lessons in financial responsibility and credit management at the gas station. Leo extended credit, up to a dollar or a dollar and a half. When your credit ran out and you were "posted," you looked for an odd job to get you off the books. Actually, Leo would sometimes let debtors work it off. No easy jobs; it was honest work—shoveling snow in the winter, raking leaves in the fall, sweeping at other times. Leo also owned a three-acre concord grape vineyard, and at harvest time you could pick grapes at ten cents a tray, which included carrying the trays down a steep hill to the road. After a while you thought twice about getting that second candy bar on credit, or even the first.

The club was an interesting experience. The members came from all over town and even from the hills. We were a mixed bag, yet I remember very few discussions that were disagreeable, and not a single fight.

Leo and Ethel's proprietorship ended in 1933. They adopted a baby boy, Carl, and the accommodations were just too small. A succession of proprietors followed them, and while the club as it had existed in the Hemmers' time ceased to exist, each of the new proprietors attracted a following that reflected his own interests.

Newman Worden was the Hemmers' immediate successor. He was

a highly skilled mechanic and a longtime employee of the Curtiss Company. Si, as we called him, welcomed the boys, and the card games continued. But Si had a passion for square dancing, and it wasn't long before the station closed on weekend nights and several carloads of enthusiasts, inspired by Si, would head off for the Grange halls up in the hills for an evening of boisterous "Swing your partners."

In the summer of 1934, the club members seemed to split into two factions: those who loved to square dance and the others who preferred slow or close dancing to the romantic sounds of the orchestra that played at the Keuka Hotel's dance hall, which was built out over the lake. We had discovered girls. Mrs. Bessie Young, the hotel's owner, brooked no nonsense and there was no teenage drinking, which is why the hotel, like the Babcock Theater, was on any parent's OK list.

That fall I went off to Ridley School in Canada, and it was there I heard that Newman Worden had died of a heart attack. His successor was Bill Hall, who had been a chauffeur for Curtiss ("GH," as he fondly called him) and was also an assistant to Charlie Faucett, the village undertaker. On the day of a funeral, Bill would dress in his dark coat, striped gray trousers and a derby hat and meet Charlie at his establishment. They would load the casket into Charlie's 1920s hearse, then adjourn across the village green to Marsh Rouin's Park Inn for a stiff beverage. They would then repair to the hearse and drive to the funeral. They were an impressive sight, the two of them sitting bolt upright, looking straight ahead, derbies squared.

Bill's assistant, Willard French, was a high school classmate. When Bill retired to Elmcroft, his elegant white-pillared mansion just south of town, Willie took over as manager. He was a fan of motorcycles—Harleys, although he tolerated Indians—and a skilled mechanic, so the station became a mecca for anyone whose 'cycle or jalopy needed tuning up, if not total resuscitation.

I ran into Willie French again one day after the war, in the late 1960s, when I landed at Costa's Airport near Corning. He was tinkering with a light plane he owned. We got to talking about the Hemmers and the old days, and we had an idea.

After they adopted Carl, the Hemmers moved into a small house in Pleasant Valley and Leo went back to house-painting. He'd held various civic offices and had been mayor, a good one, for several years. But a venture in the hardware business had come to naught and at length he'd liquidated and retired.

He and Ethel were getting on in years, but they were up and about, and Willie and I said, how about a reunion of the Hemmer club, a thirty-fifth reunion, it would be. Some were gone. Jack Seely had been killed in the war. "Jerk" Sick had moved away, but there were several of us around, and we decided on a surprise party for the Hemmers at the Hereford's Pleasant Valley Manor.

There were two disappointments in the planning stage. We simply couldn't locate Coach Paulson. And we couldn't locate a tape of an Amos and Andy show.

But on the appointed evening, Norm and Harriet Emilson invited the Hemmers to dinner at their house and volunteered to pick them up. But they delivered them instead to the Manor, where seven members of the old club, myself included, greeted them.

The Hemmers were totally surprised and really overwhelmed. We had turned the clock back thirty-five years, and for that evening we reverted back to the boys we'd been then. We drank a toast to those who were no longer with us, and there were tears. There were more when Leo, cigar in hand, stood up and tried to thank us, not just for the night but for all those nights back at the club. And at the end, one of the old gang stood up and, glass raised in a toast, said, "Yowsah, Kingfish, yowsah."

Graham

1872–1956

WE MEET MANY people in a lifetime. Occasionally one individual becomes indelibly engraved in your memory. For me, Graham Palmer was one of those individuals. As nearly as anyone I knew, he was a living legend.

He was a fine specimen of a man, well over six feet tall, with a bushy mane of hair and an imposing mustache. He was striking to meet, and he looked like the rugged individualist he certainly was. Most lives in our time follow a general pattern. You go to school, enter and follow a line of work and rise or fall, prosper or fail, as the fates dictate. But Graham made his own pattern. There was a drumbeat sounding in his life, but he alone heard it. More than anybody I can think of, he was his own man.

By the time I first met Graham in the mid 1930s, I already knew something about his background. He was born in Pleasant Valley in 1872, and in the late 1870s he was sent off to school a couple miles up the Valley road. He wasn't escorted by one of his parents, just dispatched. On the way to the one-room schoolhouse he passed a water-powered sawmill, and it fascinated him. But he continued on to school, where he spent a frustrating morning. When the teacher rang the bell for noon recess, Graham left and just kept on going, thus completing his formal education.

He retraced his steps to the sawmill, where he made himself useful clearing away the slab wood and piling it up. It wasn't the actual sawing operation that interested him; it was the water wheel and the intricate arrangement of gears and pulleys that made the mill function which engrossed him and determined the course his life would take.

I first made contact with Graham because of a twisted sailboat rudder. The girl whose sailboat had the broken rudder was with me when we stopped in front of his house, which sat in a clearing below the valley road. As I got out of the car, a head and a bare upper torso appeared above the ridge of the roof.

"Drive up to the Fish Hatchery and turn around and come back," the voice from the roof commanded. I did as I was told and when we got back ten minutes later, Graham was standing by his front door, barefoot and wearing only a pair of pants held up by suspenders. I learned later that Graham preferred to work in the nude in warm weather, both in his shop and outdoors. In all the years I knew him, I could never get used to seeing him standing *au natural* in front of a rapidly-turning lathe or with a whirring grinder bombarding him with sparks.

(Uncle Kid stopped to see him once about repairing a violin and found him buffbare as usual, but wearing carpet slippers. Kid kidded him about the slippers and Graham explained that the shavings hurt his feet.)

At the time of our first meeting Graham was helping the local wineries keep their French-made champagne machines operating. They were all built on the metric scale, which was no problem for Graham, formal schooling or not. He was a master machinist as well as a superior craftsman with wood. He made beautiful violins. During the early 1900s, he had carved propellers for a number of Glenn Curtiss's aeroplanes. There was nothing he couldn't fix or fabricate.

The machines in his shop were many years old, and I suspect that many if not all of them had come from the Curtiss Aeroplane and Engine Company on the hill behind Hammondsport, with Curtiss's blessings to be sure. The lathe, shaper, milling machine, and drill press were all driven by one large electric motor through a series of belts, pulleys, shafts, and more belts. When the machines were operating the whole building shook, but the work he turned out was superb.

During the years immediately after World War II I became a friend and confidant of Graham. He was alone evenings and I got in the habit of visiting him several times a week, using the excuse that I had a project that required his expertise. Actually the first time I'd sought his guidance was in 1939. I'd seen a fine gun cabinet at Abercrombie & Fitch selling for seventy-five dollars. With Graham's help, we made it for less than five dollars.

My first postwar project was an English butler's tray. I had acquired a reproduction of a seventeenth century map of the world at a stall on the Left Bank of the Seine in Paris, and I thought it would be ideal for the tray, and it was.

I discovered that Graham enjoyed a little libation of an evening, and was especially fond of Italian vermouth. It was not a favorite of mine, since one of my chores was making the herbal flavorings for it at the winery. But I brought a bottle to our first session about the tray. Graham drank most of it himself, straight, and we did not accomplish a lot. I brought half-bottles after that.

That first night, he asked me what kind of wood we should use. I said mahogany and he said he had just the piece. He disappeared up the steps into the loft and returned a few minutes later festooned with cobwebs and carrying a dark and dusty piece of wood. It had a history. He and Glenn Curtiss had been walking on the beach near Miami in the 1920s and came upon the piece of wood. Curtiss wondered where it had floated in from and Graham, discussing wave action, tides, winds, and currents, announced it was mahogany from Honduras. The two men lived in different worlds but they met on terms of mutual respect, and Curtiss did not doubt that Graham was right. What Graham was doing in Miami he never explained. The historic piece made a gorgeous tray.

His shop was at the back of the house, which consisted of a combination living room-dining room-kitchen, heated by a wood burning stove. The bedroom opened off this room and there was an eight-by-ten-foot alcove with its three walls lined with the special tools he used to carve and shape the violins. I was fascinated with the special knives that were mounted on the walls. Graham had made each of them from Swedish tool steel and fitted each with a curly maple handle and a brass ferule, finished off with his trademark, a rope twist carved on the end of the handle.

The alcove held a couple of chairs and it was here we talked in the evenings. Although his formal schooling was nil, he could and would quote from the classics and the Bible, although he was an avowed agnostic. One of the several town legends about Graham concerned the time he was standing in the meat market behind the Episcopal rector, who was buying a pound of bacon. "Why Dr. Somerville, I'm surprised," Graham said. "Don't you follow the edicts of the Bible?" "What do you mean," cried Dr. Somerville. "Touch not the meat of the swine," said Graham, quoting chapter and verse.

One day in Uncle Charlie's office, Graham let drop that he had once been married, which none of us had known. Actually, another part of the legend was that he had been a great Lothario who had snuck out of more bedroom windows than a metropolitan burglar.

I was less sure of that after one of our nights, when Graham told me the story of his brief marriage. He was working at a machine shop in Auburn, married a Corning girl, and they set up housekeeping in an apartment in Auburn. One evening he left his night shift job early and discovered his wife bedded down with the day foreman (who had put Graham on the night shift to make the liaison possible). Graham hadn't been detected and he made no outraged scene. But the next morning, he persuaded his wife to visit her folks for a week, as she'd wanted to, and he put her on the train to Corning. Then he went to the furniture store and told them to reclaim all their installment plan goods, went to the landlord and canceled their lease, packed his tools and caught a train to Syracuse, and then proceeded to Providence, Rhode Island, where he worked for ten years for Browne and Sharpe, which made fine instruments and machine tools.

I had the feeling that the story I'd just heard was known by very few individuals and I had just been admitted to a select inner circle. I often wondered what wife Nellie thought when she got back to Auburn, but of course Graham didn't know either.

We had just started a maintenance department at the winery when Uncle Charlie advised me that Graham had told him because of his arthritis he could no longer operate his machine shop and wanted to sell all the equipment. Charlie had offered him $3,000. I wasn't enthusiastic, and told Charlie that only Graham himself could do good work on that ancient equipment. Charlie said the winery was committed and he didn't want to hear any more about it. I thought we had to get out of the deal, much as I loved Graham, and it turned out to be quite simple.

I went up to Graham's and said, "We've got to have an inventory." "A what?" says Graham. "A list of the equipment you're selling us," I said. "Not by a damn sight," he said. "You're getting what you see." I said we needed a detailed list. "Then I withdraw the offer. Besides, Taylors has offered me a thousand dollars more," he said, sly devil that he was. "I'm sorry to hear that," I said with my fingers crossed behind my back, and drove to the cellar to break the news to Uncle Charlie.

Graham didn't believe in banks, or checks, and he took the four thousand from Taylors in cash and locked it in a small safe in the living room. Not long after the sale, he fell seriously ill with pleurisy, the second cousin to pneumonia. Hospitals were another institution Graham had no use for, so we had to figure out how to care for him at home. The doctor knew a male orderly from the VA hospital at Bath who would look in on him twice a day. His nearest neighbors, the Obrochtas, agreed to give him breakfast and lunch, and Jackie and I saw to his dinners. (I conferred with his longtime girl friend, Marie, but at the moment they were at odds and she'd have nothing to do with him.)

It gives an insight to Graham's character that one night Jackie, then seven months pregnant with our daughter Anne, had to deliver the dinner alone. When I next saw him alone he hemmed and hawed and finally blurted out that it would be better if Jackie didn't come up by herself, because the neighbors might get the wrong idea.

I stopped by one morning on my way to Bath. Graham had just started walking again. Now he was sitting in a chair, head in his hands, crying. "My money is all gone from my safe," he said, "every penny of it." There was the four thousand cash from Taylors, and another thousand or so he'd had before. Who else knew the combination? I asked him. Only his girl friend Marie, he said.

I knew then where the money had gone, but retrieving it would not be easy or pleasant. But there was only one way to do it: confront her. I drove to her house and knocked loudly. She opened the door and said, "How's Graham?" I said he was no longer sick but very angry because his money was missing and he wanted me to call the State Police. But I'd asked him to hold off, I said, until I'd made some inquiries. That was why I'd stopped to see her, I added. Did she know anything about the money? "Oh, no," she said. "Well, I just thought

I'd ask," I said, and headed for the door.

"Where're you going?" she asked me.

"To go and talk with the troopers," I said.

"Wait a moment," Marie said. "I want to talk with you."

She had taken the money, she admitted, but only to put it in a safe place—her checking account. As soon as Graham had gotten well she would see that it was straightened out. Gotten well or died, I thought to myself.

I said, "Just give me a check for six thousand dollars, made out to Graham, and I won't go to the BCI (the Bureau of Criminal Investigation)."

"Fifty-six hundred and fifty," she said.

"OK," I said, "make it out." She did, with tears streaming down her cheeks.

I took the check down to Graham and after writing "For Deposit Only" on the back, had Graham endorse it. He was overwhelmed when he saw it, but quickly recovered and asked me what I was going to do with it. I told him to trust me and wait and see. I went down to Ed Hunter at the Bank of Hammondsport and opened a checking account in Graham's name and returned with a checkbook, a bank book, and a signature card.

Graham needed a little convincing that his money hadn't just vanished but was available when he needed it. I showed him how to make out a check (for five dollars) and enter the stub. He was skeptical but he went along with me.

Along with his doubts about banks, hospitals, and religion, Graham had no use whatever for bureaucracy in any form, which led to what I think of as my final service to him.

An old family friend had given Cousin Caroline a remarkable present, a 1928 Stutz roadster, canary yellow with robin's egg blue fenders, red spoked wheels, and pigskin upholstery. Graham caught sight of it one day when he was visiting at the Farm on some antique repair business, and he fell in love with it. The Stutz required a lot of mechanical attention and spent more time in garages than on the road, which is probably why Graham was able to convince Caroline to sell it to him.

It became his pride and joy. For him it ran like a top, and he kept it spotless and shiny. He drove it for years and was still driving it one day after the war when I stopped to see him and found him in a foul mood. The insurance company bureaucrats were demanding what he called "damn fool information they didn't need."

I offered to help. They needed his driver's license number. I checked his papers and the license had expired three years before. He'd been driving since 1901, he said angrily. Why start worrying now? A friend at the Motor Vehicle Bureau said there was no way out—he'd have to take out a learner's permit and do the driver's test, the works. I wasn't brave enough to tell Graham myself. I turned to one of his good friends, George Pratt, a circuit court judge in Corning. Judge Pratt came up and broke the bad news to Graham, whose mustache bristled alarmingly, and the judge dumped the problem back in my lap. I would nursemaid Graham through the registration process and then through the test. We made it through registration with a minimum of profanity.

A few days later I drove the Stutz up to Bath with Graham for the test. Sam Balcom, an old family friend, happened by in slippers and his Cornell sweater. He lived near the courthouse and knew everybody, including the examiner, with whom he had a word.

Sam reported later that at the eye exam, Graham not only read the bottom line but the "Printed in USA" legend in tiny type. The examiner himself had to approach within inches to read it himself. "Don't you wear glasses?" the examiner asked. "Only when I want to see something," Graham said. He had ignored the booklet full of rules and regulations. I just pleaded, "Stick your arm out anytime you do anything!"

When the inspector saw the Stutz (now thirty-some years old) he said, "What in the world is that?" "The best damn car you'll ever ride in," Graham replied. The examiner just got in the car and said, "Let's go." Graham started the engine, stuck out his arm, and away they went. They returned from the other direction, slowed, Graham stuck out his arm again and they pulled to a stop.

Graham passed the test. The examiner's only comment was that he needed a central rearview mirror.

A rugged individualist to the end, Graham had fought the bureaucracy to a draw.

Danny

Hammondsport, 1988

THE FIRST THING I saw was an unfamiliar crown of silver hair. But then I saw the twinkling blue eyes and the freckles. It was Danny Hodge, and no mistake, and the first time we'd seen each other since before the war. (I suppose you have to specify World War II these days.) We'd come close a couple of times, but the timing was never quite right. Ed Percy would say, "Danny was in town last week and asking for you."

When we finally did meet, Danny's first question was, "Remember the time you saved my life?" Yes, Danny, I remember that, and a good many other things.

Danny and his family moved to Hammondsport from New York City at the beginning of the 1930s. His father had been a cab driver. His business had been hit hard by the beginnings of the Depression, and he was thinking the economics of a small town might be better. Danny had four sisters, and he was the apple of their eye. He brought with him the belief that your fists were the key to your survival. He was quite surprised that no one was interested in meeting him in the alley. We didn't even have an alley.

What Danny discovered was what his contemporaries in a small, rural, upstate village did for amusement. He was introduced to the woods, Cold Brook stream, and the lake. He became an ardent fisherman and trapper and, when he was old enough, a hunter. He joined the Boy Scouts.

We were in the same class in school and we soon got together in various undertakings. Our first joint effort was an ambitious trap line which started behind Uncle Charlie's farm and went almost to the top of Loughlin Glen. We'd hope to trap some coons, but our only victim was a hapless woodchuck who ought to have been hibernating. It wasn't badly hurt, so we decided to take it home and make a pet of it. We grabbed it by the scruff of the neck and carried it, growling and snapping, all the way to Danny's house. We placed it in a barrel with some water and bread crusts.

The next day, Danny came to school with a long face. It seemed there had been an accident. His dog, a greyhound, had discovered our new pet and eaten it.

Danny also became very interested in fishing, and was good at it. He was soon as familiar with Cold Brook as Charlie and other Snell boys were. He knew all the deep holes where the big brown trout would lie on hot days. Some mornings we'd get up before dawn, walk to the dam and fish down the stream, hoping, if it was a school day, we wouldn't be too late.

At one time, Danny was operating a set line—a heavy cord with a number of leaders and hooks. Set lines were usually checked at night, since they were illegal in bodies of water inhabited by trout, as our lake was. We heard the story the next morning at school. Danny had been checking his line when he realized that he'd hooked a good-sized fish. He gave a heave and the next thing he knew, a three-foot-long eel was thrashing and snaking around in the bottom of the boat. An eel is not a thing of beauty in broad daylight, let alone on a dark night by flashlight. Danny had never seen one before. He cut the leader and threw it back, and in a while was able to stop shuddering.

Another incident that brought Danny immortal fame happened when he was out hunting partridges alone. Deer were by no means as plentiful then as they are now, and there was no deer season. Danny was climbing a steep, narrow trail when a deer came loping down the trail, heading right for him. He threw up his gun and fired. The gun was loaded with birdshot, but the charge hit the deer right in the chest and it dropped dead at Danny's feet. He was fined seventeen dollars and fifty cents for shooting protected game. No plea of self defense was possible.

Danny loved sports, and what he lacked in finesse he made up in speed and, especially, in spirit. If there was one sport in which he had a natural aptitude, it was fighting, and that was the spirit he took into every game and sport he played. In basketball we played a man-to-man defense, and Danny was all over his man, usually fouling out before the end of the game.

The life-saving incident he reminded me of took place during a Boy Scout outing. The citizens of the village had helped the local troop convert an old icehouse in the glen into a fine Scout house, complete with a large stone fireplace, the only source of heat. Our project, on that memorable Saturday afternoon, was to lay in a supply of wood.

Earlier that fall, Danny and I had been hunting above the big basin in the glen, just below the main falls. The walls of the glen must be three hundred feet high there. We remembered that there were a lot of wind-fallen trees and limbs up there. We volunteered to go up and slide them over the edge of the glen, so that other Scouts at the bottom could drag them to the cabin.

It was quite a climb, but we reached the top at last. The rim above the edge wasn't level. It pitched down quite steeply. We had an ax and trimmed off the limbs before dragging the trees to the edge of the steep lip and letting them slide down. We had rigged up a safety rope so we could free any logs that got hung up. There was also a spot near the edge where we could watch the logs fall. And quite an exciting sight that was. Some of the logs shattered as they hit—perfect for kindling.

We had trimmed a fair-sized pine and started it down, but it got stuck on a sumac. Danny went down the steep bank, holding on to the log, and then pushed the sumac, which is a brittle wood. It snapped, freeing the log. Luckily it didn't snag on Danny. He fell over and landed on his stomach. He started sliding, feet first, toward the edge, not ten feet below him.

Strictly by instinct, I grabbed the safety rope and, letting it slide through my hand, went down the slope. When I reached Danny I closed my hand on the rope and grabbed him by the collar, stopping his slide. I will always remember how his freckles stood out on his pale face. The other thing I'll never forget is that when I looked at my right hand holding the rope, there was less than six inches of rope left.

Danny and I shared many adventures and for the most part they were fun, and some were funny when you looked back at them. I'm thinking of the night we were ice-skating on the frozen Inlet, playing tag, and with Danny chasing me, we both skated off the ice into the lake.

Wars and jobs separate the closest of friends, as they did Danny and me, but when we did get together, the easy camaraderie was there as it always had been. Danny's gone now, but I've shared these memories with his three surviving sisters.

Back to Flying

A Crisis Over California

Tehachapi, California, 1961

THE AOPA (Aircraft Owners and Pilots Association) was going to have a "No Engine Course" at their annual flight safety fly-in convention in Palm Springs. The Holiday Flying School, operated by Fred and Goldie Harris in Tehachapi, would supply some personnel and aircraft. I, representing Schweizer, would give briefings and do whatever else I could do.

The idea of the No Engine Course was to show power-plane pilots that airplanes don't just fall out of the air when the engine quits; they're both controllable and maneuverable. The course consisted of a lecture and five flights in a sailplane. (It was a nice way to introduce them to soaring, of course.)

Fred needed some help ferrying aircraft from Tehachapi down to the Springs and I volunteered. I was to be towed to Palm Springs, 160 miles away, in a Schweizer two-place trainer, the 2-22. One of Fred's regulars, a meteorologist named Darryl Wilkins, would pilot the Super Cub tow plane.

It was a lovely day for flying—high scattered clouds and excellent visibility—but we wanted to get off as quickly as possible, before the big thermals started developing. We had a fair headwind to start with, and it began to pick up. When we passed over Gus Breiglib's Gliderport operation, our ground speed was practically zero. As we approached the San Gorgonio Mountains, Darryl radioed me that we would have to climb because of the downward flow of the air in the lee of the mountains.

Our route would take us between Lake Arrowhead and Big Bear.

We were at about a thousand feet and still climbing. As we approached the southern slope of the mountain, I got my first glimpse of the Los Angeles basin. It looked like a bowl of dirty whipped cream: the infamous Los Angeles smog. The sheer slopes of the mountains seemed to slide down and disappear into a white void.

The air had grown fairly rough. Then, just as we came nearer the mountain, the tow plane shot up as if it had been fired from a gun. I pulled the stick back in an effort to keep up with it. The next moment the Cub was caught in a downdraft and went plunging down. As I rammed the stick forward my primary concern was not over-running the towplane and hitting it, but the fact was that neither of us was wearing a parachute.

With me going up and Darryl going down it was only a second or two before the tow line snapped and I was on my own. It was too turbulent to have any feeling whether you were going up or down and my variometer wasn't working. There was nothing behind me but rocks and cliffs and I couldn't get back to the airport at Big Bear. There was nothing to do but head into the cotton wool. Fortunately, as I moved away from the face of the mountain, the turbulence subsided, so I continued out and away to where the valley should be.

As we moved south, Darryl came on the air and assured me that there were any number of landing strips somewhere below. I said, "Great! Locate one and circle above it!" The air was quite calm as I descended. At about 600 feet above ground level, which was the upper reaches of the smog, I could make out roads and buildings below and, wonder of wonders, a cropduster airplane parked alongside a field. I made a circuit and landed. I called Darryl, who had seen me enter the muck. I told him the field was adequate but there was a ditch almost in the middle. He landed without incident, however. We retied the ring and took off and we were soon above the smog and headed for Banning Pass.

When we reached the pass, the smog ended, and you could see the demarcation line between the smog of the basin and the clear air of the desert. In the distance I could see the green oasis that was the Palm Springs area, all date groves, golf courses, and tree-lined streets.

Darryl brought me over the center of the field at two thousand feet, where I released and called the tower. I identified myself as a

Schweizer sailplane, gave the registration number and requested landing instructions. I was told that the runway was twenty-seven and that I was number four to land, following a Cessna 310. I called the tower back and repeated that I was a sailplane and wanted to land on the ramp. Negative, the tower said. The active is twenty-seven and you are now number five. Follow the Bonanza! The top speed of a 2-22 was about the same as the stalling speed of a Bonanza. I was now down to about 500 feet.

I looked for an off-field alternate, but it was either rough desert or somebody's back yard. The moment of truth arrived and I literally drove into that string of traffic behind a Commanche. I had so much speed I was still flying when I came to the offramp. No problem: lift it up a bit and turn the corner and then set it down.

A "follow me" Jeep came charging out. "Why didn't you say you were a glider," the driver said. "We thought you were saying Cessna!" Fred operates a soaring school from that airfield, but he calls them gliders not sailplanes, and that was the term the tower knew.

A couple of the pilots complained about the way I had sneaked in front of them, but in the circumstances, I don't really think apologies were called for.

A Canadian Junket

August 1964

DURING THE ANNUAL plant shut-down, I planned a combination business and vacation trip in the 1-30. My ultimate goal would be the Alexander Graham Bell Museum at Baddeck on Cape Breton Island, Nova Scotia. En route I would visit Schweizer dealers at Sugarbush, Vermont and West Lebanon, New Hampshire, and on my return, stop at New England Light Aircraft at Salem, New Hampshire.

At that time the 1-30 had a ninety horsepower Lycoming engine, which limited its range to 150 still air miles (no headwinds, that is). That meant the pilot had to plan his routes and refueling stops with care, and pay close attention to the strength and direction of the wind.

I took off from Elmira and made a first stop at Ballston Spa, where the Mohawk Club flew. I went on to Sugarbush, where I stayed overnight. The next day I made my stop at West Lebanon, circled Mt. Washington to admire the views of it and the White Mountains. It was a beautiful day and I was heading northeast and checking my ground speed when I got a hell of a kick in the butt. The plane dropped abruptly and just as abruptly bounced up again. I hit the top of the canopy and on the way back down my camera, which was hung around my neck, contacted my nose. Was it the vortex left by a large, fast aircraft or what? We still had all of our surfaces, but it seemed like a prudent idea to land at Augusta, Maine, to check things out and top up the tank.

The airport operator helped me check over the 1-30, but the only damage was to my nose. The operator thought it was a bounce off the

White Mountains, an example of clear air turbulence. I took off again for St. Johns, New Brunswick, where I cleared customs and then flew on to Moncton.

In Canada only the largest city airports have fixed base operators as we know them in the States. Private transient planes are handled by the flying clubs, and the club's chief flying instructor is usually the person in charge. Moncton also had a control tower and a flight service station operated by the Department of Transportation. The local club was friendly and cooperative.

When I said I was heading for Baddeck, the chief flight instructor pulled out some charts to help me lay out my course. There was lots of open space on those charts but very few airports. The closest to Baddeck was at Sydney, about fifty miles northeast of Baddeck. There was a small airport shown at Trenton, halfway between Moncton and Sydney. The distance between Moncton and Sydney was some 290 miles, which meant that refueling midway was crucial.

The strip at Trenton belonged to a mining company, and the instructor very kindly called and determined that I was okay to land, and that there was 80 octane fuel available. We went across the field to check the weather and found it would be fine the next day, but iffy thereafter.

A club member drove me to a hotel in town and picked me up again the next morning. He and the instructor helped me with the preflight check, gave me a prop as we say, and I was off. Meteorology was right; it was a beautiful day. I flew the north coast, with Prince Edward Island on my left and tiny fishing villages, Pugwash and Malagash, below.

When I landed at Trenton, a French-Canadian attendant greeted me and, moving to the pump, said, "You need fuel?'' "Eighty octane," I said. "Mon dieu," he said. He led me to the porch of a building and one of the rustiest fuel tanks I ever saw. We manhandled it over to the plane and he fetched a hand pump and a wrench. I proposed we take a break for a cup of coffee. I had no idea how much rust there might be in the fuel, and I thought a pause would let it settle. Did he have a chamois or a fine strainer? Evidently not, our language communications were imperfect.

I had him hold the pump well off the bottom and I strained the fuel through my handkerchief. There were a few specks of rust on it. When I took off I spiraled up directly over the field. The country I'd passed over was very picturesque but didn't offer much by way of emergency landing fields. But I reached 5,000 feet without a sputter, so I headed off on course.

I passed Antigonish on St. George Bay and on to Cape Breton Island. Flying up the eastern shore of Bras d'Or Lake I could see Baddeck to the west and just ahead, Sydney Airport, south of the city. As I touched down, the ship gave a slight lurch to the right. I thought it was a gust of wind, but it was soon clear that the right rudder was out. Luckily the wind wasn't strong, so by going very slowly and using gentle bursts of power, I reached the flying club area without a single pirouette.

The local chief flight instructor came out and asked what the problem was. I said the right disc brake had gone and probably needed a new puck. The CFI was also the chief engineer, so we pushed the 1-30 into the maintenance hangar—where it developed that they had every size puck except the one I needed. But by using a truck brake shoe, a hacksaw, and a grinder, we made one, and it worked.

I asked the CFI where to tie down and he asked my why. I said I proposed to rent a car and drive to Baddeck to visit the museum. "Why don't you fly down?" he said. "No airport," I said, "Of course there is," said he. "Show me," I said, spreading the chart. He said it wasn't on the map, but on the point just south of the Bell mansion. "A fellow used to fly a Bonanza in and out of there all the time," he said. He added that there was a fire patrol strip just two miles east of the village. So there it was, a chance to fly into one of the most important historical sites in the history of aviation. And with its ninety-horsepower engine, the 1-30 had good performance on short takeoffs and landings. Assured by the CFI, I went to Flight Service to file a flight plan and check the weather. A strong northeaster would be coming through within the hour and would probably close down the field.

I hadn't had anything to eat since breakfast, so I grabbed a quick sandwich and hurried back to the plane. With the CFI assuring me there'd be no problems, I took off in increasingly gusty wind and headed southeast.

Pushed by a stiff tailwind down the north end of Bras d'Or Lake, I could soon make out the point of land on which stood Dr. Bell's stately summer residence. His laboratory was located nearby. It was here that the Aerial Experimental Association was founded in 1907.

The mansion was impressive. Much less impressive was the air strip described by the CFI at Sydney. There was indeed a field below and west of the house, but as I flew over I saw a man crossing the field. And he was either the shortest midget in Canada or the wheat in the field was the tallest. The wheat was up to his armpits, and it was obviously impossible to land there. I flew on to look for the fire patrol strip and could find no sign of it at all. It simply didn't exist.

I began to realize that I'd been had, or been fed some ludicrously out-of-date information. I was just able to raise the Sydney tower and they reported that the ceiling was below 300 feet, visibility less than a half-mile, winds gusting to sixty miles an hour. Field closed!

What next? Since I was flying at 500 feet and unlikely to visit the vicinity again, I took a picture of the striking tetrahedral-styled building. Out of the corner of my eye I saw a racetrack. I remembered childhood tales of barnstormers taking off and landing on racetracks. I said to myself, why not? But my guardian angel intervened; when I flew over for a closer look I saw that a water line was being laid and a ditch went right across the center of the straightway.

By this time I'd been circling Baddeck for fifteen minutes. My fuel was not good for more than the hundred miles back to Trenton, if that, so I gave up on Baddeck and started heading downwind, climbing gradually to get a little altitude (money in the bank) under us.

I made it back to Trenton late in the afternoon. I really don't believe my French-Canadian friend was all that delighted to see me, certainly not as delighted as I was to see him. But out came the rusty barrel and the pump. We had a cup of coffee. Out came the dirty handkerchief and I was on my way again. I got back to the Moncton Flying Club just at sunset—six hundred miles and ten hours after I left.

I hope Dr. Bell knows that I tried.

Four Letters

To William Hunter, a Champlin Family Genealogist

12 Feb. 93

Dear Bill,

During the past fifty plus years I have flown many different types of aircraft for a total of more than eight thousand hours. Some were quite sophisticated, but they never gave me as much trouble as the machine I'm trying to control now! Please forgive the mistakes and errors....

When the Elwood turned up as Ellwood I realized that you are the person who C.D.C. 3rd had contacted me about and I had supplied the basic information which you enclosed.

First of all, regarding W. Ellwood D. Sr.; he was born in Buffalo as you know. He attended Ridley College in St.Catharines, Ont., where he played on the first football team. He then attended the University of Toronto where he again played on the Varsity first team. He was a classmate and friend of John A.D. McCurdy who, upon graduation, returned to his home in Baddeck, N.S. and became associated with Dr. Alexander Graham Bell. Dr. Bell was experimenting with man-carrying kites and turned to Glenn H. Curtiss of Hammondsport for a suitable power plant.

To shorten it a bit, McCurdy was making exhibition flights in Buffalo, where WED Sr., resided. They met at the airfield and McCurdy suggested that Gink (WED Sr.) come to Hammondsport and take up aviation, which he did and thus met Gladys Champlin. They were married in London, England, which is another story.

I'm a little awed when I read my brothers' war records, for I had a quite lackluster one myself.

I also attended Ridley College as did Duane, and then Cornell University. I then joined the family's Pleasant Valley Wine Co. in 1938. In August of 1941, because of my school associations, I enlisted in the R.C.A.F. I completed my pilot training at #2 S.F.T.S., Uplands, Ottawa. I went overseas in Sept. 42 on the Q.E. In '43 I was on the way to becoming a Spitfire Photo Recon Pilot when I was transferred to the U.S.A.A.F. I ended up in Troop Carrier! I have five battle stars on my E.T.O. ribbon, the British '39–'43 star and was chasing down a couple of Air Medals for my grandchildren.

I married Jacqueline Leigh-Mallory on 20 May 1944. Brother Duane was our best man. We have two children: Jacqueline Anne, born 6 May 1946 and Trafford Leigh-Mallory, born 28 June 1948. My wife contracted multiple sclerosis in 1949. She entered a nursing home in 1975. Margaret Underhill and I were married in Aug. '82.

The winery was bought out in '57 and I went to work for Schweizer Aircraft Corp. of Elmira, N.Y. as Sales Manager and a test-demonstration pilot. Schweizer bought the Teal Amphibian in which Bill Champlin of Rochester had a major financial interest. At the time I put him in touch with C.D.C. 3rd.

By the summer of '80 my hearing had deteriorated (?) to the point I didn't feel I should fly instruments and decided to retire. I moved back to Hammondsport and to keep occupied began doing volunteer work for the Glenn H. Curtiss Museum, and have been at it ever since in various capacities.

We have several good friends in Ottawa and visit back and forth quite frequently. One couple is Bob and Ruth Bradford. He retired as director of the National Air Museum in Rockford.

I'm sorry this is so long winded. If you have an opportunity, please put Hammondsport on your visit list. We have lots of room in the summer and would like to meet with you. In the meantime if you have any questions let me know.

All the best,

Tony

To Tony's son, Trafford

27 Feb. 93

Trafford, my boy,

I was starting a tale about the time our Cousin Harry and I went to Lake Placid to learn to drive bobsleds. However in view of the day's events I thought I would break off and write you a few lines.

Yup, we are still here. Mardo's mother is still in and out of the hospital at the moment. I've been spending my mornings at the museum, working on the old Citizens Hose cart. Have taken the wheels off, scraped, sanded, and primed them. Also the steps where the people rode on the way to a fire if they had horses. Otherwise they pulled it themselves.

We visited a man in Geneva, who has horses and buggies. He is the one who gave me the name of Abner Lapp, down your way and still hope to visit.

The lake has finally frozen in front of the house and the ice should be thick enough after another zero night. However it depends on whether I feel up to lugging the boat out of the shed and rigging it. I had quite a trying afternoon.

This morning I went to the head of the lake and parked by the Curtiss Memorial with the idea of walking down and checking on the cottage, particularly the stream for ice build-up. The snow was crusted and just too deep, so I went home for lunch and to get my X country skis.

It was a beautiful day, sunny but with a fair north wind. There was a sheet of new, clear ice running from the Keuka Maid down past Phil and Caroline's. The wind made it ripple. Mandy [their beloved

Scottie] was with me and unfortunately she spotted a muskrat out on the ice. I finally got her to come back and got down to the cottage. Everything looks okay except that there is a lot of snow in the creek.

I decided to go back via the path and give the muskrat a wide berth. As I said, it was a beautiful day and I was considering going on up to the country club and doing some more skiing. I was on the driveway level and had to get down to the parking lot level. I decided that the sloping ramp was the best bet—the one that has the big rocks at the bottom. Well, it wasn't.

Being my usual sensitive self, I traversed it, rather than running it straight down. I picked a wide gap between two big boulders and away I went. Unfortunately there was another boulder just beneath the snow and my skis came to an abrupt halt, but I didn't.

I never hit anything so hard in my life, right on top of my head. I was sure I had broken nearly every bone in my body, but I hadn't. I lay there a few moments till the stars disappeared and the sun came out again. I took off my skis and started looking for Mandy. There she was, way out on the ice where we had seen the muskrat. I was not in the best of spirits when I had to slog through the deep snow and out on the lake to retrieve her.

By this time I had lost all interest in any further skiing and only wanted to get home and around a good belt of Scotch and a good hot bath, but I did have to stop at Richard's for a green pepper as I was putting chili together for dinner. I had already put in a teaspoon of curry instead of chili powder.

When I arrived home Mardo pointed out that I had lost about four square inches of skin from the top of my head. So I took two belts of Old McPherson, but still only one very hot bath.

Anywho it's been a long day and I wanted to bring you up-to-date, so to speak. Will give you a call if anything develops. Our love to you all.

Dad

To Tony's daughter, Anne

4 March 1993

Dear Anne,

I am enclosing a copy of a letter to Traff which is self-explanatory and will send him a copy of this.

Obviously last weekend wasn't a particularly good one for me, as you can see from the other letter. Actually the Scotch and the hot bath both were successful, but from there on it was all down hill.

The next day, Sunday, was a beautiful day, clear and cold, with a good north wind. I enlisted some help and unlimbered the ice boat. The ice was beautiful and I spent at least an hour going back and forth across the lake and then quit for lunch. Mardo arrived back from seeing her mother in Corning. (She's 94, you know.)

After lunch and some of the Sunday papers it was just too nice to stay inside, so I went outside for some more iceboating. I made several runs and was bringing it back in so Mardo could take a spin, but I got careless. I was coasting in at about 20 mph, not paying much attention, when the right rear runner dropped through a thin spot—and we came to an abrupt stop. I was sitting up and not braced. I slid forward and the tiller caught me in the solar plexus.... Although I never have been, it felt as though I had been kicked by a mule. Key-ryst it hurt, and I couldn't breathe.

We were able to unstick the boat and stow the sails. Went back in the house to recuperate (?) but after a while I let Mardo run me to the Emergency room at the hospital. Broke two ribs.

The long and the short of it was that I spent three days there, feeling sorry for myself, but more so for Mardo, who now has patients in two hospitals, thirty miles apart.

I got sprung last night. It's easier to be miserable at home than it is in a hospital, but a lot tougher on Mardo.

Your mother has received the dispatches from the front, but I wanted you to get it from "the horse's rump."

Love,

Dad

To Charles Champlin

20 March 1993

Dear Chuck,

I appreciated your very kind letter. I have enjoyed living a fairly adventurous life, but I'm going to have tone it down and take Mardo's hint. For my sixty-fifth birthday she gave me a windsurfer, for my seventy-fifth, a croquet mallet. It used to be that you bruised easily but healed quickly, but recently it seems you bruise easier but the healing is much slower.

I have heard that events happen in threes. I believe it now. The third egg hit the fan the day after I came home from the hospital. It was the most traumatic one for me, including the ski and iceboat incidents. We were sitting in the den when I happened to look out of the window. Mandy was running out toward the end of the point. We have a muskrat in residence out there and Mandy had spotted it. The weather had been very warm and the ice was rotted. Mardo went running out to call the dog back.

What followed was like a slow motion sequence. Mandy started out on the ice after the muskrat, which had come up through a hole about twenty-five feet from shore. When Mandy wouldn't come back when Mardo called, Mardo started out on the ice. The storm windows were on so I couldn't call. Then first Mandy and then Mardo disappeared from sight, into the lake! Luckily I had been using a length of rope in the garage and didn't have to hunt for one. I made my way out to the point as quickly as I could. Luckily they had come back up in the holes and not under the ice. Mardo had boosted Mandy up onto the ice and she had run ashore. Mardo was in the lake hanging on to the edge of the ice. I waded out until I was knee-deep and threw her the rope. She was so cold she couldn't hold the rope in her hands but she managed to wind it around her arms, and I pulled her in. A close call.

Had a great blizzard last weekend. Went to Richards Sat. AM and stocked up. Went home, battened the hatches, and rode it out. Thank heavens didn't lose power and had a well-stocked bar. Two feet of snow. Didn't get plowed out until Tuesday.

Best to all,

Tony